Limited Classical Reprint Library

STUDIES IN
BIBLICAL
ESCHATOLOGY

by

H. A. Ironside and F. C. Ottman

Foreword by
Dr. Cyril J. Barber

Printed by Klock & Klock in the U.S.A.
1983 Reprint

FOREWORD

The study of prophecy has fallen upon hard times. Prophecy "buffs" have often brought discredit to the discipline of biblical eschatology due to their insistence upon identifying minute historic details and absorption in the subject to the exclusion of other facets of God's revelation.

The true task of biblical prophecy has been to "discern the signs of the times"--to see what God is bringing to pass as the history of peoples and societies unfolds--and to point to our accountability to Him. Because approximately 25 percent of Scripture was prophetic at the time of its writing, we should be prepared to lay aside some of our prejudices and realize how important to God is the subject before us. By means of His Word, He has revealed Himself and His will to us. His Word will be fulfilled. The more we are able to identify with His plan for the world, the greater will be our ability to cooperate with Him in the outworking of His purpose.

While it is true that works on biblical eschatology are eagerly read by some Christians and ignored by others, a very large segment of Christendom reads only those works written by people who adhere to the point of view which they have espoused. The general tendency, therefore, is to find out if the writer's perspective is the same as that held by the reader. If it is, then his work is read. If not, then it is passed over as scarcely worthy of their consideration.

Hopefully this book will not fall into either of these categories.

Dr. Henry Allan Ironside (1878-1951) was a great expositor. Many of his books were originally messages which he delivered to different audiences. They were put into more permanent form when God's people found that they had received edification and enlightenment from them

In 1943, Dr. Ironside published *The Great Parenthesis*. In many respects, this work is a masterpiece. For example, Dr. Ironside takes certain prophecies such as Daniel 9:24-27, Isaiah 61:2-3, the Olivet Discourse, Acts Discourse, Acts 15:7-29, *et cetra* and explains why in each of these statements there is a gap or parenthesis before something in the plan and purpose of God is enacted.

Far from neglecting Dr. Ironside's contribution, present day believer's should welcome it as a powerful apologetic for the authenticity of God's Word.

A man of equal learning and accomplishment was Dr. Ford C. Ottman (1859-1929). Dr. Ottman contributed many fine commentaries which are still eagerly prized by expositors. In 1911 he published *God's Oath* in which he demonstrated from Scripture the way in which the prophetic word has been fulfilled in the past. On the basis of the hermeneutics of fulfilled prophecy, he began working with the unfulfilled portions of God's revelation.

In this book, Dr. Ottman deals convincingly with the promises of God to Abraham, David and the Prophets. He treats, in addition, the parables of Matthew 13 and shows from all of these Scriptures the need for God's Word to be fulfilled in keeping with His covenants to His ancient people Israel.

Whether one agrees with all that Drs. Ironside and Ottman have related or not, the fact remains that they have made a contribution to biblical scholarship which is at once sincere, and they believe, scriptural. We need to demonstrate the same kind of sincerity and objectivity in interacting with what they have written. We should be prepared, therefore, to heed the admonision of the Apostle Peter, who wrote, *"No prophecy recorded in Scripture was ever thought up by the prophet himself. It was the Holy Spirit within these godly men who gave them true messages from God"* (II Peter 1:20-21. Living Bible). And seeing Drs. Ironside and Ottman sought faithfully to uphold the truth of Scripture as they saw it, we too may derive some blessing as we contemplate afresh these riches from God's inspired Word.

Cyril J. Barber
Author, *The Minister's Library*

THE

GREAT

PARENTHESIS

by

H. A. Ironside

This edition reprinted from
Zondervan Publishing House
Grand Rapids, 1962 Edition

ISBN: 0-86524-143-0

Printed by Klock & Klock in the U.S.A.
1983 Reprint

PREFACE

The contents of the present volume are really an enlargement of lectures on Bible prophecy that have been given at various conferences during the past few years. It was never convenient to have these stenographically reported at the time of their delivery, and so the substance of the addresses has been very carefully gone over and is now presented for the consideration of those who are interested in the revelation which the Spirit of God has given concerning things to come. It is the author's fervent conviction that the failure to understand what is revealed in Scripture concerning the Great Parenthesis between Messiah's rejection, with the consequent setting aside of Israel nationally, and the regathering of God's earthly people and recognition by the Lord in the last days, is the fundamental cause for many conflicting and unscriptural prophetic teachings. Once this parenthetical period is understood and the present work of God during this age is apprehended, the whole prophetic program unfolds with amazing clearness.

It is not with any pretension of having discovered something new that I have prepared this volume. I am glad to acknowledge my indebtedness to many sober, spiritually-minded teachers of the Word who in years gone by saw clearly many truths as to God's prophetic plan which later writers and teachers have obscured in large measure. While I do not expect all my readers to agree with me, I humbly ask that, like the Berean Jews of old, they do not reject this testimony without careful inquiry, but that they search the Scriptures to see whether these things are so. Personally, they have been a part of my own thinking for so many years and have meant so much to me in my study of the Word of God that I am eager to have others enter into them, too. On the other hand, I have no desire to press anything that is not substantiated by Scripture. "We can do nothing against the truth, but for the truth." And in the Old Testament it is written: "To the law and to the testimony: if they speak not according to this word, it is because there is no light in them."

H. A. IRONSIDE.

Chicago, Ill.

CONTENTS

CHAPTER I

INTRODUCTION

It is noticeable that every major conflict between nations for many centuries past has resulted in a greatly increased interest in the study of the prophetic Scriptures. When men see everything shaking to pieces which they have supposed to be firm and stable, it is not to be wondered at that they begin to inquire concerning those things which cannot be shaken, as set forth in God's Holy Word. Unfortunately, we are all creatures of limitations, and our thinking and our outlook are very likely to be bounded in great measure by the circumstances of the times in which our lot is cast. Thus there has ever been an inclination on the part of many students of prophecy to try to fit the events of which they themselves have cognizance into the prophetic picture as given in the Word. Ever since the Napoleonic wars, for instance, how many efforts have been made to identify certain outstanding characters as the Beast or the Antichrist, and how often have predictions been confidently made that events going on at a particular time were heading up to Armageddon and would bring within a very few months or years the end of the present age, the return of Christ, and the setting up of His Millennial Kingdom!

It is always right to be watching and waiting for the coming of the Lord. This we are commanded to do. "That blessed hope and the appearing of the glory of our great God and Saviour Jesus Christ" should ever be the lodestar of our souls as we journey on over the sea of life; and surely every instructed Christian, saddened and wearied by man's vain efforts to bring about and insure a lasting peace on earth, must look with eager, glad anticipation to the promised Second Advent of the Prince of Peace, who is to reign in righteousness and bring deliverance to the troubled world.

But time and again prophetic teachers have attempted to work out various systems of chronology drawn partially or wholly from Scripture or in other cases drawn from some fanciful interpretation of the Great Pyramid in Egypt, the stars in their courses, or even the predictions of charlatans like Nostradamus, Mother Shipton and others. Most of these systems prove popular for a time, but as a rule their overconfident exploiters set the dates for the fulfillment of their hopes so close at hand that they themselves live to see their prophecies proved utterly false. Others pass away before their predictions are shown to be wrong, and yet in many instances these attempted efforts to set the time for Messiah's Second Advent are worked over by others and added to in such a way as to modernize them and apply them to new and changed conditions, but all at last are proved to be false.

The reason for this is, as I honestly believe, that we are living in a period concerning which we have absolutely no chronology in the Word of God, and certainly nothing in the Great Pyramid, to guide us. I only refer to the Pyramid because so many have based their faith upon what they fancy to be its corroboration of their theories. I do not for one moment believe it is the predicted altar to be set up at the border of the land of Egypt, for it is not an altar at all, but a great mausoleum. The Word of God needs no outside corroboration. It is complete in itself. "All scripture is given by inspiration of God, and is profitable for doctrine, for reproof, for correction, for instruction in righteousness: that the man of God may be perfect, thoroughly furnished unto all good works." If the Word of God can perfect the man of God completely, then he needs not to add anything to it in order to obtain this desired end.

It is a recognized principle in the ways of God with men to present certain privileges to them or give certain promises which, however, are contingent as to the time of fulfillment upon the faith and obedience of those to whom they are given. Some outstanding promises do not come under these limitations. God's covenant with Abraham was one of pure grace. Nothing that has happened since or can happen will change it in the least degree. Through Abraham's glorious Seed, our Lord Jesus Christ, all nations shall yet be blessed in accordance with the promise. But other promises have been given which were dependent upon faith and obedience for their fulfillment. One has only to think of God's promises to Israel that they should inherit the land of Palestine and possess it in spite of all the efforts of their enemies to dislodge them, provided they walked in obedience to His Holy Word. This they failed to do, and therefore they lost their land, but the same God who told them that this would be the result of their waywardness, has also declared that the time will come when they will return to that land and will become a regenerated nation who will worship the Lord in the beauty of holiness.

It has often been pointed out by others, but is well worth repeating, that the Old Testament seer might be likened to a man standing on one of our Western plains looking off toward a great mountain range. Many miles before him is a vast mountain which for the moment fills all his vision. Clouds cover the top of it, so that it seems to pierce the heavens, but suddenly the clouds are lifted and in the blaze of the westering sun he sees another and higher peak beyond, covered with snow, which seems to shine in resplendent glory. What the man gazing upon this scene cannot see, however, is the valley or the lower ranges of mountains that come in between these two peaks. The one may be many miles beyond the other. In between may be lesser hills, valleys, rivers, villages and farms, but all of these are unseen by the man upon the plain.

Let us imagine a cross surmounting the first peak, and call this the vision of the coming of the Lord Jesus Christ to suffer and to die for our sins. Then imagine that the glory surrounding the second and higher peak takes the form of a crown of light, and think of it as indicating the Second Coming of our Lord Jesus to reign in power and glory over all this lower universe. Peter spoke of the "sufferings of Christ, and the glory that should follow." These two mountains illustrate both. But now, in between them we have all the events of the present age of grace, and these could not be seen by the Old Testament prophets for it was not yet the will of God to make them known. These are the mysteries kept secret from the foundation of the world, which began to be made manifest by our Lord Jesus as He told of the mysteries of the kingdom of heaven; and then were more fully unfolded in the unique revelation of the mystery of the Church, the body of Christ, given to the Apostle Paul, and the unfolding of the mystery of iniquity and of Babylon the Great through Paul and John. Other mysteries there are linked with these, and nearly all of them have to do with what is going on between the First and Second Comings of our Lord.

The chronological periods given in the prophets, otherwise called "the times and the seasons," have to do with God's earthly people Israel, and therefore with events up to the cross when the Lord was rejected, and other events which will not begin to take place so long as the Church is in this scene, for that Church is in itself the unfolding of the mystery which has been hid in God from before the foundation of the world, and is now made manifest for the obedience of faith among all nations.

It is my purpose in these chapters to show that this hidden period of time which has now extended over nineteen centuries was intimated by the Old Testament prophets and has been confirmed in the New Testament, but that through losing sight of it, many have missed the mind of God entirely in regard to the working out of His great plan for the blessing of Israel, the salvation of the nations, and the unique place which the Church as the body of Christ has in the counsels of God, and will have for all eternity. I believe it can be shown from Scripture that this Great Parenthesis is the true key to a right understanding of prophecy. This key once laid hold of will save from much blundering, and certainly should deliver the people of God from discouragement when it almost looks as though God's plans have gone awry and are not working out according to His mind. The fact is, He is working everything according to the counsel of His own will, but many of us have failed to understand what that counsel involves.

With these preliminary thoughts in mind then, shall we go on to examine a number of Scriptures in which the Great Parenthesis is clearly indicated, and as we do so, may God grant that it be in dependence upon His Holy Spirit, to keep us from missing His mind, and to lead us, in accordance with the promise of our Lord, into all truth, as He takes of the things of Christ and shows them to us and makes known unto us things to come.

Chapter II

THE GREAT PROPHECY OF THE SEVENTY WEEKS

We have in the ninth chapter of the book of Daniel the most remarkable time prophecy of the Holy Scriptures. Sir Edward Denny was, I think, perhaps the first prophetic student to designate this chapter, "The Backbone of Prophecy." He may, of course, have borrowed the term from someone else, but if so, the present writer has never found it used by anyone who wrote earlier than this particular teacher. The term is well given, for if we understand the outline indicated here, we shall find that all the prophetic Scriptures fall into place without forcing them, and that so simply as to make it evident that we have here the backbone of the entire prophetic system of the Bible.

Those who have given much study to the book of Daniel will remember that the chapter begins with an account of Daniel's personal exercises. He tells us that he had been studying the books of some of the prophets who had gone before him. He refers to the book of Jeremiah for one (Chap. 29:10-14), and probably the second book of Chronicles (36:21), for another. In these books he learned that God would accomplish seventy years in the desolations of Jerusalem. It had been definitely foretold that following the destruction of the city and Temple and the enslavement of God's earthly people in Babylon, a period of seventy years would

15

elapse ere they would be restored to their own land and be permitted to rebuild the Temple, and eventually the city of Jerusalem itself.

Daniel had been carried away in one of the first of the campaigns against Palestine. He was then but a youth, and now had become an old man. He realized, therefore, that the seventy-year cycle must be nearly completed. This stirred his heart to prayer — which in itself is most suggestive. How often people take up the study of prophecy from a purely intellectual standpoint, and yet surely there is nothing to move our hearts toward God like occupation with His marvelous purpose in regard to the coming of His own blessed Son into the world again and the setting up of His glorious kingdom.

Daniel felt in his soul that the people were not in a fit state for restoration, and he took the place of confession before God. He himself was perhaps one of the holiest men living at that time, and yet, as he prostrates himself before the Lord, he identifies himself with the sins of his people as he cries, "I and my people have sinned." As he pours out his heart in contrition, he counts on God to work deliverance, and in answer to his prayer, a messenger is sent from the Throne of God, even Gabriel himself, the same glorious being who appeared to him on a later occasion, and who at the beginning of New Testament times was chosen to convey to the blessed Virgin Mary the wondrous news that she was to be the destined mother of the promised Messiah.

There is something moving in the way the Spirit of God directs attention to the time when Gabriel first appeared to Daniel. We are told that he "touched him about the time of the evening oblation." That is, it was the time when, if things had been right in Israel, the evening sacrifice would have been offered on the altar at Jerusalem; but that altar was cast down; the Temple was in ruins. No smoke of sacrifice ascended to God from that holy place. Yet Daniel never forgot the time when the oblation should have been placed upon the altar.

Of course, that offering spoke of the sacrifice of our Lord Jesus which was yet to take place. God Himself saw in every victim placed on Jewish altars a type of the Person and work of His own beloved Son; and everything that God will yet accomplish for Israel, for the Church, and for the nations, will be based upon the finished work of Calvary's cross. Our Lord there "tasted death for every man." Actually, the last word is in the neuter in the original. Our Lord tasted death for every *thing*. The blessing of the entire universe is contingent upon the work which He accomplished on the cross.

Now let us note the message or the prophecy that Gabriel brought to Daniel. We read in verses 24 to 27:

"Seventy weeks are determined upon thy people and upon thy holy city, to finish the transgression, and to make an end of sins, and to make reconciliation for iniquity, and to bring in everlasting righteousness, and to seal up the vision and prophecy, and to anoint the most Holy. Know therefore and understand, that from the going forth of the commandment to restore and to build Jerusalem unto the Messiah the Prince shall be seven weeks, and threescore and two weeks: the street shall be built again, and the wall, even in troublous times. And after threescore and two weeks shall Messiah be cut off, but not for himself·

and the people of the prince that shall come shall
destroy the city and the sanctuary; and the end thereof shall be with a flood, and unto the end of the war
desolations are determined. And he shall confirm the
covenant with many for one week: and in the midst
of the week he shall cause the sacrifice and the
oblation to cease, and for the overspreading of
abominations he shall make it desolate, even until
the consummation, and that determined shall be
poured upon the desolate."

There are a few items here which become a little
clearer if we turn to other translations. For instance, in
verse 25, the latter part, the Revised Version reads: "It
shall be built again, with street and moat, even in troublous times." Some versions read in place of "troublous
times," "the *narrow* times." Then in verse 26, the marginal reading seems better than the received text: "After
the sixty-two weeks shall Messiah be cut off, and shall
have nothing." The latter part of verse 26 is given in
the Revised Version as: "Even unto the end shall be
war; desolations are determined." And in verse 27, the
last half of the verse reads in the Revised Version:
"Upon the wing of abominations shall one come that
maketh desolate." Other slight differences are found in
various versions, but they need not occupy us now.

Let us weigh carefully just what is here revealed.
Remember in the first place, Daniel had understood by
books the number of the years in which God would
accomplish the desolations of Jerusalem. His prayer
of confession is with that in view. God meets him by
informing him through His angel that not at the expiration of seventy years but at the close of seventy weeks
will all Israel's sorrows come to an end. The word

translated *week* is recognized by scholars generally as a generic term simply meaning a *seven*. It could be used for a seven of days, a seven of months, or, as is undoubtedly the case here, a seven of years, since it was of years that Daniel was thinking. Seventy weeks of years, then, would be 490 years.

Now let us observe exactly what the angel says. "Seventy sevens are determined," or "cut off" (that is, cut off from the entire period of time). These seventy seven's, or 490 years, are set apart in the divine reckoning for what the angel calls, "Thy people and thy holy city," that is, Daniel's people, certainly the people of the Jews, and his holy city, Jerusalem, the literal capital of the land of Palestine.

Now, what will take place at the expiration of this period of 490 years? The angel adds: "To finish the transgression, and to make an end of sins, and to make reconciliation [or atonement] for iniquity, and to bring in everlasting righteousness, and to seal up the vision and prophecy, and to anoint the most Holy." Notice carefully each of these expressions. At the end of 490 years, Israel's transgression will be finished, and their sins brought to an end, because their Messiah will have made reconciliation or atonement for iniquity. The long period of Israel's sufferings under the heel of the Gentiles will be completed, and everlasting righteousness will be brought in. This refers clearly to the setting up of Messiah's kingdom. Then the vision and prophecy will be sealed up. That is, all will be fulfilled so that vision and prophecy will no longer be needed; and last of all, the most Holy will be anointed. This must refer,

I believe, to the Shekinah glory returning to Israel when the people are gathered back in their own land and Jehovah's Temple is rebuilt. The glory has been missing ever since the destruction of Jerusalem by Nebuchadnezzar. It was not seen in the temple of Zerubbabel nor in the temple of Herod, but it will return when Israel's mourning shall be ended and, as a repentant people, they will be brought back to God. Thus far, then, the promise of verse twenty-four.

Now, if we can find out just when the 490-year period was to begin, it ought to be an easy thing to count 490 years from that point and then to ask, "Have all these promises been fulfilled?" The starting point is given in the next verse. "Know therefore and understand, that from the going forth of the commandment to restore and to build Jerusalem" — let us stop there for a moment. This is clearly the time from which we are to begin to count. When did a commandment go forth to restore and to build Jerusalem? Right here there is a difference of opinion among sober teachers of prophecy. Some insist that the reference is to the commandment given in the seventh chapter of the book of Ezra, which was approximately 457 B.C.; but a careful examination of that decree will make it evident that it did not really have to do with restoring and building the city of Jerusalem at all, but was rather a confirmation of the earlier decree of Cyrus to rebuild the Temple and reinstate the worship of God in Israel. It seems far more likely that the commandment referred to is actually that given in the second chapter of the book of Nehemiah. There we have in very truth a commandment to restore and build

Jerusalem, and that commandment was given about 445 B.C.

We are not told whether the sevens of years are to be counted according to sun time or lunar time, and for our present purpose it is not necessary that we should go into the problem here. Sir Robert Anderson, in his masterly work, *The Coming Prince,* has taken it up in great detail, and has presented a chronological system which seems fully satisfactory, though all are not prepared to accept it. Those who are interested may consult that work at their leisure. I shall not deal with chronology as such here. I only desire to emphasize that evidently we have in Nehemiah 2 the starting point for this time prophecy.

But now let us go on with the quotation of the rest of the verse: "From the going forth of the commandment to restore and to build Jerusalem unto the Messiah the Prince shall be seven weeks, and threescore and two weeks." Here, then, we have sixty-nine weeks — not seventy. In other words, 483 years — not 490. For some reason the angel separates the last week of seven years from the sixty-nine which were to be completed at the coming of Messiah the Prince. And these sixty-nine weeks are divided into two periods — seven weeks, or forty-nine years, and sixty-two weeks, or 434 years. Undoubtedly the division here is in order to prepare our minds for a further division between the sixty-ninth and the seventieth weeks.

We are told: "The street shall be built again, and the wall, even in troublous times," or, as other translations read, "in the narrow," or "the straitened times." The reference is evidently to the seven weeks as distinguished from the threescore and two weeks. The former period is called "the narrow times," and during those forty-nine years the city of Jerusalem was rebuilt and the people gathered back to it. They were troublous times in measure, but the reference is evidently not so much to the distress of the people at that time as to the fact that the city was built in the narrow period.

The sixty-two weeks begin immediately after the expiration of the seven weeks, and we are told in verse 26: "And after threescore and two weeks shall Messiah be cut off and have nothing." If Sir Robert Anderson be correct in his system of chronology, this tremendous event occurred within a literal week after the exact close of the sixty-nine weeks of years. He points out that sixty-nine years of 360 days each, expired when our Lord was welcomed into Jerusalem by the children and others who cried, "Hosannah; Blessed is he that cometh in the name of the Lord." However, we are not told that Messiah would be cut off at the exact time of the expiration of the sixty-two weeks, but "*after* threescore and two weeks shall Messiah be cut off." This part of the prophecy has been fulfilled to the letter. "He came unto his own, and his own received him not." He presented Himself to Israel as their promised King-Messiah. They said, "We will not have this man to reign over us," and demanded that He be crucified. Pilate asked, "Shall I crucify your King?" They exclaimed, "We have no king but Caesar." And so the Messiah for whom the nation had waited so long was crucified. Following that, if we are to take the seventieth week as an immediate continuation of the period which ended at the cross, in seven years from the time of the Saviour's crucifixion all the promises made to Israel should have been fulfilled!

The fact is, they were not fulfilled. Israel did not recognize their Messiah. They do not know Him yet as their Sinbearer. Their transgression has not been finished. An end of sins for them has not been made. They do not know anything yet of atonement for iniquity. Everlasting righteousness has not been brought in. Vision and prophecy have not been sealed up. The most Holy has not been anointed by the return of the Shekinah. What then? Has the prophecy failed? Has God's Word been proved to be false? Impossible! We know that He cannot deny Himself. But it is right here that we find one of the great and important truths of the Word.

Between the sixty-ninth and the seventieth weeks we have a Great Parenthesis which has now lasted over nineteen hundred years. The seventieth week has been postponed by God Himself who changes the times and the seasons because of the transgression of the people. As I have put it elsewhere, though some have objected to the expression, the moment Messiah died on the cross, the prophetic clock stopped. There has not been a tick upon that clock for nineteen centuries. It will not begin to go again until the entire present age has come to an end, and Israel will once more be taken up by God.

Let us turn again to the prophecy and see definitely what is there predicted. After the declaration to Daniel that Messiah would be cut off and have nothing after the conclusion of the 483-year period, we read: "And the people of the prince that shall come shall destroy the city and the sanctuary; and the end thereof shall be with a flood, and unto the end wars and desolations are determined." Now what exactly is it that is here predicted? Messiah was cut off. He had nothing so far as the kingdom so long promised and expected was concerned. Shortly after His crucifixion, the Roman people came and destroyed the city and the Sanctuary. We are not told just when this would take place. Actually, it was forty years after. Also observe that it is not said here that the prince would come and destroy the city. A prince is in view who is yet to play a large part in prophecy. He, however, has not appeared yet, but his people, that is, the Roman people, were used as the scourge of God to punish Israel for their sins, and they destroyed Jerusalem and the Temple of Jehovah.

Then we have all the present age put into three lines: "The end thereof shall be with a flood, and unto the end wars and desolations are determined." That is, as by an overflowing flood the people of Israel were to be destroyed by their enemies, scattered throughout the world, and until the end, that is, the seventieth week, which remains unfulfilled, there shall be wars and desolations. This is exactly what our Saviour Himself tells us, as recorded in Matthew 24. During all the present age, "ye shall hear of wars and rumors of wars: see that ye be not troubled: for all these things must come to pass, but the end is not yet." That end is again the seventieth week.

Throughout the book of Daniel we have the expression frequently, "the time of the end." The same expression is found elsewhere in the prophetic Scriptures. The time of the end is the last seven years of the times which God has allotted to the people of the Jews, which has not yet begun to run its course. We shall see as we continue our studies what God is doing in this intervening period which we have designated, "The Great Parenthesis."

When this time of waiting comes to an end, then the prince whose people have already appeared shall himself appear; that is, the great Roman leader of the last days, called in Revelation 13, "the Beast" because he is emphatically the embodiment of every evil principle in all the empires of the world. When he appears, he will pretend at first to be the friend of the Jews, and we read in verse 27: "He shall confirm the covenant with many for one week: and in the midst of the week he shall cause the sacrifice and the oblation to cease, and for the overspreading of abominations he shall make it desolate, even until the consummation, and that determined shall be poured upon the desolate," or, as some read, "the desolator." Strange is it that many have supposed it was Prince Messiah Himself who was to confirm a covenant for one week. But when did He ever make such a covenant? The blood of the covenant which He shed upon the cross is not to confirm a covenant for seven years, but it is the blood of the everlasting covenant.

In the last days when God takes Israel up again and is about to bring them into fullness of blessing, a Roman prince will arise who will make a covenant with the nation for seven years, promising them protection and liberty in religion as they return to their land. For three and one-half years he will permit this to go on, but in the midst of the week he will violate the covenant and demand that all worship to Jehovah cease, and the Antichrist will be manifested in his true character. This will result in what is known in Scripture as the time of Jacob's trouble, or the Great Tribulation, and it will go on for three and one-half years until judgment is visited upon the desolator, and God's earthly people are delivered. The greater part of the book of the Revelation, in fact virtually everything from chapter four to the end of chapter nineteen, has to do with events which will take place in heaven and on earth during this last unfulfilled seventieth week of Daniel. When this is seen, all is wonderful harmony, and the prophetic Scriptures are plain.

CHAPTER III

THE ACCEPTABLE YEAR OF THE LORD

When once the break in the prophetic plan is seen as set forth in Daniel 9, one recognizes the fact that provision is made for this in prophetic interpretation throughout the entire Word of God. Prophecy has to do first with events connected with the nations in contact with Israel before and up to the coming of and rejection of the Messiah. Then there is a long interval during which, we learn from the New Testament, God is doing a work never mentioned in Old Testament times. Following this we have prophecies relating to the coming judgments at the time of the end and the Second Advent in power and glory of our Lord as He takes possession of the kingdom so long predicted.

A very striking instance is that of Isaiah 61; of which a portion was read and commented on by our Saviour at His first return visit to Nazareth, where he had been reared, after His baptism by John and the temptation in the wilderness. We are told by Luke that when He went into the synagogue on the Sabbath Day, and stood up to read, there was delivered unto Him the book of the Prophet Esaias, and when He had opened the book, He found the place where it is written:

> "The Spirit of the Lord is upon me, because he hath anointed me to preach the gospel to the poor; he hath sent me to heal the brokenhearted, to preach deliverance to the captives, and recovering of sight

to the blind, to set at liberty them that are bruised,
to preach the acceptable year of the Lord" (Luke
4:16-19).

In the opening words of the next verse we read: "And
he closed the book, and he gave it again to the minister,
and sat down." There is something here that is very
significant. By turning back to Isaiah 61, we find that
He finished reading at a comma, for there in verse 2 we
read:

> "To proclaim the acceptable year of the Lord,
> and the day of vengeance of our God; to comfort all
> that mourn; to appoint unto them that mourn in
> Zion, to give unto them beauty for ashes, the oil of
> joy for mourning, the garment of praise for the
> spirit of heaviness; that they might be called trees
> of righteousness, the planting of the Lord, that he
> might be glorified" (Isaiah 61:2-3).

The remainder of the chapter speaks of the wonderful
blessing which will come to the land of Palestine and
the people of Israel in the last days.

Now when our Lord ceased reading in the middle of
verse 2, He evidently had a very definite reason for it,
and that reason is closely linked with what we have
already been considering in our study of the great prophecy of the seventy weeks. One might suppose, if he had
never considered the matter before, that the entire
prophecy of Isaiah 61 would be continuous. There is
nothing in this Old Testament passage to indicate otherwise; but by closing the book when He did, our Lord
distinguished very definitely between His ministry connected with His First Coming and that which is to take
place when He comes the second time. He ceased read-

ing as He uttered the words, "To proclaim the acceptable year of the Lord." This introduced the Gospel Era. He did not read further because the day of vengeance of our God was not due to begin at that time, and, in fact, it has not yet begun.

In other words, our Lord put the entire dispensation of the grace of God in which we live into a comma. That comma represents a period of nearly two thousand years, at least. How much more, we cannot say. Not one other part of the prophecy has been fulfilled since the Lord closed the book. When Daniel's last seventieth week begins, then the fulfillment of the rest of the prophecy will start, and soon every promise to the people of Israel will be confirmed.

The Lord Jesus came in lowly grace, preaching good tidings unto the meek. He came binding up the broken-hearted, proclaiming liberty to captives and the opening of prison to those who were bound. He preached the acceptable year of the Lord, but Israel rejected Him. They did not recognize in the lowly Nazarene the King whom they were expecting, and so they fulfilled other Scriptures in rejecting Him.

This left God free, if I may put it that way, to open up secrets that had been in His heart from before the foundation of the world, and so we have the glorious age of grace in which we live, the calling out of the Church from Jew and Gentile to be the body and bride of Christ, and to share His throne with Him in the coming age. During all this time Israel nationally is rejected. It is folly to maintain, as some do, that the British nation and kindred peoples are really Israel and that a distinction is now to be made between Israel and the Jews. Before the Assyrian and Babylonian captivities, God made this distinction, but since that time we find the terms "Jew" and "Israelite" used interchangeably. This will be seen clearly when we come to consider the great parenthetical portion of the Epistle to the Romans, chapters 9 to 11. During all this time Israel nationally is set to one side. They are "lost," as it were, among the Gentiles. Individual Israelites may be saved by grace in the same way as individual Gentiles, but God is not dealing with the chosen nation as such.

When this age comes to an end and the Church of God has been caught away to be with the Lord, then will follow the awful period of judgment so frequently referred to in the prophetic Scriptures, "the day of vengeance of our God." It will be the day when God will deal in judgment with apostate Christendom and apostate Judaism, when the vials of his wrath will be poured out upon the guilty nations who have rejected His Word, rejected His Son, and blasphemed His Holy Spirit. That day of vengeance is referred to again and again in the Scriptures under various names. It is called "the great and dreadful day of the Lord," "the time of Jacob's trouble," "the great tribulation," "the coming hour of temptation," and various other terms are also applied to it. It has nothing to do with the trials and tribulations through which the Church of God is now passing. For the Church, the entire period of her testimony here on earth is one of tribulation, even as our Lord said: "In the world ye shall have tribulation, but in me ye shall have peace." And the Apostle Paul tells us: "Ye must

through much tribulation enter the kingdom of God."
But this is to be distinguished from what is emphatically
called *the Great Tribulation,* which takes place after the
Rapture of the Church and is the time when God will
deal in wrath with the guilty nations of the world.

However, following this day of vengeance comes the
time when the Lord will comfort all that mourn. He will
return in power to Israel, and the remainder of this sixty-
first chapter of Isaiah will have its glorious fulfillment.
Note what is predicted in verses 3 to 7. In that day
Zion's mourning will be turned to joy; for the ashes of
her blighted hopes will be given the beauty of acceptance
with God. She will exchange the spirit of heaviness for
the garment of praise, and restored Israel will be called
"trees of righteousness, the planting of the Lord"; and
all this that He might be glorified.

Then will come the blessing of the land, when God's
promise to Abraham that the land should be his and in
possession of his seed forever, will be literally fulfilled.
"And they shall build the old wastes, they shall raise up
the former desolations, they shall repair the waste cities,
and the desolations of many generations shall come to
an end."

Israel will no longer be despised and hated by the
nations. The Jew will not be looked upon with contempt
and disapproval. Strangers from among the Gentiles,
sons of the alien, will delight to serve God's ancient
people who themselves will be named the priests of the
Lord, and will be recognized as the ministers of our God.
Because of all the anguish and wretchedness they have
endured throughout the centuries, they will receive in

return of the riches of the Gentiles, and will grow in the favor God shall put upon them. Verse 7 is very significant. God will make up to them in a marvelous way for all that they have endured throughout the years of their wanderings, and this in their own land, where everlasting joy shall be upon their heads.

It will be at that time that the promise given through Jeremiah will be fulfilled. In the thirty-first chapter of his prophecy, we have a corroborative passage that is linked definitely with this passage in Isaiah.

"The Lord hath appeared of old unto me, saying, Yea, I have loved thee with an everlasting love: therefore with lovingkindness have I drawn thee. Again I will build thee, and thou shalt be built, O virgin of Israel: thou shalt again be adorned with thy tabrets, and shalt go forth in the dances of them that make merry. Thou shalt yet plant vines upon the mountains of Samaria: the planters shall plant, and shall eat them as common things. For there shall be a day, that the watchmen upon the mount Ephraim shall cry, Arise ye, and let us go up to Zion unto the Lord our God. For thus saith the Lord; Sing with gladness for Jacob, and shout among the chief of the nations: publish ye, praise ye, and say, O Lord, save thy people, the remnant of Israel. Behold, I will bring them from the north country, and gather them from the coasts of the earth, and with them the blind and the lame, the woman with child and her that travaileth with child together: a great company shall return thither. They shall come with weeping, and with supplications will I lead them: I will cause them to walk by the rivers of waters in a straight way, wherein they shall not stumble: for I am a father to Israel, and Ephraim is my firstborn. Hear the word of the Lord, O ye nations, and declare it in the isles afar off. and say, He that scattered Israel will gather him, and keep him, as a shepherd doth his flock. For the Lord hath redeemed Jacob, and ransomed him from the hand of him that was stronger than he. Therefore they shall come and sing in the height of Zion, and shall flow together to the goodness of the Lord, for wheat, and for wine, and for oil, and for the young of the flock and of the herd: and their soul shall be as a watered garden; and they shall not sorrow any more at all. Then shall the virgin rejoice in the dance, both young men and old together: for I will turn their mourning into joy, and will comfort them, and make them rejoice from their sorrow. And I will satiate the soul of the priests with fatness, and my people shall be satisfied with my goodness, saith the Lord" (Jeremiah 31:3-14).

Then the new covenant will be confirmed with the house of Israel and with the house of Judah according to the promise of verses 31 through 34:

"Behold, the days come, saith the Lord, that I will make a new covenant with the house of Israel, and with the house of Judah: not according to the covenant that I made with their fathers in the day that I took them by the hand to bring them out of the land of Egypt; which my covenant they brake; although I was an husband unto them, saith the Lord: but this shall be the covenant that I will make with the house of Israel; After those days, saith the Lord, I will put my law in their inward parts, and write it in their hearts; and will be their God, and they shall be my people. And they shall teach no more every man his neighbour, and every man his brother, saying, Know the Lord: for they shall all know me, from the least of them unto the greatest of them, saith the Lord: for I will forgive their iniquity, and I will remember their sin no more" (Jeremiah 31:31-34).

This is the covenant referred to in the eighth verse of Isaiah 61, where God says: "I will direct their work in truth, and I will make an everlasting covenant with them." The closing verses of the chapter set forth the delight that God will have in His people in that day:

"And their seed shall be known among the Gentiles, and their offspring among the people: all that see them shall acknowledge them, that they are the seed which the Lord hath blessed. I will greatly rejoice in the Lord, my soul shall be joyful in my God; for he hath clothed me with the garments of salvation, he hath covered me with the robe of righteousness, as a bridegroom decketh himself with ornaments, and as a bride adorneth herself with her jewels. For as the earth bringeth forth her bud, and as the garden causeth the things that are sown in it to spring forth; so the Lord God will cause righteousness and praise to spring forth before all the nations" (Isaiah 61:9-11).

Let us suppose that we were living in Old Testament times before the First Coming of our Lord Jesus to the earth, and that we were earnest students of the prophetic Word. Imagine, for instance, that we were puzzling over this wonderful portion of Isaiah's prophecy. Could we, by any possibility, realize through reading it that there was a great parenthesis between the two clauses, "the acceptable year of our Lord," and "the day of vengeance of our God"? Daniel 9 is the key that unlocks the truth here as elsewhere, but this was not known at the time that Isaiah wrote. Therefore, we are told in the First Epistle of Peter, chapter 1, that the Old Testament prophets wrote of the coming of Christ, but were utterly unable to understand the times and the seasons connected with this glorious truth. Peter writes:

"Of which salvation the prophets have inquired and searched diligently, who prophesied of the grace that should come unto you: searching what, or what manner of time the Spirit of Christ which was in them did signify, when it testified beforehand the sufferings of Christ, and the glory that should follow. Unto whom it was revealed, that not unto themselves, but unto us they did minister the things, which are now reported unto you by them that have preached the gospel unto you with the Holy Ghost sent down from heaven; which things the angels desire to look into" (I Peter 1:10-12).

In other words, these Old Testament prophets wrote as they were borne along by the Spirit of God, and then, after putting pen to papyrus, they sat down and studied their own writings, pondering them thoughtfully, wondering just what all these marvelous promises could mean, and when they would be fulfilled. They wrote, as Peter again tells us, of the sufferings of Christ and the glories that should follow, but of the interval between the two they knew nothing.

The strange thing is that many Christians ignore it today, and by failing to recognize the importance of this Great Parenthesis, they are in continual perplexity as to the time when prophecy is to be fulfilled.

CHAPTER IV

FURTHER INSTANCES OF THE HIDDEN INTERVAL

It is not alone in one or two outstanding passages that we find the evidence of the hidden interval between the rejection of Christ and His Second advent, but when once we have recognized the break between the sixty-ninth and seventieth weeks in the time prophecy of Daniel 9, we discern the same thing in passage after passage. In this present chapter it is not my intention to go into any great detail in regard to these, but to point out a number of instances which we shall see, I believe, harmonize perfectly with what has already come before us.

Let us look again at the book of Daniel itself. Throughout that book a period is brought before us called "the time of the end," or "the latter times." When we once get the key to the meaning of this in chapter 9, then everything dovetails perfectly with what is there brought before us. In chapters 2 and 7 we have marvelous visions giving us outlines of the entire period which our Lord designated as "the times of the Gentiles." This expression covers all the years during which Israel and Palestine are under Gentile domination. The Lord said: "Jerusalem shall be trodden down of the Gentiles, until the times of the Gentiles be fulfilled." The expression "trodden down" does not necessarily imply rigorous rule or persecution, but simply that the Gentiles will be in the place of authority. This began with Nebuchadnezzar, and will continue until our Lord returns in triumph and the kingdoms of this world become the kingdom of our God and His Christ.

In Daniel 2 we have "the times of the Gentiles" represented by a great, heroic, human figure composed of gold, silver, brass, iron and clay. The four great world empires, three of which had passed away before Christ came, and the last of which was then in existence, are clearly Babylon, the head of gold; Media-Persia, the breast and arms of silver; Graeco-Macedonia, the body and thighs of brass; and Rome, the legs of iron. The last condition, however, of "the times of the Gentiles," is symbolized by the feet with ten toes, part of iron and part of miry clay or brittle pottery. It is very evident that this last condition has not yet been fully developed. It, therefore, belongs to the time of the end, and will not come into actual existence until the Church of the present age has been caught away to be with the Lord. Then there shall arise ten kingdoms on the basis of the old Roman Empire, which will form an alliance, offensive and defensive; and the prophecy says: "In the days of these kings shall the God of heaven set up a kingdom, which shall never be destroyed."

This is seen even more clearly in the seventh chapter. There, when a man of God has a vision of "the times of the Gentiles," he sees the nations as four great, ravenous beasts, so terrible that there is nothing on earth exactly like them. The last of these beasts represents, like the iron in the image, the Roman Empire, but the final condition of that empire is pictured by ten horns which, of course, correspond to the ten toes on the image.

A careful consideration of verses 23 to 27 will make this clear:

> "Thus he said, The fourth beast shall be the fourth kingdom upon earth, which shall be diverse from all kingdoms, and shall devour the whole earth, and shall tread it down, and break it in pieces. And the ten horns out of this kingdom are ten kings that shall arise: and another shall rise after them; and he shall be diverse from the first, and he shall subdue three kings. And he shall speak great words against the most High, and shall wear out the saints of the most High, and think to change times and laws: and they shall be given into his hand until a time and times and the dividing of time. But the judgment shall sit, and they shall take away his dominion, to consume and to destroy it unto the end. And the kingdom and dominion, and the greatness of the kingdom under the whole heaven, shall be given to the people of the saints of the most High, whose kingdom is an everlasting kingdom, and all dominions shall serve and obey him" (Daniel 7:23-27).

Notice that the Great Parenthesis occurs between verse 23, which pictures to us the Roman Empire as it was in the past, and verse 24, in which we have its final condition. The ten horns we are told are ten kings that shall arise. I will not go into detail here as to the conflict among the kings, resulting in the subjugation of three and the coming to the front of one who will have international authority and think to change times and laws, but I would simply emphasize the fact that this is in full accord with what we find elsewhere in Scripture, as to the manifestation of the last great Gentile ruler who will defy God Himself and seek to destroy everything that is of God in the earth, but when the judgment falls, his dominion will be taken away and then the long promised kingdom of righteousness will be set up under the whole heaven and shall be given to the people of the saints of the most High. This is a remarkable expression. It does not say it shall be given to *the saints of the most High.* The saints of the most High would be those in the heavens, but *the people of the saints of the most High* will be Israel here on earth. They shall enter into and enjoy the kingdom, for all dominions shall serve and obey Christ. Notice that the prophecy does not give us any inkling of what will take place between the rise of the fourth beast and the appearance of the ten horns. All that is included in the present age, and was unseen by prophetic eyes in Old Testament times.

This is corroborated again in chapter 8, which is largely occupied with the conflicts between Persia and Greece, but down to verse 22 we have fulfilled prophecy. Beginning with verse 23 we are carried on to the latter time of the Grecian kingdom when the transgressors are come to the full and "a king of fierce countenance, and understanding dark sentences, shall stand up." This is the last king of the north, who will be the bitter enemy of the people of Israel in the last days, and will vie with the Roman leader in attempting to dominate the land of Palestine. We are told of his activities in verses 24 and 25:

> "And his power shall be mighty, but not by his own power: and he shall destroy wonderfully, and shall prosper, and practise, and shall destroy the mighty and the holy people. And through his policy also he shall cause craft to prosper in his hand; and he shall magnify himself in his heart, and by peace shall destroy many: he shall also stand up against

the Prince of princes; but he shall be broken without hand" (Daniel 8:24-25).

I have gone into this prophecy in my book, *Lectures on the Book of Daniel*, but what I want my readers to see now is that the Great Parenthesis occurs in between verses 22 and 23. All the long period between the last state of the Grecian Empire and the latter times is passed over in silence; yet what momentous events have taken place in those centuries which have already gone!

In chapter 11 we again see the same remarkable prophetic structure. Down to verse 35 we have a marvelous outline of that which has long since been fulfilled in history — the wars between the Seleucidae and Ptolemies, culminating in the resistance and victory of the Maccabees with the assistance of the ships of Chittim, bringing the Roman legions to support the Jewish nationalists. The moral conditions prevailing for a century or more afterwards are given to us in verses 32 to 35, the last verse reading as follows:

> "And some of them of understanding shall fall, to try them, and to purge, and to make them white, even to the time of the end: because it is yet for a time appointed" (Daniel 11:35).

That is, Israel will suffer under Gentile domination until their miseries will be brought to a head and to a conclusion in the time of the end.

The entire present dispensation comes in between verses 35 and 36, the thirty-sixth verse introducing immediately the willful king, the Antichrist of the last days, who will do according to his own will, and exalt himself, and magnify himself above every god, and speak marvelous things against the God of gods, and prosper until the indignation be accomplished, that is, until the vials of the wrath of God have all been poured out upon the earth. The remainder of the chapter has to do with events which will be fulfilled in the last half of the seventieth week of chapter 9, and when we pass into chapter 12, we have the Great Tribulation in all its intensity, followed by Israel's awakening and reward in the Kingdom Age.

The book of Hosea contains moral instruction for the people of Israel designed to awaken them to a recognition of their sad departure from God, so that in the main it does not deal with future events. But there are some remarkable passages in this little book in which we find the same structure that we have been considering. In the earlier verses of chapter 3 we have Jehovah's love for Israel and her unfaithfulness. Then verse 4 is really a description of her condition throughout the entire present parenthetic age. We read:

> "For the children of Israel shall abide many days without a king, and without a prince, and without a sacrifice, and without an image, and without an ephod, and without teraphim" (Hosea 3:4).

We have no details here as to the great historical events that would take place during the long period of Israel's rejection by God following their rejection of Messiah, but in a few graphic sentences we note the things of which they would be deprived.

Verse 5 carries us into the last days:

> "Afterward" (that is, after the long parenthetic period during which they are wandering among the

> nations) "shall the children of Israel return, and seek the Lord their God, and David their king; and shall fear the Lord and his goodness in the latter days" (Hosea 3:5).

The parenthetic interval is found again between the last verse of chapter 5 and the first verse of chapter 6. In verse 15 of chapter 5 we hear Messiah Himself speaking, after His own people have refused to recognize Him. He says:

> "I will go and return to my place, till they acknowledge their offense, and seek my face: in their affliction they will seek me early" (Hosea 5:15).

The first part of this verse was fulfilled literally when the Lord Jesus ascended to heaven. There He has taken His place at the Father's right hand, and He waits until Israel will be brought to recognize their sins and to call upon Him in repentance. But nearly two thousand years have passed since our Lord returned to the Father's house. Meantime Israel remains an unbelieving generation, as the Lord Himself predicted they would, but as soon as the present interval has passed and the Church of God has been caught up to be with the Lord, they themselves will begin to fulfill the opening verses of chapter 6:

> "Come, and let us return unto the Lord: for he hath torn, and he will heal us; he hath smitten, and he will bind us up. After two days will he revive us: in the third day he will raise us up, and we shall live in his sight. Then shall we know, if we follow on to know the Lord: his going forth is prepared as the morning; and he shall come unto us as the rain, as the latter and former rain unto the earth" (Hosea 6:1-3).

This will be the day of Israel's repentance. If we remember Peter's words that one day is with the Lord as a thousand years and a thousand years as one day, there may be something more significant in the expressions used in verse 2 than some of us have realized. I do not for a moment favor any date-setting system, and yet one may well raise the question as to whether the two days of that verse might not have reference to the two thousand years of Israel's rejection, and the third day speak of the thousand years of Christ's reign in righteousness.

When we turn to the book of Psalms, we find many similar passages setting forth in juxtaposition the sufferings of Christ and the glories that shall follow. To attempt to point them all out would mean to write a book on the Messianic Psalms, but I would draw attention here to several of them, and the thoughtful reader who searches the Scriptures in dependence upon the Spirit of God will have no difficulty in finding many more.

Psalm 22 has well been called "the Psalm of the Cross" or "the Psalm of the Sin Offering." It begins with our Lord's cry of abandonment: "My God, my God, why hast thou forsaken me?" It ends, if the last words are literally translated, in a cry of triumph: "It is finished." In verses 1 to 21 we have our Lord's sufferings on the cross. Verse 22 tells of His resurrection and His appearance among His own. The Great Parenthesis occurs between verses 22 and 23, for throughout the remainder of the Psalm we have set forth the coming of the kingdom and the deliverance of Israel, based upon that which our Lord endured in His hours of anguish on the tree.

Psalm 110 is frequently referred to in the New Testament, and is recognized by all instructed readers as being definitely Messianic. In the first verse we see our risen, glorified Lord taking His place at the right hand of God. Then comes the prophetic interval for which we have been looking, and following that from verse 2 to the end of the Psalm we have the return of the Lord in power and the establishment of His kingdom on Mount Zion.

I take time to refer to only one other Psalm, and that because of the striking way in which it is used by the Apostle Peter in the New Testament. In I Peter 3:10-12, the Apostle quotes from Psalm 34:12-16:

> "For he that will love life, and see good days, let
> him refrain his tongue from evil, and his lips that
> they speak no guile: let him eschew evil, and do
> good; let him seek peace, and ensue it. For the eyes
> of the Lord are over the righteous, and his ears are
> open unto their prayers: but the face of the Lord is
> against them that do evil" (I Peter 3:10-12).

Now observe how Peter ends his quotation. He says: "The face of the Lord is against them that do evil." Just as Christ Himself stopped reading from Isaiah 61 at a comma, so does the Apostle here, for when we turn back to Psalm 34 we find the complete statement reads: "The face of the Lord is against them that do evil, to cut off the remembrance of them from the earth" (Psalm 34:16). Why did Peter stop in the middle of the sentence? Because, guided by the Holy Spirit, he recognized that the time had not yet come for God to cut off the wicked in judgment from the earth. In other words, he left room for the present age of the times of the

Gentiles to come in between the two parts of the last half of this verse.

To these instances might be added, as I have already intimated, many others; but I trust that these are sufficient to prove the point I am trying to make, namely, that the prophetic Scriptures cannot be understood properly unless this parenthetic period is taken into account, but when once it is seen and recognized as the divine order in God's revelation to mankind, all becomes luminously clear.

CHAPTER V

OUR LORD'S GREAT PROPHECY

In the light of what we have been considering, let us turn now to our Lord's great prophecy uttered on the Mount of Olives shortly before His crucifixion. We find this prophecy recorded in the three Synoptics, namely, in Matthew 24, Mark 13, and Luke 21. It will help us to understand these words aright if we remember that they were uttered just as the sixty-ninth week of Daniel 9 had come to a close. As yet the disciples knew nothing of the long interval that was to elapse ere the seventieth week would be fulfilled. They had already understood to some extent, and yet very feebly, that their Master was about to suffer and to die, but not until after His resurrection did they really comprehend what He meant when He told them that the Son of Man was to be crucified and the third day rise again. They were in the position of a godly Jewish remnant waiting expectantly for the manifestation of the kingdom. They had this and this only in mind when they asked the question: "Tell us, when shall these things be? and what shall be the sign of thy coming, and of the end of the age?"

I take it that most of my readers are well aware of the fact that the expression, "end of the world," as given in the Authorized Version is somewhat misleading. The marginal reading is correct. The end of the age, they knew, would be at the close of the seventieth week, and they were asking the Lord definitely how they might know when that time was about to expire. This is corroborated when we turn to Acts 1, and find these same disciples inquiring of the risen Lord: "Wilt thou at this time restore again the kingdom to Israel?" All their expectations were centered in that kingdom. They knew nothing of the present interval which we speak of as "the dispensation of the grace of God." The mystery of the Church, the one body, had not yet been revealed. Though our Lord had spoken on two occasions of the Church, as recorded in Matthew 16 and again in chapter 18, it is evident that this did not mean to them anything more than the congregation of the righteous. The full revelation of what was in the Lord's mind was to be given later.

In answer to their question, the Saviour did not reprove them because they interpreted Old Testament prophecies literally and looked for an earthly kingdom to be set up at the end of the age, but He told them: "It is not for you to know the times and the seasons which the Father hath put in his own power. But ye shall receive power, after that the Holy Ghost is come upon you, and ye shall be witnesses unto me both in Jerusalem and in all Judaea, and in Samaria and unto the uttermost parts of the earth." What all this implied they did not at first understand. Doubtless He explained many things to them during the forty days between His resurrection and His ascension, as intimated in Acts 1:2-3, but His program for this age was unfolded little by little until the full revelation of the dispensation of the mystery of the one body was given to the Apostle Paul and through him imparted to others.

So then, as we consider Matthew 24, we should try
to put ourselves in the place in which the Apostles were
at that time in order that we may get their mental attitude and understand what it was concerning which they
asked Him; then we shall understand His answer.

He knew that Israel's day was over for that time. He
had already said to them, "Your house is left unto you
desolate." When the disciples looked admiringly upon
the great buildings of the Temple and its surroundings
and exclaimed, "Master, see what great buildings are
here," He replied, "There shall not be left here one stone
upon another, that shall not be thrown down." This must
have amazed them, for they doubtless supposed that in
a very little while He would proclaim Himself as King-
Messiah and that that very Temple would be the center
of Jehovah's worship when the King should reign in
Zion.

And so they asked in surprise for information regarding three things. First, "Tell us, when shall these things
be?" that is, "When will Jerusalem be destroyed? When
will the Temple be thrown down?" We do not get the
answer to that in Matthew 24. When we turn to Luke
21, verses 20 to 24, we find that question fully answered.
Christ's words are as follows:

> "And when ye shall see Jerusalem compassed with
> armies, then know that the desolation thereof is nigh.
> Then let them which are in Judaea flee to the moun-
> tains; and let them which are in the midst of it depart
> out; and let not them that are in the countries enter
> thereinto. For these be the days of vengeance, that
> all things which are written may be fulfilled. But
> woe unto them that are with child, and to them that
> give suck, in those days: for there shall be great dis-

tress in the land, and wrath upon this people. And they shall fall by the edge of the sword, and shall be led away captive into all nations: and Jerusalem shall be trodden down of the Gentiles, until the times of the Gentiles be fulfilled" (Luke 21:20-24).

The second and the third questions are intimately linked together. The disciples inquired, "What shall be the sign of thy coming, and of the end of the age?" They rightly linked Messiah's manifested presence in and to Israel with the end of the age. It is this double question that the Lord answers in the words recorded in Matthew 24 and in the last part of Luke 21, as also in Mark 13. In other words, let us bear in mind that our Lord was not giving His apostles an outline picture of what would take place during the past nearly two thousand years, the great interval between His First and Second Comings. He was speaking to them as to a Jewish remnant who were waiting for the kingdom, who knew that sixty-nine weeks of Daniel's prophecy of the times and the seasons had expired, and who were concerned as to the fulfillment of the brief period that was left and the ushering in of the kingdom. In verses 4 to 8 we have what in a general way covers this entire dispensation:

"And Jesus answered and said unto them, Take heed that no man deceive you. For many shall come in my name, saying, I am Christ; and shall deceive many. And ye shall hear of wars and rumors of wars: see that ye be not troubled; for all these things must come to pass, but the end is not yet. For nation shall rise against nation, and kingdom against kingdom: and there shall be famines, and pestilences, and earthquakes, in divers places. All these are the beginning of sorrows" (Matthew 24:4-8).

But these will be the actual conditions prevailing in the first part of Daniel's seventieth week, for the Great Tribulation in its intensity occupies only the last three and one-half years, or 1,260 days. The first half, or forty-two months, will be taken up with providential judgments leading up to that awful hour of trial. At first the distress on earth will be occasioned by the disrupted condition of things when, following the Rapture of the Church, God once more takes up Israel, and the Gentile nations will be in turmoil and conflict. This will be followed by a time of great testing for the remnant of Israel, who will be called out in that day to be God's witnesses in the earth. It is particularly to these that verses 9 to 14 apply:

> "Then shall they deliver you up to be afflicted, and shall kill you: and ye shall be hated of all nations for my name's sake. And then shall many be offended, and shall betray one another, and shall hate one another. And many false prophets shall rise, and shall deceive many. And because iniquity shall abound, the love of many shall wax cold. But he that shall endure unto the end, the same shall be saved. And this gospel of the kingdom shall be preached in all the world for a witness unto all nations; and then shall the end come" (Matthew 24:9-14).

Notice that He speaks here of the good news which these Jewish messengers are to carry throughout the world, called distinctively "the gospel of the kingdom." There is, of course, only one Gospel, but that Gospel presents different aspects at different times. The Gospel is God's message concerning His blessed Son. It was proclaimed in the Garden of Eden when God declared: "The seed of the woman shall bruise the serpent's head."

It was preached to Abraham when He said: "In thy seed shall all the nations of the earth be blessed." The Old Testament prophets were Gospel preachers as they told of the coming Messiah. When John the Baptist appeared, his voice rang out, proclaiming: "Repent ye: for the kingdom of heaven is at hand." On the other hand, let us never forget that it was also John the Baptist who preached the Gospel of grace when he said, "I saw and bear record that this is the Son of God. Behold the Lamb of God, which taketh away the sin of the world." The Lord Jesus went about proclaiming the Gospel of the kingdom. He presented Himself to Israel as God's King, but they refused Him. Then He turned to the weary multitudes and said, "Come unto me, all ye that labour and are heavy laden, and I will give you rest." And we must not forget that though John's Gospel was written several decades later than the Synoptics, yet it records the preaching and teaching of our blessed Lord in regard to the Gospel of grace while He was going about through the land of Palestine proclaiming the kingdom.

Here in Matthew 24 we have no apparent break in the testimony. If we can understand that the Great Parenthesis comes in between our Lord's rejection and the beginning of the fulfillment of this Olivet Discourse, everything will be clear. In that day of trial, God will raise up a special testimony in Israel even as we are told in the book of Daniel. "They that be wise shall shine as the brightness of the firmament; and they that turn many to righteousness as the stars for ever and ever . . . Many shall be purified, and made white, and tried;

but the wicked shall do wickedly: and none of the wicked shall understand; but the wise shall understand" (Daniel 12:3, 10). These wise ones in Israel will proclaim the Gospel of the kingdom. Their witness will go on until all nations have heard the testimony. Then the final end of the age will come.

In writing as I have done, I trust no one will misuse the truth which I am here seeking to present by endeavoring to excuse themselves from present missionary activity on the ground that it will be Israel's business to proclaim the Gospel of the kingdom in a coming day. Our Lord seems to have purposely led Mark to record His saying a little differently. In Mark 13:10 we read: "And the gospel must first be published among all nations." This is a very broad statement, and we know from what the Spirit of God afterwards revealed that it is our responsibility to carry the Gospel everywhere during this intervening period before Israel's remnant testimony will be given to the people of the end-times.

Verse 15 of our chapter brings us to the midst of the week and introduces the last three and one-half dreadful years. Notice our Lord's words:

> "When ye therefore shall see the abomination of desolation, spoken of by Daniel the prophet, stand in the holy place, (whoso readeth, let him understand:) then let them which be in Judaea flee into the mountains: let him which is on the housetop not come down to take anything out of his house: neither let him which is in the field return back to take his clothes. And woe unto them that are with child, and to them that give suck in those days! But pray ye that your flight be not in the winter, neither on the sabbath day: for then shall be great tribulation, such

as was not since the beginning of the world to this time, no, nor ever shall be. And except those days should be shortened, there should no flesh be saved: but for the elect's sake those days shall be shortened. Then if any man shall say unto you, Lo, here is Christ, or there; believe it not. For there shall arise false Christs, and false prophets, and shall shew great signs and wonders; insomuch that, if it were possible, they shall deceive the very elect. Behold, I have told you before. Wherefore if they shall say unto you, Behold, he is in the desert; go not forth: behold, he is in the secret chambers; believe it not" (Matthew 24:15-26).

The abomination of desolation spoken of here is not to be confounded with the transgression of desolation of Daniel 8:13. That had to do with the polluting of the Sanctuary by the setting up of an idol in the Holy Place in the days of Antiochus Epiphanes, but this reference is to Daniel 12:11-12:

"And from the time that the daily sacrifice shall be taken away, and the abomination that maketh desolate set up, there shall be a thousand two hundred and ninety days. Blessed is he that waiteth, and cometh to the thousand three hundred and five and thirty days" (Daniel 12:11-12).

That is, the setting up of the abomination of desolation, whatever its full meaning may be, will be the signal for the remnant of the latter days, to let them know that in 1,260 days the Great Tribulation will be over, and in thirty days more the new order of things will have come in. The additional time, bringing the waiting period up to 1,335 days, may have to do with the reinstitution of Jehovah's worship in Jerusalem. These verses we have quoted above have nothing to do

with the destruction of Jerusalem in the past, as one
may see by comparing them with Luke 21, but they
describe a future siege of Jerusalem, when the Roman
prince and the Antichrist have been manifested. Then
shall be great tribulation such as was not since the
beginning of the world, no, nor ever shall be. Then
Satan will raise up false Christs and false prophets to
seek to deceive the waiting remnant, but the Lord has
forewarned them not to believe the lying testimonies of
Satan-inspired leaders in that day.

His Coming will be in manifested glory at the close
of the tribulation period, as we read in verses 27 to 31.

> "For as the lightning cometh out of the east, and
> shineth even unto the west; so shall also the coming
> of the Son of man be. For wheresoever the carcass is,
> there will the eagles be gathered together. Immedi-
> ately after the tribulation of those days shall the
> sun be darkened, and the moon shall not give her
> light, and the stars shall fall from heaven, and the
> powers of the heavens shall be shaken: and then shall
> appear the sign of the Son of man in heaven: and
> then shall all the tribes of the earth mourn, and they
> shall see the Son of man coming in the clouds of
> heaven with power and great glory. And he shall
> send his angels with a great sound of a trumpet, and
> they shall gather together his elect from the four
> winds, from one end of heaven to the other" (Mat-
> thew 24:27-31).

I am not attempting a careful exegesis of this chapter,
but am merely drawing attention to its broad outlines.
A few things, however, should be noticed before leaving
it. The twenty-eighth verse evidently refers to the city
of Jerusalem which will be the carcass in that day, and
against it the eagles, or "vultures," the carrion-devouring

armies of the nations, will be gathered. There will be portentious signs in the heavens when the Son of Man appears in glory. The tribes of the land will mourn, as Zechariah has foretold in his twelfth chapter, And men will "see the Son of man coming in the clouds of heaven with power and great glory." This is something altogether different from the Rapture of the Church as portrayed in I Corinthians 15 and in I Thessalonians 4. There is no gathering of saints to Him in the heavens here, but He sends forth His angels with the great sound of a trumpet, and they gather His elect together from the four winds, from one end of heaven to the other. These are not the heavenly saints but the earthly elect, the 144,000 of Israel and the great number of redeemed Gentiles as set forth in Revelation 7. They will be gathered to Christ Himself when He appears in Jerusalem and His feet stand upon the Mount of Olives, before His foes are dealt with in judgment.

It will not be necessary for our present purpose to pursue the further study of this chapter, interesting as it is. The inquiring reader can find many excellent helps if he desires to go into the matter carefully.* My object has been simply to show that the key to our Lord's prophecy is the ninth chapter of the book of Daniel. The Great Parenthesis there indicated, if taken into account when reading this remarkable chapter, makes everything perfectly plain.

* I am glad to recommend three excellent books on the Gospel of Matthew: *Lectures on Matthew*, by William Kelly, and the expositions by Dr. A. C. Gaebelein and Dr. E. Schuyler English. Any of these will prove helpful to the student of prophecy who desires a careful explanation of this portion of the Word.

CHAPTER VI

THE FIRST CHURCH COUNCIL;
THE PARENTHESIS RECOGNIZED
BY THE APOSTLES

Acts 15 is the great dispensational chapter of that book. It occupies a unique place in the New Testament, and is a very distinct help in the understanding of God's present work of grace and His future plans for Israel and the world.

When Paul returned to Antioch at the conclusion of his first missionary journey, we are told that the whole Church was gathered together, to whom he and Barnabas "rehearsed all that God had done with them, and how he had opened the door of faith unto the Gentiles" (Acts 14:27). For some time afterwards they continued in that same city, teaching and enjoying the fellowship of the saints, but soon a discordant note was introduced, destroying the spiritual harmony which up to that time had prevailed.

We are told in the first verse of chapter 15: "And certain men which came down from Judaea taught the brethren, and said, Except ye be circumcised after the manner of Moses, ye cannot be saved." It is evident that these men maintained they acted under apostolic authority and were the official representatives of the Church at Jerusalem. They were evidently rigid Jews of the Pharisaic type who had professed conversion to Christ and had been identified with the churches in

56

Judaea. Having only the Old Testament, they based all their conclusions upon it. We need to remember, in order not to judge them too harshly, that so far as we have definite information, not one book of the New Testament had yet been written. There is a bare possibility that Matthew or Mark or perhaps both might be exceptions to this, but of that we have no proof. When these brethren or others referred to the Scriptures, it was necessarily the Old Testament which they had in mind. From the Old Testament they learned that God had made a covenant of grace with Abraham, had promised that all nations would be blessed through his Seed, and had given the ordinance of circumcision as the outward sign that was to separate the covenant people from the rest of the world.

Of course, from the beginning the apostles had taught, as Peter did, the setting aside of the nation of Israel because of their rejection of Messiah, and called upon those who trusted Him to separate themselves by baptism from the apostate part of the nation, and thus save themselves from that untoward generation and the judgment soon to fall upon it; but we can well understand that many Jewish believers might not have grasped the full implication of this, nor have recognized the fact that God was doing an altogether new thing not predicted in Old Testament times.

There is, therefore, no reason to question the sincerity of these Judaean emissaries who doubtless thought that Paul and Barnabas were playing fast and loose with the divine order in not insisting that the Gentile believers accept the sign of the Abrahamic covenant and thus identify themselves with the remnant of the chosen people.

There was evidently considerable discussion in the Antiochian Church regarding the whole matter, as a result of which Paul and Barnabas were asked to go with some others directly to Jerusalem and confer there with the apostles and elders about this question. As they made their way toward their appointed destination, they passed through Phenice and Samaria, declaring whenever they came in contact with Christian assemblies how God had wrought in power in converting the heathen from among the Gentiles. The news of this brought great joy, we are told, unto all the brethren. It is evident that the questions raised by the men from Judæa had not come before these churches as they made no mention of bringing such demands to bear upon the young converts, but simply rejoiced in what God had done for them.

In verse 4 we are told that "when they were come to Jerusalem, they were received of the church, and of the apostles and elders, and they declared all things that God had done with them." This was evidently in a large open meeting where a great number of the Jerusalem Christians gathered together to receive them and to welcome them in their midst. In this meeting no doctrinal matters or questions of ceremonial observances were discussed until after Paul and Barnabas had given their testimony to the way in which God had wrought through their ministry to the Gentiles. After this we are told: "There rose up certain of the sect of the Pharisees which believed, saying, That it was needful to circumcise them,

and to command them to keep the law of Moses."
These men, like the others who had appeared at Antioch,
felt sure of their ground for they could appeal directly
to Old Testament Scripture, and they took it for granted
that God was now doing what He had promised to do
through the prophets, that is, to give the knowledge of
His salvation to the Gentiles, but that they would receive
blessing through Israel and would be united to them as
children of the covenant by taking upon them the outward sign to which they referred. See Isaiah 56:6;
60:3-5; Zech. 8:23, to which many other passages might
be added.

Apparently the leaders decided not to debate the
question at that time nor to attempt to handle it in a large
open meeting, for in verse 6 we read: "The apostles and
elders came together for to consider of this matter."
This would be much wiser, of course, than putting the
question up to the entire body of believers, many of
whom would have a very imperfect understanding of the
Gospel itself and a very slight knowledge of the Holy
Scriptures. The apostles appointed by the Lord Jesus
to carry the message into all the world and those who
had been selected as elders to guide the affairs of the
local churches met in council with Paul and Barnabas
and their associates to go into the matter dispassionately
and carefully.

We can see, as we read on, that even these brethren
were not of one mind, for we are told that there was
"much disputing." How long this went on we do not
know, but eventually the Apostle Peter took the floor

and reminded them how God had in a very clear and definite way sent him to the Gentiles in the house of Cornelius, but that there had then been no commandment to circumcise the believers or to put them under the yoke of the law of Moses. I quote Peter's address in full so far as we have it here. Doubtless verses 7 to 11 give us but an abbreviation of what he presented to the assembled company:

> "Men and brethren, ye know how that a good while ago God made choice among us, that the Gentiles by my mouth should hear the word of the gospel, and believe. And God, which knoweth the hearts, bare them witness, giving them the Holy Ghost, even as he did unto us; and put no difference between us and them, purifying their hearts by faith. Now therefore why tempt ye God, to put a yoke upon the neck of the disciples, which neither our fathers nor we were able to bear? But we believe that through the grace of the Lord Jesus Christ we shall be saved, even as they" (Acts 15:7-11).

Observe how carefully the Apostle Peter presented his case. It was God who had chosen him to go to the Gentiles, that through his lips they should hear the word of the Gospel and put their trust in the Lord Jesus Christ. As he was preaching, Cornelius and his household believed the message, and immediately God, who reads the hearts, recognized their faith and gave them the Holy Spirit in the same way in which He gave it to the one hundred and twenty of Israel on the day of Pentecost. The fact that these were uncircumcised Gentiles and that those were circumcised Jews made no difference whatever to God. It was the state of the heart upon which He looked, and so Peter insists that He did not distinguish between the two groups, but purified their hearts by faith, that is, regenerated them when they believed the Gospel. If this satisfied God, why should it not satisfy the Jewish Christians? Were they not tempting God when they sought now to put the yoke of the law upon the neck of these young believers from among the Gentiles, a yoke which they themselves, as Jews, had always found burdensome?

Then Peter closes in a remarkable way. He says: "We believe that through the grace of the Lord Jesus Christ we shall be saved, even as they." We might well expect that he would have turned it completely around. He might have said: "We believe that they shall be saved even as we"; but he does not do that. He declares that the Jews, despite all their privileges, are to be saved on the same basis of pure grace as idolatrous or philosophical Gentiles who put their trust in the Lord Jesus Christ.

This was evidently so convincing that the legalists were nonplused and for the moment knew not how to reply. Taking advantage of the silence, Barnabas and Paul, one after the other, addressed the audience. Note that Barnabas came first in this case as he was well known to the Jerusalem Christians and was highly esteemed for his godliness and righteous life. Paul, who was doubtless more or less under suspicion on the part of some, followed. Both gave the same marvelous testimony to the mighty wonder-working power of God as He wrought among the Gentiles. In this they corroborated the testimony given by Peter.

We can imagine the rigid Pharisaic Christian Jews silenced but unconvinced. In their own minds they would be saying, "But we have the Word of God on our side. Regardless of the remarkable experiences Peter and Barnabas and Paul can relate, it is very definitely stated in Scripture that those whom God recognizes as His covenant people are to be marked out from the rest of the world by the covenant sign. Moreover, who has been authorized to set aside the commands of the Law, a Law given by God Himself when He appeared to Moses on Sinai?" They knew, of course, that there were many promises in the Old Testament of blessing for the Gentiles. They knew that the day was yet to come when all the nations of the world would recognize in the Lord Jesus Christ God's King, but when that day came, Israel was to have the pre-eminent place. There was no proof that God's attitude would be changed in regard to the matters in question. The presumption was that all the Gentiles would in a certain sense become as Jews when together they should all enjoy the blessings of Messiah's reign. Yet these brethren must have been puzzled to explain the way in which God was now working among the Gentiles and His apparent indifference regarding what to them seemed so important.

James, however, had the key to the entire situation. We have a brief outline of his speech given in verses 13 to 21:

"Men and brethren, hearken unto me: Simeon hath declared how God at the first did visit the Gentiles, to take out of them a people for his name. And to this agree the words of the prophets; as it is written,

After this I will return, and will build again the tabernacle of David, which is fallen down; and I will build again the ruins thereof, and I will set it up: that the residue of men might seek after the Lord, and all the Gentiles, upon whom my name is called, saith the Lord, who doeth all these things. Known unto God are all his works from the beginning of the world. Wherefore my sentence is, that we trouble not them, which from among the Gentiles are turned to God: but that we write unto them, that they abstain from pollutions of idols, and from fornication, and from things strangled, and from blood. For Moses of old time hath in every city them that preach him, being read in the synagogues every sabbath day" (Acts 15:13-21).

He refers to what Peter had already told them, but he uses an expression which is of great interest to us, and was indeed the explanation to the present work of grace. "God," he says, "at the first did visit the Gentiles, to take out of them a people for his name." Now this is not the conversion of the Gentiles as predicted in the Old Testament. The taking out of a people, instead of the conversion of the nations as such, was something very different from that revealed by the prophets. This spoke of a special election from among the Gentiles and that doubtless for a particular purpose. This is the work that God is doing now. While the messengers of the Gospel are to carry it to all nations, God's present object is not the conversion of the nations through this testimony but that all men may have an opportunity to come to Christ if they will, but He who knows the end from the beginning has foreseen the fact that only a small number comparatively would actually receive the message in faith, and trust the Lord Jesus Christ as their

Saviour. This company is designated throughout the book of Acts as the Church of God, and of the Church of God as such we hear nothing in the Old Testament prophecies.

But now observe how James harmonizes the present work of God in taking an elect people out from among the nations and the prophecies of the conversion of all the nations in some future day. He refers his hearers to the prophecy of Amos as recorded in chapter 9, verses 11 and 12: "After this I will return." This is not exactly the way Amos wrote it, but James is quoting from the Septuagint, and he recognizes the correctness of the expression. "After this," that is, after the present work of God in taking a people out from among the nations is concluded, Messiah will return again. Then when He comes back He will build once more the Tabernacle of David which has been for so long set aside. He will raise up the throne of David again and fulfill the prophecies made to that man after His own heart. It will be in that day that the residue will seek after the Lord and all the Gentiles upon whom His Name will then be called.

This made everything clear. James, you see, recognized and explained the Great Parenthesis in God's dealings with Israel. He showed that the Church of God had been called out and was bearing its witness in that parenthetic period. When it shall come to a close, the Lord will return again and fulfill all the prophecies connected with Israel's restoration and the salvation of the nations of the world. And so he exclaims, "Known unto God are all his works from the beginning of the world."

God is working according to a plan, and that plan was partly unfolded in Old Testament times, but now has been fully made known. In the light of the revelation thus given, James suggested that no further pressure should be brought upon the Gentiles to make them conform to Jewish rites or ceremonies, but that they should be called upon simply to abstain from the evils connected with idolatry, from the immorality that was so common among the nations, and from unclean foods which to their Jewish brethren were abhorrent. If any of the Gentile believers wished to know more of the teachings of the Law, they could easily find enlightenment, for in virtually every city there were synagogues in which the Law of Moses was read and taught, and any who desired could go in to hear.

This settled the matter at least for the present, and a letter was drawn up and sent out to the Gentiles to put their minds at rest regarding the teaching of the legalists who were seeking to turn them away from their liberty in Christ. We have the letter given in verses 23 to 29:

"And they wrote letters by them after this manner; The apostles and elders and brethren send greeting unto the brethren which are of the Gentiles in Antioch and Syria and Cilicia: Forasmuch as we have heard, that certain which went out from us have troubled you with words, subverting your souls, saying, Ye must be circumcised, and keep the law: to whom we gave no such commandment: it seemed good unto us, being assembled with one accord, to send chosen men unto you with our beloved Barnabas and Paul, men that have hazarded their lives for the name of our Lord Jesus Christ. We have sent therefore Judas and Silas, who shall also tell you the same things

by mouth. For it seemed good to the Holy Ghost,
and to us, to lay upon you no greater burden than
these necessary things; that ye abstain from meats
offered to idols, and from blood, and from things
strangled, and from fornication: from which if ye
keep yourselves, ye shall do well. Fare ye well"
(Acts 15:23-29).

It must have been with great joy and light hearts that
Barnabas and Paul and their companions left Jerusalem
and returned to Antioch. The truth for which they had
been contending for so long was now acknowledged by
the brethren at Jerusalem, and they could go on preaching with the full assurance that their testimony was en-
dorsed by those who had been in Christ before them.
They immediately gathered the C h u r c h together, to
whom the letter was read, and all rejoiced for the consolation that it brought. It is true that later on further
trouble developed, because legalism is a form of leaven,
and it is in the nature of leaven to work; and so we have
the Epistle to the Galatians, written to Gentile believers
some years later in order to counteract the contentious
propaganda of certain Jews who still insisted on pressing
upon the Gentiles the necessity of conforming to the Law
of Moses. That letter is in itself the very best answer
to legality of every description.

The pitiable thing is that in the centuries that have
elapsed since, the Judaizing of the Church has gone on in
an amazing way until in many places the Gospel of the
grace of God is looked upon as though it were a strange
new heresy, whereas the effort of men to procure justification by human merit and sanctification by attention to
religious rites and ceremonies is accepted as the ortho-

dox position. It only shows how hard it is for these poor hearts of ours to abide in the truth of the grace of God. We so readily seek some other ground of approach to God and fitness for His presence than that of pure, unadulterated grace as set forth in the work of our Lord Jesus Christ and the purifying power of the Holy Spirit. One great reason for this is that so many fail to differentiate between the covenant of works given at Sinai and the grace of God as revealed in the Lord Jesus Christ. We read in John 1, verse 17: "The law was given by Moses, but grace and truth came by Jesus Christ." That Law, Paul tells us in the Galatian letter, was a child-leader designed to guide the steps of the people of God in the days of their nonage until Christ Himself should come. Now that He has come there is no further need of the child-leader, but all that is required both for justification and sanctification is found in the risen Christ, who, of God "is made unto us wisdom, and righteousness, sanctification and redemption" (I Cor. 1:30).

Chapter VII

THE PARENTHETICAL PERIOD IN ISRAEL'S ECCLESIASTICAL YEAR

Before going on to examine the parenthetical part of the Epistle to the Romans which deals with God's past, present and future ways with Israel, there is another Old Testament Scripture to which we should turn our attention for further corroboration of the undisclosed present period which we have been considering.

In the twenty-third chapter of the book of Leviticus we have the feasts or "set times" of Jehovah. This chapter has well been called Israel's ecclesiastical year, using the term "ecclesiastical" in the sense in which it is often used today as designating the special festivals of the professing Church. So far as Christians are concerned, the Word of God does not indicate any such festivals for their observance, and the more we make of them the more we are likely to come under the censure of the Apostle to the Gentiles as set forth in the Epistle to the Galatians: "Ye observe days, and months, and times, and years. I am afraid of you, lest I have bestowed upon you labour in vain" (Galatians 4:10-11).

But with Israel it was otherwise. In the legal dispensation God Himself appointed certain weekly and annual festivals which were to be faithfully observed during all that dispensation, and each of which had a typical significance. In the third verse of this twenty-

third chapter of Leviticus we have the "sabbath of rest,"
which is called a "holy convocation," in which no work
was to be done.   This, of course, was the weekly "set
time" and was observed with a double purpose. First,
it was a recognition of Jehovah's creation rest as indicated in Exodus 20, verses 8 to 11:

> "Remember the sabbath day, to keep it holy. Six
> days shalt thou labour, and do all thy work: but the
> seventh day is the sabbath of the Lord thy God: in
> it thou shalt not do any work, thou, nor thy son,
> nor thy daughter, thy manservant, nor thy maidser-
> vant, nor thy cattle, nor thy stranger that is within
> thy gates: for in six days the Lord made heaven and
> earth, the sea, and all that in them is, and rested
> the seventh day: wherefore the Lord blessed the sab-
> bath day, and hallowed it" (Exodus 20:8-11).

Then in Deuteronomy 5, where we have the reitera-
tion of the Ten Commandments, another reason is given
for the observance of the Sabbath. We read in verse
15: "And remember that thou wast a servant in the
land of Egypt, and that the Lord thy God brought thee
out thence through a mighty hand and by a stretched out
arm: therefore the Lord thy God commanded thee to
keep the sabbath day." This second reason makes one
thing very definite, namely, that the Ten Commandments
as such were never given to the Gentiles but solely to
Israel, the covenant people. Of course, when the Gentiles became familiar with them, it was their responsibility to maintain the high moral standards there set
forth, but nowhere are we told that the Sabbath was a
sign of God's covenant with the nations.

It had both a backward and a forward aspect. Looking forward, it typified the rest that remains for the
people of God, a Sabbath Rest which will be enjoyed
eternally by all who know Christ as Saviour, as indicated in Hebrews 4, verses 4 to 9.

The reason that the Sabbath occupies the first place
in this list of the feasts of Jehovah is because God's
first thought for mankind is His last. He has ever had
before Him the time when in the new heavens and the
new earth He will dwell with His people in a condition
of perfection, after all the varied experiences through
which men shall pass during their sojourn in this world.

In verse 4 we read: "These are the feasts of the Lord,
even holy convocations, which ye shall proclaim in their
seasons." The word *feasts* here is somewhat misleading. We think of a feast as a time of merriment and en-
joyment, possibly even as an occasion when we regale
ourselves with toothsome viands; but no such thought
is necessarily connected with the word used here. It
would be better to translate it "set times" or "appointed
seasons," because some of these so-called feasts were
actually fasts, when the people were to refrain from food
and drink as they meditated upon their sins and transgressions. They were, however, definite, appointed
seasons to be observed from year to year.

As we read through the chapter, we notice that three
of these "set times" were to be observed in the spring of
the year, and all of these were types of great events
which have already had a glorious fulfillment. First we
are told:

"In the fourteenth day of the first month at even
is the Lord's passover. And on the fifteenth day of
the same month is the feast of unleavened bread unto
the Lord: seven days ye must eat unleavened bread.
In the first day ye shall have an holy convocation: ye
shall do no servile work therein. But ye shall offer
an offering made by fire unto the Lord seven days:
in the seventh day is an holy convocation: ye shall
do no servile work therein" (Lev. 23:5-8).

The Passover and the Feast of Unleavened Bread were
intimately connected. We do not have to guess at the
meaning of either for when we turn to I Corinthians 5,
verses 6 to 8, we read:

"Your glorying is not good. Know ye not that a
little leaven leaveneth the whole lump? Purge out
therefore the old leaven, that ye may be a new lump,
as ye are unleavened. For even Christ our passover
is sacrificed for us: therefore let us keep the feast,
not with old leaven, neither with the leaven of malice
and wickedness; but with the unleavened bread of
sincerity and truth" (I Cor. 5:6-8).

The Passover, then, typified the death of our Lord
Jesus Christ, God's unblemished, spotless Lamb who
gave Himself for us in order that divine judgment might
never fall upon us. To Israel in Egypt, in connection
with the first Passover and the sprinkling of blood, Jehovah said: "When I see the blood, I will pass over
you." This points to the cross of Christ, and is the great
truth that gives rest to every believing heart.

The fourteenth day of the first month was in the early
spring, for Israel's sacred year began at that time. The
month Abib, or "Green Ears," answers, generally speaking, to the last part of our March and the first half of
April. It was then that the Passover was to be observed,

and when we come to the New Testament we find that our Lord Jesus Christ observed this feast Himself with His disciples on the first evening of the fourteenth of Abib, and in the morning of the same day He was nailed upon the cross, and in the afternoon He died as the great Paschal Lamb. The Jewish day was from sunset to sunset, and the Passover was to be slain between the two evenings, as we are told in Exodus 12; so our Lord ate the Passover and died as the Paschal Lamb between the two evenings. Thus the type was completely fulfilled.

Now we who have put our trust in Him are called to purge away all leaven, and leaven is ever in Scripture a type of evil. Our Lord warned His disciples to beware of the leaven of the Pharisees, which is hypocrisy and self-righteousness; of the leaven of the Sadducees, which is false doctrine; and of the leaven of Herod, which is worldliness and political corruption. And· in the passage already referred to in First Corinthians, we read of the leaven of malice and wickedness. In Galatians and in First Corinthians, Paul uses the expression, "A little leaven leaveneth the whole lump." In the one case he refers to false doctrine which, if not checked, permeates the mass, and in the other to immorality which, if not judged in the light of the cross of Christ, will have a most devastating effect upon those who are inclined to be led astray. It is for us, therefore, as the redeemed of the Lord, redeemed not with corruptible things such as silver and gold but with the precious blood of Christ, to be careful to put all leaven out of our lives and so to walk before God in holiness and truth. This is to keep the Feast of Unleavened Bread according to the divine appointment for our dispensation.

We come next to the Feast of Firstfruits. In verses 9 to 14 we read:

> "And the Lord spake unto Moses, saying, Speak unto the children of Israel, and say unto them, When ye be come into the land which I give unto you, and shall reap the harvest thereof, then ye shall bring a sheaf of the firstfruits of your harvest unto the priest: and he shall wave the sheaf before the Lord, to be accepted for you: on the morrow after the sabbath the priest shall wave it. And ye shall offer that day when ye wave the sheaf and the lamb without blemish of the first year for a burnt-offering unto the Lord. And the meat-offering thereof shall be two tenth deals of fine flour mingled with oil, an offering made by fire unto the Lord for a sweet savour: and the drink-offering thereof shall be of wine, the fourth part of an hin. And ye shall eat neither bread, nor parched corn, nor green ears, until the selfsame day that ye have brought an offering unto your God: it shall be a statute for ever throughout your generations in all your dwellings" (Leviticus 23:9-14).

Again we are not left to our own imagination when we ask: "What is the meaning of this feast?" For when we turn to First Corinthians 15, that great resurrection chapter in which the Apostle is emphasizing the importance of the truth of Christ's having been raised from the dead, we see that in verse 20 he says: "But now is Christ risen from the dead, and become the firstfruits of them that slept." Then again in verses 22 and 23:

> "For as in Adam all die, even so in Christ shall all be made alive. But every man in his own order: Christ the firstfruits; afterward they that are Christ's at his coming" (I Corinthians 15:22-23).

The presentation of the firstfruits, then, typified the rising of Christ from the dead and His acceptance by God the Father after He had completed the work upon which our redemption rests.

And notice in verse 11 of our chapter, it was on the morrow after the Sabbath that the priest was to present the firstfruits before God. Now remember that our Lord Jesus Christ died on Passover Day and was raised again at the beginning of the first day of the week following. We can see how God here pictures the setting aside of the Sabbath of the Law and the bringing in of what the Apostle John calls, in Revelation 1, "the Lord's day." From Psalm 118, we infer that the Spirit of God puts special honor upon this day because of the glorious event which was then to take place. In verse 22 we have the rejection of Christ involving His crucifixion: "The stone which the builders refused is become the head stone of the corner." His resurrection and the sanctity of the new day are implied in verses 23 and 24: "This is the Lord's doing; it is marvelous in our eyes. This is the day which the Lord hath made; we will rejoice and be glad in it."

Throughout the last Sabbath of the Jews which God ever recognized, no one on earth could possibly know whether redemption was a success or not. The body of the Lord Jesus Christ after His death upon the cross lay in Joseph's new tomb. Had He not come forth in resurrection on the first day of the week, all His declarations in regard to the great work He came to do would have been proved false. It was His resurrection which made it manifest that He was indeed the promised Saviour of

mankind. He was delivered up to death for our of-
fences and was raised again for our justification. Christ
having completed the work that saves, God bore witness
to His delight in His Son and His satisfaction in the work
he had accomplished by raising Him from the dead.
The Lord Jesus as the risen One has been accepted of
the Father, and all who believe are accepted in Him.

There is much more in this section that we could dwell
upon, but I pass over it now because my chief object is
to show how what we have here links up with what we
have already been considering.

In the next section we have the Feast of Pentecost.
Note verses 15 to 22:

> "And ye shall count unto you from the morrow
> after the sabbath, from the day that ye brought the
> sheaf of the wave-offering; seven sabbaths shall be
> complete: even unto the morrow after the seventh
> sabbath shall ye number fifty days; and ye shall offer
> a new meat-offering unto the Lord. Ye shall bring
> out of your habitations two wave-loaves of two tenth
> deals: they shall be of fine flour; they shall be baken
> with leaven, they are the firstfruits unto the Lord.
> And ye shall offer with the bread seven lambs with-
> out blemish of the first year, and one young bullock,
> and two rams: they shall be for a burnt-offering
> unto the Lord, with their meat-offering, and their
> drink-offerings, even an offering made by fire, of
> sweet savour unto the Lord. Then ye shall sacrifice
> one kid of the goats for a sin-offering, and two lambs
> of the first year for a sacrifice of peace-offerings.
> And the priest shall wave them with the bread of
> the firstfruits for a wave-offering before the Lord,
> with the two lambs: they shall be holy to the Lord
> for the priest. And ye shall proclaim on the self-
> same day, that it may be an holy convocation unto

you: ye shall do no servile work therein: it shall be
a statute for ever in all your dwellings throughout
your generations. And when ye reap the harvest of
your land, thou shalt not make clean riddance of the
corners of thy field when thou reapest, neither shalt
thou gather any gleaning of thy harvest: thou shalt
leave them unto the poor, and to the stranger: I am
the Lord your God" (Leviticus 23:15-22).

This feast took place fifty days after that of the firstfruits. The word "pentecost," of course, indicates this,
and we are told definitely that the Israelites were to
count from the morrow after the Sabbath when they
brought the sheaf of the wave offering until seven Sabbaths had passed. Then upon the morrow after the
seventh Sabbath they were to bring a new *meal* offering
unto the Lord. This is the better translation here. We
generally think of meat as flesh, but when the Authorized
Version was translated, the word still had its original
meaning of food, so that this was the food offering and
was composed of meal. Two wave loaves were to be
presented before the Lord. Unlike the ordinary meal
offering, which typified our Lord Jesus Christ and in
which there was to be no leaven, these wave loaves were
to be baked with leaven, and they are called also "firstfruits unto the Lord." It is clear, then, that they typify
not Christ Himself but believers in Christ in whom there
is a sinful nature (as there was not in Him), but that
nature has been judged in the light of the cross of Christ
and therefore the leaven is conceived of as baked. They
represent, then, redeemed sinners who have been born
of God, even as we read in James 1, verse 18: "Of his
own will begat he us with the word of truth, that we
should be a kind of firstfruits of his creatures."

Now, we have the fulfillment of this feast on the day of Pentecost as recorded in the second chapter of the book of Acts. It was then that our Lord baptized believers by the Holy Spirit, and this baptism, we are told in First Corinthians 12, verse 13, formed the one body which is the Church of this dispensation. It is well to notice the full statement in First Corinthians:

> "For as the body is one, and hath many members, and all the members of that one body, being many, are one body: so also is Christ. For by one Spirit are we all baptized into one body, whether we be Jews or Gentiles, whether we be bond or free; and have been all made to drink into one Spirit" (I Corinthians 12:12-13).

The two loaves undoubtedly picture the two groups — Jew and Gentile. Both alike were sinners; both had to judge their sins in the light of the cross; both are accepted by God in all the value of the work of His Son. There is no intimation here, however, that both would form one body, nor was that made known on the day of Pentecost, but through the Apostle Paul, as the chosen vessel of testimony to the Gentiles, this truth was later made known as the dispensation progressed.

And now we come to something of intense interest for those who have followed me in this series of studies thus far. These three feasts, which all have to do with the blessing of the people of God in this age, all took place in the spring of the year. There were no more such "set times" until the seventh month, which would answer to our September-October, and then there were three more feasts following one another in quick succession and intimately linked together. But all of them have to do particularly with God's future dealings with the nation of Israel, so that we have a period of some five months in which there were no special "set times" indicated. This long period fits in perfectly with the parenthesis in God's prophetic plan which we have seen must be taken into account in so many places if we are to rightly apprehend what God is doing now.

When the summer was over and the close of the year had come, God commanded His people to observe the Feast of Trumpets. Notice verses 23 to 25. This ordinance of the blowing of trumpets on the first day of the seventh month is observed by the Jews today for the ushering in of the new civil year as distinguished from the ecclesiastical year. It is called the Feast of Rosh-Hashana. On this day the trumpets are blown, indicating the ushering in of a new period of time. This has to do entirely with Israel. It signifies the blowing of the great trumpet when God's earthly people who have wandered from Him for so long will be called back to Himself and to their land to enter upon Millennial blessedness. Many Scriptures refer to this, a few of which we will mention here:

> "All ye inhabitants of the world, and dwellers on the earth, see ye, when he lifteth up an ensign on the mountains; and when he bloweth a trumpet, hear ye. For so the Lord said unto me, I will take my rest, and I will consider in my dwelling place like a clear heat upon herbs, and like a cloud of dew in the heat of harvest. For afore the harvest, when the bud is perfect, and the sour grape is ripening in the flower, he shall both cut off the sprigs with pruning hooks, and take away and cut down the branches. They shall

be left together unto the fowls of the mountains, and to the beasts of the earth: and the fowls shall summer upon them, and all the beasts of the earth shall winter upon them. In that time shall the present be brought unto the Lord of hosts of a people scattered and peeled, and from a people terrible from their beginning hitherto; a nation meted out and trodden under foot, whose land the rivers have spoiled, to the place of the name of the Lord of hosts, the mount Zion" (Isaiah 18:3-7).

This passage clearly refers to the call which will go out from the Lord after the Church Age is past, summoning His scattered people Israel to return to Himself and to their inheritance. Again in Isaiah 27:12-13 we read:

"And it shall come to pass in that day, that the Lord shall beat off from the channel of the river unto the stream of Egypt, and ye shall be gathered one by one, O ye children of Israel. And it shall come to pass in that day, that the great trumpet shall be blown, and they shall come which were ready to perish in the land of Assyria, and the outcasts in the land of Egypt, and shall worship the Lord in the holy mount at Jerusalem."

Surely these words need no explanation. They are absolutely clear and tell us in no uncertain way that the blowing of the trumpet has to do with Israel's return.

In the second chapter of Joel, verses 1 and 2, we see that when this trumpet is blown, the people of Israel will be in the midst of great tribulation and distress such as they have never previously known. The attempt has often been made by various interpreters of prophecy to connect the Feast of Trumpets with the Rapture of the Church because at that time we are told the Lord will descend from heaven, ". . . with the trump of God," but the context here shows us that the Feast of Trumpets does not in any sense typify anything connected with the heavenly calling, but has to do with the ingathering of Israel to their earthly inheritance. With this agree the words of our Lord which we noticed in a previous study, where He declared that at His Second Coming He would send forth His angels with a sound of a trumpet and gather together His elect from the four quarters of the earth. This makes the meaning of the Feast of Trumpets crystal clear and shows its direct application to the regathering of Israel.

If the Feast of Trumpets had to do with the Rapture of the Church, there would be no place for that which follows in Leviticus 23 because immediately afterwards we have the second "set time" in this latter series for Israel — the great Day of Atonement, when Israel shall recognize in the Lord Jesus Christ the One who made atonement for their sins but whom up to that time they will not have known. Let us read carefully verses 26 through 32:

> "And the Lord spake unto Moses, saying, Also on the tenth day of this seventh month there shall be a day of atonement: it shall be an holy convocation unto you; and ye shall afflict your souls, and offer an offering made by fire unto the Lord. And ye shall do no work in that same day: for it is a day of atonement, to make an atonement for you before the Lord your God. For whatsoever soul it be that shall not be afflicted in that same day, he shall be cut off from among his people. And whatsoever soul

it be that doeth any work in that same day, the same
soul will I destroy from among his people. Ye shall
do no manner of work: it shall be a statute for ever
throughout your generations in all your dwellings.
It shall be unto you a sabbath of rest, and ye shall
afflict your souls: in the ninth day of the month at
even, from even unto even, shall ye celebrate your
sabbath" (Leviticus 23:26-32).

These verses can have no reference to the Church
as such for already we have seen set forth in the Passover the same truth which is now brought before us
here, but the great point of the type is that inasmuch
as Israel failed to apprehend the meaning of the Passover, it will not be until the coming day of tribulation
when they are in distress and sorrow that they will
realize the fact that the Saviour whom their fathers
rejected was the One who actually made atonement for
their sins. This great Day of Atonement as observed
by Israel in the latter day is set forth in Zechariah 12,
verses 10 to 14:

"And I will pour upon the house of David, and
upon the inhabitants of Jerusalem, the spirit of
grace and of supplications: and they shall look upon
me whom they have pierced, and they shall mourn
for him, as one mourneth for his only son, and shall
be in bitterness for him, as one that is in bitterness
for his firstborn. In that day shall there be a great
mourning in Jerusalem, as the mourning of Hadad-
rimmon in the valley of Megiddon. And the land
shall mourn, every family apart; the family of the
house of David apart, and their wives apart; the
family of the house of Nathan apart, and their wives
apart; the family of the house of Levi apart, and
their wives apart; the family of Shimei apart, and
their wives apart; all the families that remain, every
family apart, and their wives apart."

In that day when Israel shall realize how terribly they
have blundered in refusing the Lord Jesus Christ when
He came in lowly grace, they will bow before God in
bitterness of soul and confess their sin.   In the first
verse of chapter 13 we are told the result:

> "In that day there shall be a fountain opened to
> the house of David and to the inhabitants of Jeru-
> salem for sin and for uncleanness" (Zech. 13:1).

In other words, Israel's cleansing will come when in
spirit they reach the true Day of Atonement and recognize the once rejected Jesus as their Saviour and Lord.
Then they will cry, in the words of Isaiah 53, "He was
wounded for our transgressions, he was bruised for our
iniquities: the chastisement of our peace was upon him;
and with his stripes we are healed." That entire wonderful chapter will open up to them in a marvelous way
as the Holy Spirit reveals to them their sin and their
Saviour.

One feast remains ere the year is closed — the Feast
of Tabernacles or of Ingathering. This was for Israel
the happiest festival of all the year. It was the time
when they dwelt in booths as a reminder of the tents
of the wilderness and when they all rejoiced together
in the good things God had given them through the
vintage and the harvest. We have quoted before and
so it will be well to quote again here the actual instruction given in this chapter in Leviticus:

> "And the Lord spake unto Moses, saying, Speak
> unto the children of Israel, saying, The fifteenth day
> of this seventh month shall be the feast of taber-
> nacles for seven days unto the Lord. On the first day

shall be an holy convocation: ye shall do no servile work therein. Seven days ye shall offer an offering made by fire unto the Lord: on the eighth day shall be an holy convocation unto you; and ye shall offer an offering made by fire unto the Lord: it is a solemn assembly; and ye shall do no servile work therein. These are the feasts of the Lord, which ye shall proclaim to be holy convocations, to offer an offering made by fire unto the Lord, a burnt-offering, and a meat-offering, a sacrifice, and drink-offerings, every thing upon his day: beside the sabbaths of the Lord, and beside your gifts, and beside all your vows, and beside all your freewill-offerings, which ye give unto the Lord. Also in the fifteenth day of the seventh month, when ye have gathered in the fruit of the land, ye shall keep a feast unto the Lord seven days: on the first day shall be a sabbath, and on the eighth day shall be a sabbath. And ye shall take you on the first day the boughs of goodly trees, branches of palm trees, and the boughs of thick trees, and willows of the brook; and ye shall rejoice before the Lord your God seven days. And ye shall keep it a feast unto the Lord seven days in the year. It shall be a statute for ever in your generations: ye shall celebrate it in the seventh month. Ye shall dwell in booths seven days; all that are Israelites born shall dwell in booths: that your generations may know that I made the children of Israel to dwell in booths, when I brought them out of the land of Egypt: I am the Lord your God. And Moses declared unto the children of Israel the feasts of the Lord" (Leviticus 23:33-44).

Surely anyone familiar with the Word of God can see in this the picture of that wonderful day when the Lord Jesus shall return in power and glory, and His earthly people will be brought into blessing here in the world and will dwell beneath their own vine and fig tree, rejoicing in the goodness of the Lord. Then the prophecy of Zechariah will have its perfect fulfillment. The Feast of Tabernacles and the deliverance of the people are identical. This is set forth clearly in Zechariah 14, verses 16 to 21:

"And it shall come to pass, that every one that is left of all the nations which came against Jerusalem shall even go up from year to year to worship the King, the Lord of hosts, and to keep the feast of tabernacles. And it shall be, that whoso will not come up of all the families of the earth unto Jerusalem to worship the King, the Lord of hosts, even upon them shall be no rain. And if the family of Egypt go not up, and come not, that have no rain; there shall be the plague, wherewith the Lord will smite the heathen that come not up to keep the feast of tabernacles. This shall be the punishment of Egypt, and the punishment of all nations that come not up to keep the feast of tabernacles. In that day shall there be upon the bells of the horses, HOLINESS UNTO THE LORD; and the pots in the Lord's house shall be like the bowls before the altar. Yea, every pot in Jerusalem and in Judah shall be holiness unto the Lord of hosts: and all they that sacrifice shall come and take of them, and seethe therein: and in that day there shall be no more the Canaanite in the house of the Lord of hosts."

And so the wonderful story comes to an end, and Israel, for so long the nation of the wandering foot, will at last have found their rest in subjection to and glad recognition of the Lord Jesus Christ who was not recognized by them when He came to fulfill the type of the Passover and the firstfruits, but who in that day will be manifested to them as the One who made atonement for their sins upon the cross and under whose righteous rule they shall find rest after all the sorrows and trials they have endured throughout the centuries since they cried, "Away with Him, away with Him; crucify Him, crucify Him."

The break between the two sets of feasts is clear and definite, and is corroborative evidence that our interpretation of the parenthesis in Daniel 9 is the very truth of God in regard to His prophetic dealings with Israel and the world.

Chapter VIII

THE MYSTERY OF THE OLIVE TREE

If my reader has followed me thus far, he will be prepared now to examine with a degree of intelligence the place that the Great Parenthesis occupies in what is itself a parenthesis — the great dispensational division of the Epistle to the Romans as set forth in chapters 9, 10 and 11. It is proper to speak of these chapters as a parenthesis because so far as the doctrinal unfolding of the truth of the righteousness of God as revealed in the Gospel is concerned, one could move on without being conscious that anything was missing between the closing verses of chapter 8 and the opening verses of chapter 12. In the first eight chapters of this epistle we have unfolded for us God's method of dealing with sin according to the righteous demands of His throne, and His Way of providing a perfect righteousness for men who have none of their own. Then in chapters 12 to 16 we see the effects of all this upon the life of the obedient believer: practical righteousness manifested in the lives of those who have been made the righteousness of God in Christ. But between chapters 8 and 12 we have a great parenthetic division in which the Apostle turns aside, as guided by the Holy Spirit, to show how the present proclamation of the Gospel of the grace of God harmonizes with God's former revelation to Israel and His electing grace in making them His covenant people.

In Romans 3 we learn that there is no difference, that all have sinned and come short of the glory of God. The Jew is shown to have no more claim upon the grace of God in Christ than the Gentile. All must come to God in exactly the same way, as needy sinners trusting His blessed Son for salvation. This would naturally raise the question in the mind of any honest Jew: But what then of the special promises made to Israel? What of the covenant entered into at Sinai? How does this affect the promise made to Abraham and to his seed? These questions and others of kindred character are answered fully and completely in chapters 9 to 11.

In chapter 9 the Spirit of God speaks particularly of the Lord's past dealings with Israel; in chapter 10, of His present dealings with them; and in chapter 11, of His future dealings, which will be in exact accord with the prophetic Word.

Turning, then, to chapter 9, we see that Israel was an elect nation. It pleased God to separate this people from all other peoples unto Himself in order that they might occupy a special place of testimony in the earth. This privilege was not given to them because of any merit of their own. It was in sovereign, electing grace that God chose Isaac and set Ishmael to one side, and again chose Jacob and set Esau to one side. God was not unrighteous in doing this. He was the Creator. Like the potter, He had power over the clay to make of it whatever He would. If any object to the truth of election in this sense, the answer to every objection is simply this: God has a right to do as He wills. He chose Israel and made that nation the depositary of His promises, and this was in order that they might be a means of blessing to the whole world.

It is a great mistake, however, to attempt to read eternal things into the ninth chapter of Romans. There is nothing in this chapter about election to eternal life or a place in heaven, and certainly nothing about reprobation to eternal judgment in hell. When hyper-Calvinists attempt to use this portion of Scripture to support their God-dishonoring views, they wrest the Word from its true setting. It is election to a place of privilege on earth, not to eternal blessedness, and the rejection of which it speaks must be looked at in the same way, as having to do with earthly things and not with heavenly. God chose Abraham to be the father of the covenant people. In the next generation He declared: "In Isaac shall thy seed be called"; and in regard to the sons of Isaac it is written: "The children being not yet born, neither having done any good or evil, that the purpose of God according to election might stand, not of works, but of him that calleth; it was said unto her [that is, unto Rebekah], The elder shall serve the younger. As it is written, Jacob have I loved, but Esau have I hated" (Romans 9:11-13). Observe, it was not said: "The younger shall go to heaven and the elder shall go to hell." God was not speaking of eternal things at all, but the elder was set aside in favor of the younger so far as privilege on earth was concerned.

The thirteenth verse must be understood relatively. Compared with the blessing God gave to Jacob, it would seem as though He hated Esau, but we need to remem-

ber that this statement was not made before the children
were born, but long years after in the book of Malachi,
chapter 1, verses 2 and 3, where God is tracing out the
history of His ways with the descendants of the two sons
of Isaac, and He shows how privileged Jacob, or Israel,
had been and how destitute of many similar blessings
Esau, or Edom, had been.

Now if God thus chose to take up the seed of Abraham
after the flesh and they failed completely as a nation
to appreciate His goodness, and when His own Son
came into the world they fulfilled their own Scriptures
in condemning Him, who shall question the righteousness of God in setting them to one side and taking up
the Gentiles and giving to them the glorious privileges
that they now enjoy?

So, in chapter 10 we have, as already intimated, God's
present dealings with Israel. He has set the nation as
such to one side during all this long parenthetic period
which we have been considering, but that does not mean
that the individual Jew is left without an opportunity
of salvation for eternity. Any Jew who will, may come
to God in Christ and find salvation on exactly the same
basis as any Gentile. So we read in verse 12: "There
is no difference between the Jew and the Greek: for the
same Lord over all is rich unto all that call upon him."
And the apostle adds in verse 13: "For whosoever shall
call upon the name of the Lord shall be saved." During
all this present period, while Israel nationally is set to
one side, God's "whosoever message" is going out to
the world, and Jew or Gentile may avail themselves of

it if they will, and if they refuse to do so, they are responsible for their own judgment.

In chapter 11 we have the future of this covenant people. We are told first that their eyes were blinded because they were so occupied with their own works that they rebelled against the grace of God. National Israel is judicially blinded to this present day, and this is in accordance with prophetic intimations, as we see in verses 7 to 12:

> "What then? Israel hath not obtained that which he seeketh for; but the election hath obtained it, and the rest were blinded (according as it is written, God hath given them the spirit of slumber, eyes that they should not see, and ears that they should not hear;) unto this day. And David saith, Let their table be made a snare, and a trap, and a stumbling-block, and a recompense unto them: let their eyes be darkened, that they may not see, and bow down their back alway. I say then, Have they stumbled that they should fall? God forbid; but rather through their fall salvation is come unto the Gentiles, for to provoke them to jealousy. Now if the fall of them be the riches of the world, and the diminishing of them the riches of the Gentiles; how much more their fullness?" (Romans 11:7-12).

God then has, if one may so say, taken advantage of the Jews' unbelief to open wide the door of grace to all men everywhere; and so the Gentiles are really indebted to the unbelieving Jews for their present wonderful opportunity. Surely it ill becomes any Gentile to look with contempt on or to speak in an unkind, derogatory way of the Jew because of his failure to understand God's plan when the Lord Jesus appeared on earth in accordance with the prophetic Scriptures! They did not understand, and so they lost a glorious opportunity, even as our Lord Himself said: "If thou hadst known, even thou, at least in this thy day, the things which belong unto thy peace! but now they are hid from thine eyes" (Luke 19:42). "Your house is left unto you desolate: and verily I say unto you, Ye shall not see me, until the time come when ye shall say, Blessed is he that cometh in the name of the Lord" (Luke 13:35).

And so with the setting aside of Israel, we have the Gospel of grace going out to the nations. Speaking from the standpoint of the Apostle of the Gentiles, Paul continues:

> "For if the casting away of them be the reconciling of the world, what shall the receiving of them be, but life from the dead? For if the firstfruit be holy, the lump is also holy: and if the root be holy, so are the branches. And if some of the branches be broken off, and thou, being a wild olive tree, wert graffed in among them, and with them partakest of the root and fatness of the olive tree; boast not against the branches. But if thou boast, thou bearest not the root, but the root thee. Thou wilt say then, The branches were broken off, that I might be graffed in. Well; because of unbelief they were broken off, and thou standest by faith. Be not highminded, but fear: for if God spared not the natural branches, take heed lest he also spare not thee. Behold therefore, the goodness and severity of God: on them which fell, severity; but toward thee, goodness, if thou continue in his goodness: otherwise thou also shalt be cut off. And they also, if they abide not still in unbelief, shall be graffed in: for God is able to graff them in again" (Romans 11:15-23).

The figure of the olive tree used here is taken from the book of Jeremiah, chapter 11 and verse 16:

"The Lord called thy name, A green olive tree, fair, and of goodly fruit: with the noise of a great tumult he hath kindled fire upon it, and the branches of it are broken."

There are three plants used in a special way as representing Israel. The *vine* speaks of them as God's testimony in the earth. The *fig tree* is the symbol of Israel nationally, and the *olive tree* tells of them as the covenant people in special relation to God. Because of their unfaithfulness and particularly their rejection of the Lord Jesus Christ, the natural branches were broken off from the olive tree of which Abraham is the root. He is the father of all that believe. Israel failed here, and so these branches were torn out of the tree of the covenant. In place of them, wild branches representing the Gentiles were grafted in, but we need to remember that these branches do not necessarily speak of individual souls actually saved, but of Gentile nations to whom privileges have now been granted which were heretofore uncovenanted so far as they were concerned. If there is real faith, they partake of the root and fatness of the olive tree. As we read in Galatians, "They that be of faith are blessed with faithful Abraham." But where the Gentiles manifest unbelief and heedlessness to the Word of God, they expose themselves to the same judgment that has already fallen upon Israel. The day will come when they will be torn out of the olive tree and their special privileges will come to an end.

Unbelieving critics have ridiculed the figure used here by the Apostle Paul, and have even taken occasion to point to it as a positive proof that the epistles are not definitely inspired by God. "How," they ask, "could God make such a mistake as that which Paul has made here? He speaks of grafting wild branches into a good tree, and every horticulturalist knows that you do not graft wild branches into a good tree, but you graft good branches into a wild tree in order to change completely the character of its fruit." But here, as elsewhere, it is the critics who are wrong. They do not read carefully enough, nor, shall I say, far enough. When we turn to verses 23 and 24, we read:

> "And they also, if they abide not still in unbelief, shall be graffed in: for God is able to graff them in again. For if thou wert cut out of the olive tree which is wild by nature, and wert graffed contrary to nature into a good olive tree: how much more shall these, which be the n a t u r a l branches, be graffed into their own olive tree?" (Romans 11:23-24).

Notice the expression, "If thou wert graffed contrary to nature into a good olive tree." Paul draws attention to the fact that the illustration he is using is not in accordance with ordinary custom, but is contrary to it, just as the matchless grace of God is contrary to the thoughts of man's legalistic heart. And if the Gentile nations have thus been so highly privileged, why should anyone wonder if, upon their failure, God should turn back again to Israel and graft in the natural branches into their own olive tree? This is exactly what He will do when the present period which we have described as the Great Parenthesis comes to an end.

And so we read in verse 25: "For I would not, brethren, that ye should be ignorant of this mystery, lest ye should be wise in your own conceits; that blindness in part is happened to Israel, until the fulness of the Gentiles be come in." We need to distinguish between "the times of the Gentiles" and "the fulness of the Gentiles." We have already seen that "the times of the Gentiles" covers the entire period during which the nation of the Jews, the city of Jerusalem, and the land of Palestine are under Gentile domination. This began with Nebuchadnezzar's conquest of Palestine and will end at the revelation of the Lord Jesus Christ from heaven at the close of the Great Tribulation, or as Daniel puts it, "the last end of the indignation." But the other term, "the fulness of the Gentiles," has to do with God's present work of grace. When He has taken out from among the Gentiles a people for His Name, when the last soul who is to be saved in this age has come to Christ, the Church will be completed and "the fulness of the Gentiles" will have come in. Then that Church will be caught up to be with the Lord before the seventieth week of Daniel begins. God will then take up Israel, and after the terrible time of tribulation spoken of specifically as "the time of Jacob's trouble," out of which Israel is to be saved, shall come to an end, the remainder of the nation will be brought into blessing. The apostate part of Israel will be destroyed as a result of the terrible experiences of the Great Tribulation. The remnant will be looked upon by God as the nation. And so says the Apostle in verse 26:

> "And so all Israel shall be saved: as it is written, There shall come out of Zion the Deliverer, and shall turn away ungodliness from Jacob: for this is my covenant unto them, when I shall take away their sins. As concerning the gospel, they are enemies for

your sakes: but as touching the election, they are beloved for the fathers' sakes. For the gifts and calling
of God are without repentance. For as ye in times
past have not believed God, yet have now obtained
mercy through their unbelief: even so have these
also now not believed, that through your mercy they
also may obtain mercy. For God hath concluded
them all in unbelief, that he might have mercy upon
all. O the depth of the riches both of the wisdom
and knowledge of God! how unsearchable are his
judgments, and his ways past finding out! For who
hath known the mind of the Lord? or who hath been
his counsellor? Or who hath first given to him, and
it shall be recompensed unto him again? For of
him, and through him, and to him, are all things: to
whom be glory for ever. Amen" (Romans 11:26-36).

Surely it is clear that these three chapters, then, fit
in perfectly with what we have found elsewhere as to
this parenthetic period between the sufferings of Christ
and the glories that shall follow. The Old Testament
reveals the truth that Israel would not recognize their
Messiah when He came and that trouble and disaster
would fall upon them because of this, but it gave no
intimation of what God would do during this time of
their setting aside in taking out a vast company of Gentiles to be associated with His Son throughout the Kingdom Age as His body and His bride. This is part of
the great secret which had been kept in His heart from
times eternal but now has been made known.

It may be well to point out what has been often noticed
by others, that a "mystery" as spoken of in the New
Testament is not necessarily something mysterious. It
is a sacred secret which man could know nothing about
until God revealed it. This mystery of the olive tree

was made known only after the rejection of Christ and the consequent setting aside of the chosen nation.

What a day it will be when, God's present program completed, He will take up Israel once more and bring them at last to confess their sin and to look up in faith to the Saviour whom their fathers rejected, and confess Him as their Redeemer and their long waited for Messiah! Then Israel shall blossom and bud and fill the face of the whole earth with fruit, for they will become God's instruments for the enlightenment of the Gentile world.

CHAPTER IX

THE REVELATION OF THE ONE BODY

It is now time that we consider the particular ministry which God has committed to His Church, those whom He is taking out from both Jew and Gentile in this parenthetic period; and for this we must turn particularly to the letters of the Apostle Paul. Our Lord, before He left this scene, intimated to His disciples that He had come not only to seek the lost sheep of the house of Israel and to bring them out of the Jewish fold that they might be gathered to Himself, but He declared: "Other sheep I have which are not of this fold: them also I must bring, and there shall be one fold, and one shepherd." This as recorded in the tenth of John was perhaps the first inkling of one phase of the great mystery that during the present age Jew and Gentile were to be dealt with alike on the basis of pure grace, and all special distinctions had disappeared. "There shall be," said Jesus, "one flock." It took the disciples some time, however, to grasp the significance of this, and God had to give to the Apostle Peter a special revelation, as we have already seen, before he had faith enough to go to a Gentile household and proclaim the Gospel to them. But when he did so and they believed, the Holy Spirit fell upon them and they were united in happy fellowship with their believing brethren from among the Jews. This was in accord with the vision that Peter had seen and the word that came to him saying: "What God hath cleansed, that call not thou common."

Just prior to this, Saul of Tarsus had been converted on the Damascus road, and at the very moment of his conversion a revelation was made to him which was doubtless unfolded much more fully afterwards but which embodied the special truth which was given to him to make known to all nations for the obedience of faith. When the risen Lord asked the question, "Why persecutest thou me?" His words implied an intimate relationship between Christians and Himself which had never been previously emphasized. It was the revelation of the mystery of the one body in embryo. That question declared the wondrous fact that it is impossible to touch a child of God on earth without affecting the Lord Jesus Christ in heaven, for every believer is a member of His body, of His flesh, and of His bones.

In the Epistle to the Ephesians, Paul tells us that this was made known to him by divine revelation. Note his words as given in chapter 3:

"For this cause I, Paul, the prisoner of Jesus Christ for you Gentiles, if ye have heard of the dispensation of the grace of God which is given me to you-ward: how that by revelation he made known unto me the mystery; (as I wrote afore in few words, whereby, when ye read, ye may understand my knowledge in the mystery of Christ) which in other ages was not made known unto the sons of men, as it is now revealed unto his holy apostles and prophets by the Spirit; that the Gentiles should be fellowheirs, and of the same body, and partakers of his promise in Christ by the gospel: whereof I was made a minister, according to the gift of the grace of God given unto me by the effectual working of his power. Unto me,

who am less than the least of all saints, is this grace
given, that I should preach among the Gentiles the
unsearchable riches of Christ; and to make all men
see what is the fellowship of the mystery, which from
the beginning of the world hath been hid in God,
who created all things by Jesus Christ: to the intent
that now unto the principalities and powers in
heavenly places might be known by the church the
manifold wisdom of God, according to the eternal
purpose which he purposed in Christ Jesus our Lord:
in whom we have boldness and access with confidence
by the faith of him" (Ephesians 3:1-12).

Observe carefully what Paul here says. The truth he
was declaring was not made known by a study of the
Bible because it was not revealed in Old Testament
times. God waited until the parenthetic period had well
begun, which we have been considering in these passages. Then after there had been a final testimony to
Israel, calling upon any who realized their need of
Christ to acknowledge Him as Saviour and Lord, God
by revelation made known unto Paul this mystery or
secret which He had hidden in His heart from eternity.
It is called here in verse 4, "the mystery of Christ,"
and the term "Christ" as used here includes both the
Lord Himself and His redeemed people — He the Head
and they the members of His body, as we read in First
Corinthians 12:12:

"For as the body is one, and hath many members,
and all the members of that one body, being many,
are one body: so also is Christ.

The way by which we enter into this relationship is
given in the following verse:

"For by one Spirit are we all baptized into one
body, whether we be Jews or Gentiles, whether we be

> bond or free; and have been all made to drink into
> one Spirit."

Drinking suggests fellowship or communion. All who are saved in this dispensation have been brought into one blessed fellowship by the indwelling of the Holy Spirit. It is the Lord Himself who baptizes into the body, but the element, if I may so say, is the Spirit — and not water. In water baptism we confess our personal faith in Christ. By baptism in the Holy Spirit the Lord has made us members of His body. The earliest members of the body, those who were baptized in the Spirit on the Day of Pentecost, were all, of course, Jews, but now Gentiles are made fellow-heirs, members of the same body, and partakers of God's promise in Christ by the Gospel.

This was not known, Paul tells us, in other ages, that is, in the former dispensations; but it has now been revealed unto Christ's holy apostles and prophets by the Spirit. Notice that although it was to Paul primarily that the revelation was given, he links up the other apostles and New Testament prophets with himself as recipients of this revelation. But in a very special sense it was given to him to minister this truth to the people of God. He speaks deprecatingly of himself as "the least of all saints," doubtless remembering the time when he persecuted the Church of God and wasted it; but he rejoices in the fact that this special grace had been given to him to preach among the Gentiles what he calls "the unsearchable riches of Christ." This is the Gospel (in all its fullness, and the end of it all is this: "To make all men see what is the fellowship of the mystery, which from the beginning of the world hath been hid in God, who created all things by Jesus Christ."

This expression "the fellowship of the mystery" is a very remarkable one. It tells us what real Christian fellowship is. We have communion one with another because we are members one of another. We have communion with the Lord because He is our Head and we are members of His body. All this is part of what our Authorized Version calls, "the eternal purpose of God." It might, perhaps, better be rendered "the purpose of the ages." Throughout all the ages God had this in mind, but He did not reveal it until the setting aside of Israel and the descent of the Holy Spirit to bring in the new dispensation.

In the Epistle to the Colossians Paul dwells on the twofold character of his ministry. He shows us there that he was a minister of the Gospel and also a minister of the truth of the mystery. In the first chapter he presents the Lord Jesus Christ as the first-born from the dead, the risen One who is now head of the body, the Church, in whom all the divine fullness is pleased to dwell. Then he adds:

> "And having made peace through the blood of his cross, by him to reconcile all things unto himself; by him, I say, whether they be things in earth, or things in heaven. And you, that were sometime alienated and enemies in your mind by wicked works, yet now hath he reconciled in the body of his flesh through death, to present you holy and unblameable and unreproveable in his sight: if ye continue in the faith grounded and settled, and be not moved away from the hope of the gospel, which ye have heard, and

which was preached to every creature which is under heaven; whereof I Paul am made a minister" (Colossians 1:20-23).

That which we could never do ourselves, He has done for us. People speak sometimes of man's responsibility to make his peace with God, but, alas, that he could never do. It is impossible for sinful man to make atonement for his own iniquities, and until that is done, man cannot be at peace with God. But the Lord Jesus has made peace through the blood of His cross. On the basis of this, the day will yet come when all things in heaven and on earth will be reconciled to God. That will occur when there will be a new heaven and a new earth wherein dwelleth righteousness.

Observe that when it is a question of universal reconciliation we have only two spheres — heaven and earth. In Philippians 2, verses 9 to 11, where God is dealing with the question of subjugation rather than reconciliation, we have three spheres — heaven, earth and the infernal regions. All will some day have to own the authority of the once crucified Saviour, but not all will be reconciled to Him.

Now those who have turned to God in repentance and trusted Christ for themselves have already been reconciled to God through the death of His Son. Many, of course, profess faith in Christ who by their after-lives prove they are not genuine in their profession, but where there is reality, this reconciliation is settled for eternity. Of this glorious Gospel, Paul says he was made a minister.

But now when we pass on to the last verses of the chapter, we find he had a ministry to saints as well as a ministry to sinners, and so he continues:

"Who now rejoice in my sufferings for you, and fill up that which is behind of the afflictions of Christ in my flesh for his body's sake, which is the church: whereof I am made a minister, according to the dispensation of God which is given to me for you, to fulfil the word of God; even the mystery which hath been hid from ages and from generations, but now is made manifest to his saints: to whom God would make known what is the riches of the glory of this mystery among the Gentiles; which is Christ in you, the hope of glory: whom we preach, warning every man and teaching every man in all wisdom; that we may present every man perfect in Christ Jesus: whereunto I also labour, striving according to his working. which worketh in me mightily" (Colossians 1:24-29).

This coincides with what we have already seen in the Epistle to the Ephesians. It was given to Paul to fulfill or complete the word of God by making known the mystery which had been hid from past ages, and generations but which was now made manifest. It was Paul's earnest desire to lead all of God's people into the truth of this mystery. However, this does not mean for a moment that some in the Early Church who had not yet received this truth were not made members of the body of Christ, even as it does not mean that thousands today who are ignorant of it are thereby not included in the body. All believers are members of the body, whether they know the truth of it or not, but they have the greater joy as they enter into and understand what God is now doing and their special place of privilege and responsibility in connection with it.

In closing the Epistle to the Romans after Paul had really completed the special unfolding of the Gospel and its blessed results in the lives of those who believe it, which was his particular object in writing this letter, he adds in an inspired postscript:

> "Now to him that is of power to stablish you according to my gospel, and the preaching of Jesus Christ, according to the revelation of the mystery, which was kept secret since the world began, but now is made manifest, and by the scriptures of the prophets, according to the commandment of the everlasting God, made known to all nations for the obedience of faith: to God only wise, be glory through Jesus Christ for ever. Amen." (Romans 16:25-27).

Notice again the expression used here, "the revelation of the mystery," which we are told, had been kept secret since the world began, or in all past ages. But it is now made manifest in prophetic writings. The expression translated in our Authorized Version "by the scriptures of the prophets" might imply that this mystery had now been discovered hidden in the books of the Old Testament prophets, but that is not what Paul wrote. He said: "It is now made manifest and by prophetic writings," that is, the prophetic writings of the apostles of the New Testament, "according to the commandment of the everlasting God, made known to all nations for the obedience of faith."

What a blessed thing it is to realize that this union of believers with Christ is something that once entered into can never be changed. It is unthinkable that the body of Christ should ever be dismembered or that anyone who was ever a member of His body should be lost at last.

Coming back again to the Epistle to the Ephesians, we find a very important exhortation in chapter 4, verses 1 to 7:

> "I therefore, the prisoner of the Lord, beseech you that ye walk worthy of the vocation wherewith ye are called, with all lowliness and meekness, with long-suffering, forbearing one another in love; endeavoring to keep the unity of the Spirit in the bond of peace. There is one body, and one Spirit, even as ye are called in one hope of your calling; one Lord, one faith, one baptism, one God and Father of all, who is above all, and through all, and in you all. But unto every one of us is given grace according to the measure of the gift of Christ."

We are called to walk worthy of our vocation, that is, the vocation or calling of members of Christ. We are to recognize a sevenfold unity. First we are told there is one body and one Spirit and one hope. The one Spirit here refers, of course, to the Holy Spirit in which we have been baptized into the body. The hope is that of the Coming of the Lord. Then we have another trio — one Lord, one faith, one baptism. The faith is that truth about Christ which we are called upon to confess. We acknowledge this in our baptism, thus owning the Lordship of Christ. We are no longer our own, but are to live as those who belong to Him. Then, finally, we have one God and Father of all, and He is above all and through all and in us all. This is the glorious truth of new creation. All believers are linked eternally with the risen Christ in glory.

So long as the body of Christ is on earth, it is our responsibility to make known the Gospel to the unsaved and the truth of this mystery to those who are already members of Christ. When the Church is taken out of this scene, God will no longer be dealing with the world in exactly the same way that He is now. There will be children of God in a coming age, but they will not be members of the Church which is Christ's body, the fullness of Him that filleth all in all. In the coming age the distinction between Jew and Gentile will be recognized once more. Restored Israel will be a priestly nation through whom the salvation of God will be made known to all the Gentiles, and they will be blessed in subjection to Israel as the special covenant people. The Church of this age will have its part with Christ in glory. When He reigns, we shall reign with Him as His body and His bride. How important, then, that we should appreciate our high and heavenly calling and seek now to glorify Him in all our ways, who has taken us into such intimate relationship with Himself.

The close of the Church's testimony on earth will come when the Lord Jesus returns for His own, before the dark days of tribulation begin. The Church must be out of this scene ere the seventieth week starts, and Israel will once more be recognized as God's covenant people. This involved another revelation which may be called "the mystery of the rapture." We read of it first of all in First Thessalonians 4, verses 13 to 18:

> "But I would not have you to be ignorant, brethren, concerning them which are asleep, that ye sorrow not, even as others which have no hope. For if we believe that Jesus died and rose again, even so them also which sleep in Jesus will God bring with him. For this we say unto you by the word of the Lord, that we which are alive and remain unto the coming of the

Lord shall not prevent them which are asleep. For
the Lord himself shall descend from heaven with a
shout, with the voice of the archangel, and with the
trump of God: and the dead in Christ shall rise first:
then we which are alive and remain shall be caught
up together with them in the clouds, to meet the Lord
in the air: and so shall we ever be with the Lord.
Wherefore comfort one another with these words."

I speak of this as the first revelation of this particular
truth because the Epistles to the Thessalonians were the
earliest of Paul's letters which the Holy Spirit has preserved for the edification of the Church. There are other
passages in preceding epistles, according to the order
given in our English Bibles, which deal with this subject,
but in point of time First Thessalonians gives the earliest
written word in regard to it. Here we learn that when
the Lord Jesus descends from heaven with a shout, He
will call all His own to meet Him in the air. This is a
very different thing from His Coming to the earth at the
close of the Great Tribulation, when Israel will be in
such distress, and He will appear in flaming fire, taking
vengeance on their enemies, those who know not God.
The two aspects of His Coming are altogether different.
The Coming of First Thessalonians 4 is only for the
saints. When He descends at the close of the tribulation
period, He will come with His saints to execute judgment
and to set up His glorious kingdom.

This special pre-Tribulation Rapture is not referred
to in the Synoptic Gospels, and we have just a hint of
it in John 14 where the Lord Jesus says: "If I go and
prepare a place for you, I will come again, and receive
you unto myself; that where I am, there ye may be also."
Paul speaks of it as that which has come to him "by

the word of the Lord." In other words, it was a special revelation made known in connection with the truth of the one body. In one of his later letters, First Corinthians, chapter 15, he gives us additional information in regard to this glorious event, and there he speaks of it very definitely as a mystery. He says:

> "Behold, I shew you a mystery; We shall not all sleep, but we shall all be changed, in a moment, in the twinkling of an eye, at the last trump: for the trumpet shall sound, and the dead shall be raised incorruptible, and we shall be changed. For this corruptible must put on incorruption, and this mortal must put on immortality. So when this corruptible shall have put on incorruption, and this mortal shall have put on immortality, then shall be brought to pass the saying that is written, Death is swallowed up in victory. O death, where is thy sting? O grave, where is thy victory? The sting of death is sin; and the strength of sin is the law. But thanks be to God, which giveth us the victory through our Lord Jesus Christ. Therefore, my beloved brethren, be ye stedfast, unmoveable, always abounding in the work of the Lord, forasmuch as ye know that your labour is not in vain in the Lord" (I Corinthians 15:51-58).

Observe that this aspect of His Return will take place at the sounding of the last trump. This is called in the Thessalonian passage "the trump of God," and it should be distinguished very definitely from the last of the seven angels' trumpets as mentioned in the book of Revelation, chapter 11. These angel trumpets will sound during the last half of Daniel's seventieth week, and the final trumpet ushers in the glorious kingdom of our Lord Jesus Christ. The trump of God is something altogether different. It is called "the last trump" because it will close the present age of grace and conclude God's ways with His people in this dispensation.

I have no doubt that those expositors are right who understand the expression "the last trump" to be an allusion to the third trump of the Roman legions. When the first trumpet sounded, whether it came in the night or in the day, the soldiers sprang to their feet and struck their tents. When the second trumpet sounded, they fell into line. At the last trumpet they marched away. And so we who believe have heard the first trumpet, awakening us when we were asleep in our sins. The second trumpet has called us to recognize the authority of our Lord Jesus Christ. Now we await the sounding of the last trump when we shall be caught away to be with Him forever. Then those who are living in their natural, mortal bodies will suddenly put on immortality. That is, the body will be changed in a moment, in the twinkling of an eye, and made like unto the glorious resurrection body of our Lord Jesus Christ. Those who have died and whose bodies have corrupted in the grave, will be raised to incorruptibility, and in their new bodies will be with and like Christ forever. This is our hope. For this we are called to wait. At any moment the Lord Jesus may return to fulfill these Scriptures. How blessed to be ready to hail Him with joy at His Advent!

Chapter X

THE MYSTERY OF LAWLESSNESS AND THE REVELATION OF THE MAN OF SIN

In his earliest epistle, the First Epistle to the Thessalonians, the Apostle Paul unfolded the precious truth of what we commonly call the "Rapture" of the Church. It is sometimes objected that the word "rapture" is not found in the Scriptures. This is perfectly true, but it does not therefore militate against the truth generally so designated. There are many other terms which are not actually found in the Bible and yet are themselves thoroughly Scriptural inasmuch as they are used to denominate doctrines which are clearly taught in the Word of God.

We do not find the word "trinity" in the Bible, but we do learn that God has revealed Himself in three Persons, the Father and the Son and the Holy Spirit, and this of course is the Holy Trinity. The word "substitution" is not found in Scripture, but when the Apostle exclaims, "The Son of God loved me, and gave himself for me," and when Isaiah declares, "He was wounded for our transgressions, he was bruised for our iniquities," both are teaching the great truth of substitution.

And so we need not be troubled because we do not find the actual word "rapture" either in Paul's writings or elsewhere in the New Testament, for to be raptured is to be caught away, and in this first letter to the Thessalonians, as well as in other passages, we learn that

110

the Church of God will be caught away to be with the Lord at His Return to the air. This is what we mean when we speak of the Rapture.

In seeking to comfort some of the troubled Thessalonians who were grieving because they had lost friends in Christ by death, the Apostle told them of a special revelation he had received of the Lord which, as we have already noticed, is identical with that mystery made known later, in the fifteenth chapter of First Corinthians. This is the Coming of the Lord for His saints at the close of the present dispensation and prior to the beginning of the period of judgment which is to follow. Some have supposed that the Church would go into that time of trial and tribulation, but they forget that it is to be the time of Jacob's trouble, not that of the Church's testing.

There are also those who, because of present war conditions, insist that we are already in the tribulation and that the Church perhaps will be here for at least the first half of it, but will be caught up in the midst of the seventieth week, before the intense judgments are poured upon the earth; but they surely forget that the seventieth week begins with the signing of a covenant between the head of the ten-kingdom empire yet to arise and someone, evidently the Antichrist, representing the people of Israel. That covenant has not yet been signed. Therefore, we are not in the first half of the week. It will never be signed so long as God is still taking out from among the Gentiles a people to His Name. It will not be until He is once more recognized as in covenant relationship with Israel and the apostate part of the people make a "covenant with death and hell," as Isaiah calls it (Isaiah 28:18), that the seventieth week will begin.

This, however, was not clear to those early Thessalonian Christians, and when trial and persecution arose, they became perplexed and forgot the clear, definite teaching of the Apostle concerning the hope of the Lord's return to take His own to be with Himself ere the judgments began, and many wondered if they were not already entering the Great Tribulation with all its terrors. To them it seemed as though nothing could be worse than what they were already enduring, and the teaching was promulgated by some among them that the actual Day of the Lord was upon them — that great and dreadful day when He will deal in judgment with the nations of the world and His wrath will be poured out upon those who have rejected His Gospel. It is even possible, nay, actually probable, as one gathers from Second Thessalonians 2, verse 3, that someone had forged a letter, pretending it came from the Apostle Paul, declaring this very thing; and so bewildered saints were in confusion of mind and had lost sight of the blessed hope which had meant so much to them in the days of their first love.

To correct all this, Paul wrote his second letter. In the first chapter of that letter he speaks of the Coming of the Lord with all His saints when He appears in judgment. Surely no one who compares this passage with First Thessalonians 4:13-18 could ever dream of confounding them. In Second Thessalonians 1:7-10 we read:

"And to you who are troubled rest with us, when the Lord Jesus shall be revealed from heaven with his mighty angels, in flaming fire taking vengeance on them that know not God, and that obey not the gospel of our Lord Jesus Christ: who shall be punished with everlasting destruction from the presence of the Lord, and from the glory of his power; when he shall come to be glorified in his saints, and to be admired in all them that believe (because our testimony among you was believed) in that day."

What a scene is this! And how different from the peace and blessedness of the picture given of the descending Christ calling His own to Himself, as we have it in the first epistle. There, there is no flaming fire, no taking vengeance upon the ungodly, but we see the Bridegroom coming for His bride, the Head of the Church calling all His members to be with Himself before the judgments fall upon the earth.

In the second chapter of this second epistle Paul comes directly to the point. Notice verses 1 and 2:

"Now we beseech you, brethren, by the coming of our Lord Jesus Christ, and by our gathering together unto him, that ye be not soon shaken in mind, or be troubled, neither by spirit, nor by word, nor by letter as from us, as that the day of Christ is at hand" (II Thessalonians 2:1-2).

He bases everything that he is about to say upon the truth he has already declared concerning the Coming of our Lord Jesus Christ and our gathering together unto Him. It is as though he were saying to these believers, "I beg of you, brethren, in view of what I have already made known to you concerning the precious truth of that which is to be the consummation of all our hopes, the coming of our Lord Jesus to the air, when the dead will be raised and the living changed and we shall all be gathered together unto Him, that you do not allow yourselves to be misled or to be troubled in mind as though the present difficulties you are passing through and the persecutions you are called upon to endure indicate that the actual Day of the Lord is almost upon you."

Notice that whereas in the Authorized Version we read in verse 2, "the day of Christ," it is in every critical translation rendered, "the day of the Lord." This was what they feared. "The day of Christ" always refers to the time when the saints will be gathered around the Lord Jesus Christ in the air and we will stand before His judgment seat. That will be the Day of manifestation for believers only referred to so frequently in the epistles, but the Day of the Lord is the time when He will be manifested in judgment. It includes the pouring out of His wrath during the Great Tribulation and the entire Kingdom Age that will follow.

If someone professed to have a revelation by the Spirit or another declared that he had found in the Word (that is, the Word of God) that the Church was to go through the Great Tribulation, or if someone else presented a forged letter as though it came from Paul himself, he would not have the saints believe it. The Coming of the Lord Jesus Christ and our gathering together unto Him must occur first. The Great Tribulation cannot begin until the man of sin has been manifested, but that will never be so long as the Holy Spirit is here in the earth working in and through the Church.

This comes out clearly in the verses that follow. He says:

> "Let no man deceive you by any means: for that day shall not come, except there come a falling away first, and that man of sin be revealed, the son of perdition; who opposeth and exalteth himself above all that is called God, or that is worshipped; so that he as God sitteth in the temple of God, shewing himself that he is God. Remember ye not, that, when I was yet with you, I told you these things?" (II Thessalonians 2:3-5).

The expression "a falling away" might better be rendered "the apostasy." It refers not to such fallings away from the truth as have taken place again and again throughout the Christian dispensation, but the complete repudiation of Christianity and everything that is of God, when Babylon the Great, the false religious system of the last days, will hold sway over all Christendom, and the man of sin, the embodiment of all impiety, Satan's pretended Christ, will be manifested. He is called definitely, as Judas was, "the son of perdition."

We are not to suppose, as some have taught, that Satan will have the power of resurrection. It is only God who raises the dead. Therefore, this son of perdition is not identical with Judas as though he were to be brought forth from the tomb and become the Antichrist, but just as Satan entered into Judas and so controlled and dominated him that he sold the Christ of God, so Satan will enter into and dominate and control this blasphemous leader of Israel in the last days that he will set himself up to destroy everything of God on the earth. His description as given in verse 4 is almost

identical with that of the willful king in Daniel 11. He
opposes and exalts himself above all that is called God
or that is worshiped. He takes his place in the Temple
of God, a Temple doubtless to be rebuilt in Jerusalem
in the end-times, and there declares himself to be divine.

Some have thought that the man of sin is to be identified with the first beast of Revelation 13, because we are
told that all men shall worship him whose names are
not written in the book of life of the slain Lamb. But
the worship here mentioned is in the sense of doing
homage, just as millions today do homage to Adolph
Hitler and look upon him as an invincible leader against
whom none can successfully fight. But the man of sin
is a religious leader, not simply the head of a state, and
is unquestionably, at least to my mind, identical with
the second beast of Revelation 13, the one who will have
two horns like a lamb, that is, who looks like the Lamb
of God (therefore is the false messiah), but who speaks
as a dragon, for he will be energized by Satan.

Paul tells the Thessalonians that when he was with
them he had mentioned these things to them, and then
he goes on to explain something that they had evidently
forgotten.

> "And now ye know what withholdeth that he might
> be revealed in his time. For the mystery of iniquity
> doth already work: only he who now letteth will let,
> until he be taken out of the way. And then shall that
> Wicked be revealed, whom the Lord shall consume
> with the spirit of his mouth, and shall destroy with
> the brightness of his coming: even him, whose coming
> is after the working of Satan with all power and
> signs and lying wonders, and with all deceivableness

of unrighteousness in them that perish; because they received not the love of the truth, that they might be saved" (II Thessalonians 2:6-10).

Let us examine these verses carefully. "You know," the Apostle says, "what withholdeth," that is, what hinders, what restrains, what keeps back the full manifestation of iniquity — the revelation of the man of sin. Paul had told them of a power that was already in the world which kept evil from rising to its full height. There has been much speculation as to what he meant by this withholder or hinderer. Some have supposed that he was speaking cryptically of the Roman Empire, intimating its destruction, and declaring that the man of sin could not be revealed until the Roman Empire fell. Those who so teach generally think of the man of sin as the Papacy. That the Papacy is anti-Christian cannot be questioned by those who believe and know the truth, but the man of sin is a definite individual, not a system, who will arise at a given time and be destroyed by Almighty power. Others have taught that the hinderer is organized government, and this with a good deal more plausibility. Their thought is that when the Church is taken out of the world, all organized government will collapse, and then out of the chaotic condition prevailing among the nations, the man of sin will arise. But we need to remember that the Apostle was inviting not only for the Thessalonians in his day but for all believers to the end of the dispensation, and when he says, "*Ye know what hindereth* that he might be revealed in his time," he is speaking to all Christians.

Let me put the question directly to my reader. Do you know what hinders or restrains the full manifestation of iniquity? I have asked this question over and over again of congregations, small and great, when Christian people were gathered together to study the prophetic Word, and always as with one voice the cry came back in answer, "Yes." And when I put a second question, "Who or what is the hinderer?" at once they replied, "The Holy Spirit." This seems to me so plain that I wonder that anyone could question it. In fact, the Prophet Isaiah declares this very definitely. In chapter 59, verse 19, he says: "When the enemy shall come in like a flood, the Spirit of the Lord shall lift up a standard against him"; or, as others have translated it, "The Spirit of the Lord shall resist him." He ever resists the powers of evil. As long as He is in the world doing His present work as the Spirit of grace, He resists the efforts of Satan to bring to the front his false Christ and to destroy God's testimony in this scene. And so we read that "the mystery of iniquity [or the secret of lawlessness] doth already work, only there is one now who hinders until he be taken out of the way [or out of the midst]."

The Lord Jesus said to His disciples, "When the Comforter is come, the Spirit of truth, He will abide with you forever." He, then, is here in the world working in and through the Church. As long, therefore, as the Church is in this scene, the Hinderer is here, holding back the evil; but Satan is working in a hidden way, duping men and women with false teachings and doing all he can to dishonor the name of the Lord Jesus Christ and to prepare them to receive the false Christ when he shall appear.

When the Holy Spirit, the Hinderer, goes up with the Church at the Rapture, then that wicked one, Satan's masterpiece, will be manifested, and for a time he will deceive the whole world, except the very elect (an election called out after the Church is gone), and even they will often be in perplexity and experience difficulty in standing against his persuasiveness. His doom, however, is certain. When the Lord descends in power and glory as indicated in the first chapter of this epistle, this evil personality will be destroyed by the brightness of His Coming.

But during the last half of the seventieth week he will deceive the nations by power and signs and lying wonders. Those who will be preserved in that day are designated in the prophets as "the remnant." This Jewish remnant will become God's messengers to the Gentiles who have not yet heard and resisted the truth, but for those who have heard and had every opportunity to be saved but persisted in refusing the message of grace, there is no possibility of salvation in that awful day. Because they refused the love of the truth when they might have known it, God shall send them strong delusion, that they should believe not merely *a* lie, but, according to the original text, *the* lie, that is, the lie of the Antichrist, that they all might be damned or doomed to judgment because they believed not the truth but had pleasure in unrighteousness.

That the believers of this dispensation will not be present on the earth in that day of Satan's power is clear from verses 13 and 14:

> "But we are bound to give thanks alway to God
> for you, brethren beloved of the Lord, because God
> hath from the beginning chosen you to Salvation
> through sanctification of the Spirit and belief of the
> truth: whereunto he called you by our gospel, to the
> obtaining of the glory of our Lord Jesus Christ"
> (II Thessalonians 2:13-14).

Caught away to be with the Lord before the judgments
fall, the believers will be with Christ in the Father's
house during the time of trouble here upon the earth.

And so it is evident that this revelation concerning
the man of sin fits in perfectly with what we have been
tracing throughout Scripture, the hidden purpose of God
to call out His people during the parenthetic period
between the sixty-ninth and seventieth weeks of Daniel's
vision.

Chapter XI

THE END OF THE PARENTHESIS

We come now to consider the book of the Revelation. Within our present limits we can do this only in outline. I have taken it up more fully elsewhere.* My one thought now is to show how the bulk of the visions of the Apocalypse fit in after the Great Parenthesis has terminated.

The Lord Himself has indicated the divisions of the book of the Revelation in chapter 1, verse 19. We are told that He said to the Apostle John: "Write the things which thou hast seen, and the things which are, and the things which shall be hereafter." A somewhat more literal rendering of the last two parts of this verse would be: "The things which are now going on, and the things which shall be after these things."

At the time that the Lord uttered these words, John had only seen the vision of chapter 1, the Son of Man in the midst of the candlesticks. Therefore, we are justified in saying that the first division of this Book would be chapter 1, verses 1 to 18. The things which are now going on would embrace the next two chapters where, under the similitude of seven letters addressed to seven actual Christian churches or assemblies existing in the last decade of the first century of the Christian Era in the reign of the Emperor Domitian, under whose

*Lectures on the Book of Revelation by the same author can be obtained from the publishers.

tyrannical sway John was banished to the Isle of Patmos, we have an outline picture of the moral and spiritual conditions which the Lord saw would prevail through seven periods of the Church's history from apostolic days to the end of its testimony on earth. These churches were all located in the Roman proconsular province of Asia, where John himself, according to the best records that we have, spent something like the last thirty years of his life. For a very definite reason the Lord selected the particular seven that we have here. There were other cities in this province in which churches were located, but they are not referred to here. Hierapolis was one of them; Colossæ was another. The seven here selected will be seen, by consulting a map, to form a kind of a rough circle, so that if one took the highway from Ephesus, he would go on to Smyrna, then Pergamos, Thyatira, Sardis, Philadelphia and Laodicea, and from there back to Ephesus.

We are told in the twentieth verse of chapter 1, which introduces this division: "The mystery of the seven stars which thou sawest in my right hand, and the seven golden candlesticks. The seven stars are the angels of the seven churches: and the seven candlesticks which thou sawest are the seven churches." The Lord, then, is seen in the midst of these churches which are in the place of witness-bearing here on the earth. If we are only to think of the state and condition of the churches in the day when the Apocalypse was written, there is no particular mystery involved, but the mystery is now readily unfolded, for as we stand almost in the middle of the twentieth century, we can look back over all the years that have gone and see how remarkably these letters fit into seven great periods of Church history.

Observe, we do not have here specific historical facts as to individuals predicted. I mention this because some have objected to what has already been said because of the fact that the great outstanding characters of Church history seem to be utterly ignored. "How," one commentator asks, "could the letter to Sardis, for instance, speak of the great State churches of Protestantism when there is no mention of Luther, Calvin, or any of the other outstanding heroes of the Reformation?" The answer, of course, is that we are not dealing here with events or persons so much as with principles. In the letter to Sardis we see the moral and spiritual condition of Protestantism, and that is what the Spirit of God sought to make known. The most convincing proof that this suggested interpretation is the correct one is this: If we were to change the order of these letters in any degree, we would have confusion, but taken as they are, everything is in perfect accord with Church history. We cannot, for instance, substitute Sardis for Smyrna, Laodicea for Thyatira, Pergamos for Ephesus, or make any other change without spoiling God's wonderful portrayal of the prophetic story of the Church.

According to this view, then, we are now living in the Laodicean period of Church history. Ephesus sets forth the early days when living apostles still ministered to the Church on earth. Smyrna pictures the moral and spiritual conditions prevailing in the days of the ten great outstanding Roman persecutions. Pergamos tells of the union of Church and State in the days of Con-

stantine and his successors. Thyatira is the Romish
apostasy from the beginning of the seventh century,
when the Pope first declared himself to be head of the
Church on earth. It was then that the Papacy as such,
with its amazing pretensions, really began. Sardis gives
us, as intimated above, the great State churches of the
Reformation with their uncounted thousands of baptized
adherents who had a name to live but were dead. Philadelphia gives us the revival period, the second reformation when God's people were called back to the
authority of His Word and the recognition of the all-
sufficiency of the Name of the Lord Jesus Christ. Laodicea closes the series. It is the latitudinarian period of
the Church, the era of modernism with its utter indifference to the truth of God and the claims of the Lord
Jesus.

This, then, completes the series, and prepares us to
consider the third division of the book, which John was
told would have to do with the things which shall be
after these things. When we open chapter 4 we read
in the first verse, translated literally: "After these things
I looked and, behold, a door was opened in heaven."
From this point on we do not find the Church referred
to again until, in the appendix to the book, in chapter
22, verse 16, we read: "I Jesus have sent mine angel
to testify unto you these things in the churches. I am the
root and the offspring of David, and the bright and
morning star. And the Spirit and the bride say, Come."
The bride is here identical with the Church and waits
with longing heart for the Return of her Lord. But chapter 4 to the end of chapter 19 has to do entirely with

events that will take place after the Great Parenthesis has come to an end.

While the seventieth week of Daniel may not begin immediately after the Rapture of the Church, we are not told of any lengthy period that will come in between that glorious event and the signing of the pact between the head of the revived Roman Empire and the Jewish people. In these stirring chapters we are occupied with events which will take place in heaven and upon earth during those last seven years, and it is very easy to see when the first three and one-half years will end and the last period, the forty-two months, or 1,260 days, of intense judgment, the Great Tribulation, begin.

In chapters 4 and 5 we see the heavenly saints in the glory with their Lord, worshiping before the throne, as represented by the twenty-four elders wearing victors' crowns upon their heads. No one wears a crown till after the Judgment Seat of Christ. Therefore, it is clear that these must represent the saints who will at that time have been raptured and who will have received their rewards at the hand of the glorified Saviour.

In chapter 6 we have the opening of the seals of the book of judgment which is also the title deed to this poor world. As the first six seals are opened, providential judgments fall upon this scene akin to those spoken of by our Lord Jesus as recorded in Matthew 24 which He designates, "the beginning of sorrows." In the book of Ezekiel, God speaks of His "four sore judgments" (Ezekiel 14:21). These refer not to his dealing with men in wrath but in chastisement, in order to bring them to repentance, if there be any disposition on their part to heed His voice. They agree perfectly with the seal judgments.

But in chapter 7 we have a parenthesis between the sixth and the seventh seals, and here we find 144,000 Israelites sealed before the Great Tribulation actually begins. The angel is instructed to "hurt not the earth, neither the sea, nor the trees, till we have sealed the servants of our God in their foreheads" (verse 3). In the latter part of the chapter we have a vision of a great multitude of Gentiles who will be saved in that day. They are pictured as they will appear when they have come through that awful time of trial, even as we read in verse 14: "These are they which came out of great tribulation [or more literally, the tribulation, the great one], and have washed their robes, and made them white in the blood of the Lamb." The Lord shows John these two groups that he may know that all the terrors of the Great Tribulation with the outpouring of the wrath of God in the earth will not hinder the Spirit of God from working from heaven upon the hearts of men and women who have not heard and rejected the Gospel in this parenthetic age but who will be still living on the earth in that day.

When the seventh seal is broken, seven angels are seen standing before God, to whom are given seven trumpets of judgment. The sounding of the first trumpet introduces the Great Tribulation; the sounding of the seventh trumpet brings it to an end and ushers in the glorious kingdom of our Lord Jesus Christ. We saw in the ninth chapter of Daniel that when the seventy weeks were finished, the vision of prophecy would be sealed up, and all would be complete. And in Revelation 10, verses 5 to 7, we read:

> "And the angel which I saw stand upon the sea and upon the earth lifted up his hand to heaven, and sware by him that liveth for ever and ever, who created heaven, and the things that therein are, and the earth, and the things that therein are, and the sea, and the things which are therein, that there should be time no longer: but in the days of the voice of the seventh angel, when he shall begin to sound, the mystery of God should be finished, as he hath declared to his servants the prophets."

The expression, "There should be time no longer," does not actually mean that eternity was about to begin, but "time" is used here in the sense of delay, as if one has an appointment at a certain hour and waits expectantly for another who has agreed to meet him, and finally, disappointed, says, "There is no more time," which simply means that he cannot longer delay. Note, then, that when the seventh trumpet sounds, the mystery of God's long toleration of evil will be ended. Everything will come out in the clear, and God's ways with men will be fully justified.

In chapter 11 we have further details as to this:

> "And the seventh angel sounded; and there were great voices in heaven, saying, The kingdoms of this world are become the kingdoms of our Lord, and of his Christ; and he shall reign for ever and ever. And the four and twenty elders, which sat before God on their seats, fell upon their faces, and worshipped God, saying, We give thee thanks, O Lord God Almighty, which art, and wast, and art to come; because thou hast taken to thee thy great power, and hast reigned. And the nations were angry, and thy wrath is come, and the time of the dead, that they

should be judged, and that thou shouldest give reward
unto thy servants the prophets, and to the saints, and
them that fear thy name, small and great; and shouldest destroy them which destroy the earth" (Revelation 11:15-18).

It is clear from this passage that the seventh trumpet
ends the Great Tribulation. It is not, as some have supposed, the same as "the trump of God" in First Thessalonians 4, otherwise called "the last trump" in First
Corinthians 15. In those passages the trump of God
sounds for the Rapture of the Church. Here the seventh
angel sounds his trumpet at the end of the tribulation
period to introduce the reign of Christ. It will be then
that all heaven will rejoice because the world-kingdom
of our God and His Christ will have come.

A second section of this third great division begins in
verse 19 of chapter 11, and goes on to the end of chapter
19, but with this we need not now be concerned. Those
who want to make a fuller study of it may do so at their
leisure, and there are many helpful books that would
assist the reverent student.

Chapter 20 gives us details as to the Millennial Kingdom, and we are carried on in the next two chapters to
the eternal kingdom. The book closes with an appendix
from chapter 22, verse 8, to the end.

There is one point that it may be well to dwell upon
inasmuch as many have been perplexed by it. Ordinarily
we speak of the Rapture as involving the first resurrection, but it is well to remember that the resurrection of
our Lord was part of that first resurrection and it also
includes the resurrection of saints who will be put to
death under the Beast and the Antichrist in the awful

days of the Great Tribulation. In chapter 20, after the binding of Satan preliminary to the setting up of the kingdom, we read, in verses 4 to 6:

"And I saw thrones, and they sat upon them, and judgment was given unto them: and I saw the souls of them that were beheaded for the witness of Jesus, and for the word of God, and which had not worshipped the beast, neither his image, neither had received his mark upon their foreheads, or in their hands; and they lived and reigned with Christ a thousand years. But the rest of the dead lived not again until the thousand years were finished. This is the first resurrection. Blessed and holy is he that hath part in the first resurrection: on such the second death hath no power, but they shall be priests of God and of Christ, and shall reign with him a thousand years."

The question has often been asked, "If the first resurrection takes place at the close of the Great Tribulation, how can it be said that the saints of this and past dispensations will be raised and living believers changed and all caught up to heaven before the tribulation begins?" In order to understand this clearly, let us examine the passage carefully.

John says, "I saw thrones, and they sat upon them, and judgment was given unto them." This has been translated, "I saw thrones, and sitters upon them to whom judgment was given." Now this is a distinct group, and refers clearly to those symbolized by the twenty-four elders who have already been before us in these marvelous visions of God. These are the saints of the Church Age and of past dispensations. Then John indicates another class. He says: "And I saw the souls of them that were beheaded for the witness of Jesus, and for the word of God, and which had not worshiped the beast, neither his image, neither had received his mark upon their foreheads, or in their hands; and they lived and reigned with Christ a thousand years." The resurrection of this group completes the first resurrection. None others of the dead will live again until the Millennium is past. Speaking of both these groups, the Spirit of God says, "This is the first resurrection," and a blessing is declared as the portion of all who participate in it and who will be priests of God and of Christ and reign with him a thousand years.

With this Millennial Kingdom, human history on this earth will be concluded. When the wicked are raised at the end of the Kingdom Age and stand before the Great White Throne for judgment, the present created heavens and earth will be destroyed by fire from heaven and will be succeeded by that

> "One far off divine event,
> Toward which the whole creation moves,"

when there shall be a new heaven and a new earth wherein dwelleth righteousness, where God will be all in all. This is the everlasting kingdom of our Lord and Saviour, Jesus Christ. It consists of two aspects — the heavenly and the earthly — but the new heavens and the new earth will be in such intimate relationship with the New Jerusalem descending from God out of heaven, linking both together, that it can be said when that eternal day begins, "God Himself shall be with them, they shall be His people, and He will be their God." Nothing will be permitted to disturb the happy relationship existing between God and His saints. The whole problem of good and evil will have been "threshed out," if I may use such a term, during the ages of time and those who are saved will be the exhibit of the grace of God through all the ages to come. Happy, surely, are those who shall have their portion with the redeemed in that glorious consummation!

Limited Classical Reprint Library

GOD'S OATH

A Study of

An Unfulfilled Promise of God.

by

Ford C. Ottman

Originally published by
George H. Doran Co.
N.Y., 1911

ISBN: 0-86524-143-0

Printed by Klock & Klock in the U.S.A
1983 Reprint

TABLE OF CONTENTS

TABLE OF CONTENTS

TABLE OF CONTENTS

God's Oath

CHAPTER I

THE OATH

God said to David, through Nathan the prophet, "Thine house and thy kingdom shall be established for ever before thee: thy throne shall be established for ever" (II Samuel 7:16).

This promise He afterward confirmed with an oath, saying, "I have made a covenant with my chosen, I have sworn unto David my servant, Thy seed will I establish for ever, and build up thy throne to all generations. My covenant will I not break, nor alter the thing that is gone out of my lips. Once have I sworn by my holiness that I will not lie unto David, His seed shall endure for ever, and his throne as the sun before me. It shall be established for ever as the moon, and as a faithful witness in heaven" (Psalm 89 : 3, 4, 35-37).

It will thus be seen, as in the covenant with Abraham, how God, willing more abundantly to

3

show unto David the immutability of His counsel, confirmed it by an oath: that by two immutable things — His word supported by His oath — in which it was impossible for God to lie, David might have a strong consolation to lay hold upon the hope set before him. (Hebrews 6:17-18).

This promise to David, so solemnly confirmed by God's oath, was absolutely unconditional and never to be abrogated.

David's successors might sin and in the event of their doing so they should be punished for their iniquities; but this would not invalidate the promise nor in any way whatsoever modify its character.

On this bedrock promise of God the whole super-structure of Hebrew prophecy concerning the Messiah is standing; and if, by any means what-soever, this rock may be blasted out of its place, the coherent testimony of the prophets will be lost to us: and, more than this, the same destructive force could be used to overthrow the rock on which God's promise to Abraham is founded and with its destruction the hope of every believer in Christ would perish.

God's promise, whether given to Abraham or to David, is not to be set aside; and the oath that insures our eternal salvation is no more valid than the oath that insures the perpetuity of David's house, kingdom, and throne.

A study of the promise given to David will furnish no inconsiderable testimony to the integrity of the Scripture. This is not unimportant when both the integrity and the authority of the Scripture are seriously questioned.

If the integrity of the Scripture be impaired, its authority is limited to what is left after the eliminating process is completed: if its authority can be subverted, its integrity is of no interest.

According to the records in our hands, Jesus declared that "Scripture cannot be broken"; and subjection to its authority is shown in the gospels to have been the governing principle of His life. If these gospel records be a true account of His words and of His works, then they that deny the integrity and the authority of the Scripture are at issue with Jesus and worthy of no further consideration.

Scripture pays tribute to none, but makes the most momentous claims on the reason and faith of all. For these claims it furnishes inherent justification that satisfies both mind and heart.

The suspicion that has been cast upon Scripture by unwarranted assumption should cause us no serious anxiety. The inherent witness of the Bible to itself is of a character so remarkable that it discredits altogether such assumptions, and at the same time furnishes a chain of argument so coherent and so logical that, except the language be perverted, the conclusion to which it leads is absolutely irresistible.

In the discussion before us there are two questions of vital importance.

First: Did God mean what He said when He commanded Nathan to say to David, Thine house and thy kingdom shall be established forever before thee: thy throne shall be established forever?

There can be but one answer to this question: God did assuredly mean exactly what He said in the literal sense of the words He used.

From this premise we propose to reason with the same candor and calmness that is required in other fields of investigation, and we expect to show from the Scripture that the words "house" and "kingdom" and "throne" are of obvious meaning; that they were of undoubted significance to David and to the prophets and to the apostles and that they must retain and convey the same significance to us.

The word "house" is used more than twenty-three hundred times in the Old Testament and almost invariably in exactly the same sense as it is generally used and understood by us.

The word "kingdom" is used scores of times in the Old Testament and never means anything other than a literal kingdom such as we understand by the use of the word now.

The word "throne" has in the Old Testament a literal significance, and in no instance is it used in the modern "spiritual" sense.

Any interpretation that would make these words mean something unsubstantial and intangible, that would have us believe that God promised to David a "spiritual" house, kingdom, and throne, is at variance with the teaching of the prophets and apostles and is thereby convicted of error.

Such a palpable misuse of terms would be tolerated in no exact process of reasoning and we protest against such misuse of words by interpreters of Scripture even though the object may be an attempt to justify the apparent collapse of the covenants.

What we think is of no consequence except to ourselves and to those whom our thought may influence; what God has said is of vital importance to all men.

The second question is this: Has God kept His promise to David?

The answer we give to this question establishes a principle of interpretation that must of necessity form and characterize our conception of divine revelation.

If we say that God has kept His promise to David, then we must assume the burden of proof, and furnish evidence that shall satisfy the demand of reason and of faith. If we say that God has not kept His promise to David, then we are under equal responsibility to furnish satisfactory evidence to establish our claim.

In either case no evidence that is not derived from Scripture must be admitted, and all other testimony must be ruled out as irrelevant and immaterial.

Preconceptions are a serious handicap to the just weighing of evidence; but if we dispossess ourselves of them and allow Scripture to speak to us in its own simple and earnest manner, we shall find that prophets and apostles, as they were moved by the Holy Ghost, have forged a chain of unbreakable links extending from the promise to the coronation of the King.

CHAPTER II

THE HOUSE OF DAVID

SAUL was the first king of Israel. After a brief reign, characterized by some brilliant victories, he was rejected by Jehovah for two reasons: first, because of his intrusion into the priest's office while he waited for Samuel at Gilgal; and, second, because of his failure to exterminate the Amalekites. On both occasions his rejection was officially announced by Samuel, who, after the second offence, was sent to Bethlehem to anoint his successor.

As the venerable prophet approached the gates of the city of Bethlehem the elders trembled at his coming, and said, Comest thou peaceably? And he said, Peaceably: I am come to sacrifice unto the Lord: sanctify yourselves, and come with me to the sacrifice. And he sanctified Jesse and his sons, and called them to the sacrifice. The sons of Jesse were in succession rejected by the prophet until David, the youngest, was brought in from the field, when the Lord said to Samuel, Arise, anoint him: for this is he. Then Samuel took the

9

horn of oil, and anointed him in the midst of his
brethren: and the Spirit of the Lord came upon
David from that day forward.

Thus the House of David, in the person of David,
was chosen by divine sovereignty for the execution
of a purpose which, in the mystery of God, still
awaits fulfilment.

With the vicissitudes of David's life and the
details of his reign — instructive as they may be —
we are not concerned. Our interest is in a certain
covenant that God made with David: a covenant,
so far as we can determine, unconditional on God's
part, and one that, after the lapse of thirty centuries, is still waiting for its accomplishment.

We propose to follow this covenant through
Scripture until we find its glorious fulfilment set
before us in the book of Revelation.

The music of David's harp caused the evil spirit
to depart from Saul. For the music of a sweeter
harp than David's the straining ears of the world
are unconsciously listening: until they hear it, the
world shall be troubled with an evil spirit from
God.

During Saul's life David, though anointed with
the sacred oil, made no claim to the throne of
Israel. Saul came to his end in the fatal conflict
with the Philistines on Mount Gilboa. His death

was the tragic culmination of failed ambition. Mortally wounded by the Philistines he tried to end his misery by falling upon his own sword, but, failing in this, a passing Amalekite slew him. Jonathan, Saul's son, lay dead on the same battlefield. Three days later the Amalekite that had slain Saul, bearing the royal crown and bracelet, came to David at Ziklag, and told him that Saul and Jonathan were dead.

David's lamentation over Saul and over Jonathan still holds its place of supremacy in the expression of human sorrow.

A civil war, disrupting the kingdom, followed the death of Saul. David was anointed king over the house of Judah at Hebron: Ish-bosheth, the son of Saul, was proclaimed king of Israel at Mahanaim. For seven years and six months the deadly strife continued between the house of Saul and the house of David: but David waxed stronger and stronger, and the house of Saul waxed weaker and weaker. Abner, the most powerful supporter of the house of Saul, was slain by Joab, the commander in chief of David's army. Abner's death was followed by the murder of his royal master. Thus the way was opened for the coronation of David as king over all Israel.

During David's residence at Hebron, while he

was as yet only the king of Judah, six sons were born to him. Of these, three appear to have died in infancy: of the other three, Amnon was murdered; Absalom perished while in rebellion against the crown; and Adonijah, having attempted to usurp the throne, was subsequently put to death by Solomon. The right of succession to the crown was thus secured to the sons born to David after he was enthroned king over all Israel. The importance of this will be shown when we discuss the right of Solomon to the throne of his father David. Every link of the royal genealogical chain must be kept intact until title, without a cloud, is conveyed to One in whom it exclusively centers.

The coronation of David as king over all Israel resulted in the establishment of Jerusalem as the political center of the kingdom. Henceforth Jerusalem, the city of the Great King, holds its commanding position in all prophecy as the prototype of the new Jerusalem, whose builder and maker is God. Likewise Mount Zion becomes the religious center of the kingdom, and holds its equally conspicuous place in prophecy until God's King is established on his "holy hill of Zion."

The children that were born to David after he was crowned king over all Israel are also enumerated. Of these, two only are of interest to us in our present investigation: Nathan and Solomon. Solomon, as we know, succeeded his father as king; but Nathan was older than Solomon and, on that ground, might have contested Solomon's right of succession. It would seem that Adonijah's attempt to seize the crown was justifiable only because of the fact that he was older than either Nathan or Solomon. But Adonijah was born while David was king of Judah only, and his claim to succeed David was not admitted on any ground. In the case of Nathan it was different. He, like Solomon, was born in Jerusalem and he might with justice urge primogeniture right to the succession. The record is silent as to any attempt on his part to do this; yet Solomon's title had the shadow of Nathan's claim upon it. The importance of this will be seen when we come to investigate the genealogy of the royal family as recorded in the gospels of Matthew and Luke.

The ark of God, so venerated by the Jews, had been captured by the Philistines, before the kingdom was established. For seven months it remained among the Philistines, when, to rid themselves of the judgments its presence imposed, they sent it upon its supernatural journey to Beth-shemesh. The men of Beth-shemesh were smitten because of their unholy curiosity, and they sent

messengers to the inhabitants of Kirjath-jearim
to come and take it away. And the men of Kirjath-jearim came, and fetched up the ark of the
Lord, and brought it into the house of Abinadab
in the hill. There the ark remained for many
years — in fact during the entire reign of Saul,
and until David, after centralizing the government
at the conclusion of the civil war, brought it to
Jerusalem. The judgment that fell upon Uzzah
in the transference of the ark from the house of
Abinadab to the house of Obed-edom lent additional sacredness to this ancient symbol of God's
presence among the people. From the house of
Obed-edom it was taken by David to Jerusalem,
all Israel celebrating the event "with shouting, and
with sound of the cornet, and with trumpets, and
with cymbals, making a noise with psalteries and
harps." So they brought the ark of God, and set
it in the midst of the tent that David had pitched
for it: and they offered burnt-sacrifices and peace-
offering before God. In the tent that David had
prepared, the ark remained until it was transferred
to the temple by Solomon.

The installation of the ark was the most im-
pressive feature of the dedication of the temple.
The elders of Israel, and all the heads of the tribes,
the chief of the fathers of the children of Israel were

assembled; and the Levites bore the ark from the tent to the temple. Sacrifices were offered of sheep and oxen, "which could not be told nor numbered for multitude." Then the ark was placed in the most holy place, under the wings of the cherubim; and, as the music, instrumental and vocal, blended in one glorious harmony, the glory of the Lord appeared, and filled the house of God.

The ark, whether in the tabernacle or in the temple, was a symbol of the presence of God among the people and, therefore, a type of our Lord Jesus Christ who "tabernacled among us (and we beheld his glory, the glory as of the only begotten of the Father), full of grace and truth."

Ezekie! witnessed the departure of the glory from the temple of Solomon. It left the cherubim, lingered a moment on the threshold of the temple, and then, leaving temple and city behind it, passed over the valley of Jehosaphat to the mount of Olives. That glory never returned, save in the person of our Lord Jesus Christ, who, in like manner, left the city and the temple, crossed the valley of Jehosaphat to the mount of Olives, ascended up into heaven, and carried the glory with Him there. And yet Ezekiel tells us of another temple to which the glory shall return. It is the temple of the Kingdom-Age that is yet to be. Ezekiel has given

us a detailed description of that temple in sublime
language measurable only by like language found
in the book of Revelation. He saw the glory of
the Lord return to that temple — a prophecy of
the future surpassing the power of the imagination
of man to represent. He saw the glory of the God
of Israel come from the way of the east. He heard
a voice as the voice of many waters. He beheld
the earth lighted with glory. His vision was like
the vision he had at the river Chebar. He fell
upon his face. Then the glory of the Lord came
into the house by the way of the gate whose prospect is toward the east. Then the spirit bore the
prophet up and carried him into the inner court;
and, behold, the glory of the Lord filled the house.

The glory shall return to the temple, but not in
connection with the ark of the covenant. The ark
in its materials, acacia wood and gold, was only
a type of Christ: the incorruptible wood being
the symbol of His humanity, the gold the symbol
of His deity. The mercy seat, of pure gold, placed
above the ark, was the symbol of God's throne
in Israel.

Jeremiah, referring to the time when Ezekiel's
temple is to be built, says: "It shall come to pass
in those days, saith the Lord, they shall say no more,
The ark of the covenant of the Lord: neither shall

it come to mind: neither shall they remember it: neither shall they visit it: neither shall that be done any more.   At that time they shall call Jerusalem the throne of the Lord; and all nations shall be gathered unto it, to the name of the Lord, to Jerusalem."

This may, and doubtless does, account for the absence of the ark in Ezekiel's vision.   The glory returns in the person of the Prince.   The shadow gives way to the substance.   But the Prince foreshadowed by the ark is the Prince of the House of David.   In Him God's covenant with David is to be fulfilled.

CHAPTER III

THE COVENANT

DAVID, having captured the stronghold of the Jebusites, made Jerusalem the capital city of the kingdom. He then began the building of a royal palace. He entered into treaty relations with Hiram, the king of Tyre, who furnished cedar from Lebanon, and sent workmen whose skill had long since made famous the Zidonian artisan.

Having finished the palace David remembered the ark of God. It seemed to him incongruous that he should be living in a house of cedar while the ark, the symbol of God's presence and blessing, should be left in a tent. He spoke of this to Nathan the prophet, who, divining the purpose in the king's mind, said to him, "Go, do all that is in thine heart; for the Lord is with thee."

The same night the word of the Lord came to Nathan, saying, Go and tell my servant David, Thus saith the Lord, Shalt thou build me an house for me to dwell in? Whereas I have not dwelt in any house since the time that I brought up the

children of Israel out of Egypt, even to this day,
but have walked in a tent and in a tabernacle.   In
all the places wherein I have walked with all the children of Israel spake I a word with any of the tribes
of Israel, whom I commanded to feed my people
Israel, saying, Why build ye not me an house of
cedar?   Now therefore so shalt thou say unto my
servant David, Thus saith the Lord of hosts, I
took thee from the sheepcote, from following the
sheep, to be ruler over my people, over Israel: and
I was with thee whithersoever thou wentest, and
have cut off all thine enemies out of thy sight, and
have made thee a great name, like unto the name
of the great men that are in the earth.   Moreover
I will appoint a place for my people Israel, and will
plant them, that they may dwell in a place of their
own, and move no more; neither shall the children
of wickedness afflict them any more, as before-time,
and since the time that I commanded judges to be
over my people Israel, and have caused thee to rest
from all thine enemies.   Also the Lord telleth thee
that He will make thee an house.   And when thy
days be fulfilled, and thou shalt sleep with thy
fathers, I will set up thy seed after thee, which shall
proceed from thee, and I will establish his kingdom.
He shall build an house for my name, and I will
establish the throne of his kingdom forever.   I will

3

be his father, and he shall be my son. If he commit
iniquity, I will chasten him with the rod of men,
and with the stripes of the children of men: but
my mercy shall not depart away from him, as I
took it from Saul, whom I put away before thee.
And thine house and thy kingdom shall be established forever before thee: thy throne shall be established forever.

This covenant of God with David is absolutely
unconditional. The insertion of any subsequent
condition could not abrogate nor in any way impair
it. Paul insists upon this principle when discussing
another unconditional covenant that God made with
Abraham. Christ is no less Son of David than he
is Son of Abraham; and, by parity of reasoning
found in Paul's epistle to the Galatians, we may
say, concerning the covenant with David, Though
it be but a man's covenant, yet if it be confirmed,
no man disannulleth, or addeth thereto. Now to
David and his seed was the promise made. He
saith not, And to seeds, as of many; but as of one,
And to thy seed, which is Christ. And this I say,
that the covenant, that was confirmed before of
God in Christ, a condition of whatsoever kind in-
serted thereafter cannot disannul, that it should
make the promise of no effect.

Disobedience in the family of David was to be

followed by retribution; but there is not the slightest hint that such disobedience, however obstinate or protracted, should invalidate the covenant.

The terms of the covenant are perfectly plain and beyond the possibility of misunderstanding.

Thine house and thy kingdom shall be established forever before thee; thy throne shall be established forever.

To distort these words into a meaning other than they convey is a dangerous assumption and relegates to the realm of imagination the interpretation of God's word. It is evident that David accepted these terms at their face value. In his prayer of thanksgiving, following Nathan's announcement, he says, "Thou hast confirmed to thyself thy people Israel to be a people unto thee for ever: and thou, Lord, art become their God. And now, O Lord God, the word that thou hast spoken concerning thy servant, and concerning his house, establish it for ever, and do as thou hast said. And let thy name be magnified for ever, saying, The Lord of hosts is the God over Israel: and let the house of thy servant David be established before thee. For thou, O Lord of Hosts, God of Israel, hast revealed to thy servant, saying, I will build thee an house: therefore hath thy servant found in his heart to pray this prayer unto thee.

And now, O Lord God, thou art that God, and thy
words be true, and thou hast promised this goodness
unto thy servant: therefore now let it please thee
to bless the house of thy servant, that it may continue for ever before thee: for thou, O Lord God,
hast spoken it: and with thy blessing let the house
of thy servant be blessed for ever."

No presumed difficulty of precise application
can justify the perversion of the meaning of this
covenant as given to and accepted by David.

David's house, David's kingdom, David's throne
are unambiguous terms: they can be neither twisted
nor tortured into a meaning other than they convey.
No one would venture to maintain that the covenant
of God with David was fulfilled at any time during
the monarchy: he would venture less to maintain
that it had been fulfilled since. If David's pos-
terity, in their present dispersion, with the kingdom
vanished, and the throne in ruins, and all this sup-
planted by a spiritual kingdom over which Christ
reigns from the throne on which He is now seated,
can be taken as a fulfilment of God's promise to
David, then words have lost their meaning and
the Bible is an insoluble enigma. Nothing but a
misapprehension of God's plan and purpose concerning Israel can account for the vicious interpretations that make such lucid promises void.

There may be difficulties in adhering to a literal interpretation of this covenant, but we need not anticipate them. They arise largely through our refusal to allow Scripture to speak to us in its own earnest and simple manner. We shall, for the present at least, accept the terms of the covenant as they were accepted by David, and consider the difficulties incidental thereto when we meet them.

David's trust in this covenant was unwavering to the last. He had no conception of the establishing of any kingdom other than his own. To what extent he understood the scope of his own prophetic utterances cannot be determined. That he foretold the death, resurrection, and subsequent assumption of the throne by Messiah is evident from Peter's reference to him. (Acts 2 : 25–31).

The Messianic Psalms do not indicate that their inspired authors had a very clear conception of what they foretold. Peter speaks of the prophets "searching what, or what manner of time the Spirit of Christ which was in them did signify, when it testified beforehand the sufferings of Christ, and the glory that should follow."

David may have been perplexed about "the suffering and the glory"; but he had an unfaltering faith that God would establish the kingdom of Israel according to the terms of the covenant. He knew

also that his house would fail: of this we have
touching testimony in his dying words; but, even
in his last moments, he reposed an unchangeable
trust in the covenant.　In these "last words" of
David there is a direct claim to divine inspiration.

"The Spirit of the Lord spake by me, and his
word was in my tongue."

Such is the preface to his last words.　Then follows
a description of that "Ruler over men," who is yet
to arise, "as the light of the morning, when the
sun riseth, even a morning without clouds."　Sor-
rowfully the dying king continues: "Although
my house be not so with God; yet he hath made
with me an everlasting covenant, ordered in all
things, and sure: for this is all my salvation, and all
my desire, although he make it not to grow."

The lapse of centuries, the modern trend toward
materialism, and the advent of a peculiarly in-
sidious form of hostile criticism have wrapped
us round in a pall of darkness.　But the light of
God has not failed.　The lamp of prophecy is still
burning in the darkness, even though the darkness
comprehendeth it not.　It is our own fault if we
fail to see it or refuse to follow whither it leads.
But we need not fear to follow.　It will keep us
in the company of prophets and apostles whose
range of vision swept the utmost bounds of the

everlasting hills. It will guide us through the gloom of night into the sun-lighted glory of unending day. It will usher us into the presence of Him in whom and through whom God intends to keep His "everlasting covenant" with David, which ever has been, and ever shall be "ordered in all things, and sure."

CHAPTER IV

THE COLLAPSE OF THE KINGDOM

THE momentous period of years from the accession of Solomon to the Babylonian captivity marks an era of persistent and ever deepening decline in the Jewish monarchy.

The earnest endeavors of kings like Hezekiah and Josiah to effect a reformation failed to arrest the growing apostasy. They relieved the moral gloom of the age, but — as flashes of lightning — this caused the darkness, from which the temporary emergence came, to appear more terrible and hopeless. The only star that shone through that dark night, to cheer and bless and guide those in whom faith remained, was the promise of the dawn — however far in the future it might be — of "a morning without clouds."

It could be said respecting the kings themselves that the best of them were bad and the worst of them were inconceivably wicked.

Even before David died the smoldering spirit of discontent flamed out in rebellion, and a revolution was averted only by the immediate coronation of Solomon. Of him it is said: "Solomon the son of David was strengthened in his kingdom, and the Lord his God was with him, and magnified him exceedingly."

A king never came to a mighty throne with greater promise than Solomon. When he failed, the fate of David's throne — in its ordinary succession — was sealed, for God had said to Solomon: "Wisdom and knowledge is granted unto thee; and I will give thee riches, and wealth, and honor, such as none of the kings have had that have been before thee, neither shall there any after thee have the like" (II Chron. 1: 12). Yet the certainty of the failure of the descendants of the royal line of Judah must be manifested in their history.

The fame of Solomon brought the queen of Sheba from her far distant country that she might behold his wisdom. The unequaled splendor of his reign, in all that makes the throne of kings mighty and their word potent in the councils of the world, is appraised by the detailed delineation of it in the inspired chronicle. Yet Solomon failed. Ascending the throne girded by omnipotence itself, he ended his career, shorn of his strength, bereft of his glory, with his heart turned away from Jehovah, and the anger of God kindled against him.

The monumental work of Solomon was the building of the temple upon which he lavished the accumulated treasure of his kingdom. The dedicatory service was of unparalleled sublimity. Fire from heaven, consuming the burnt offering, attested the acceptance of his prayer of consecration: and the glory of the Lord filled the house. Then the Lord appeared to Solomon by night and, in words that alone have made his early years gloriously memorable, said unto him: "If thou wilt walk before me, as David thy father walked, and do according to all that I have commanded thee, and shalt observe my statutes and my judgments; then will I stablish the throne of thy kingdom, according as I have covenanted with David thy father, saying, There shall not fail thee a man to be ruler in Israel. But if ye turn away, and forsake my statutes and my commandments, which I have set before you, and shall go and serve other gods, and worship them; then will I pluck them up by the roots out of my land which I have given them; and this house, which I have sanctified for my name, will I cast out of my sight, and will make it to be a proverb and a byword among all nations." Here is given a solemn ratification of the covenant that God made with David. That covenant is unconditional and irreversible. No subsequent insertion of any condition can annul it. God has committed Himself to its final fulfilment; though the vicissitudes of kings and thrones may obstruct and put off the day to distant years.

The divine conditions which were made to Solomon were applicable to him alone. Disobedience should deprive him of the blessing: it could not affect — because it had no reference to — David. The apostasy of Solomon could not abrogate the covenant made with David. The imposition of conditional obedience on David's successors would delay the execution of the covenant, but this could not set the covenant aside nor make it ineffective. One greater than Solomon, a Son of David, would yet appear; and through His perfect obedience the promises of God should be made good. The covenant shall then be fulfilled. The awful failure of all others, who by right sat upon the throne of Judah through the long intervening years, ought to have prepared the heart of Israel for Him.

The death of Solomon was quickly followed by the disruption of the kingdom. The ten tribes were irrecoverably lost to the house of David, and utterly banished from human history in the Assyrian captivity; but they are not irrecoverably lost to God. If their defection and ruin were irrevocable, that would mean an irreparable breach of the covenant; but prophecy gives frequent and ample and glorious assurance that their dispersion and dissolution leave the covenant unimpaired.

Over the southern kingdom, now left alone as the people of God and heir to the promise, there rolls with ever-increasing volume and darkness the cloud of the imminent Babylonian captivity. The history of her kings is the record of her successive stages toward that event.

When Rehoboam reached the zenith of prosperity, and seemed safe from the power of Jeroboam, he forsook the law of the Lord, and carried all Judah with him. God then visited him with exemplary chastisement. Shishak, king of Egypt, came against him with an immense army and spoiled the kingdom. Repentance of the king and of the princes of Israel caused the Lord to intervene in their behalf, and He stayed the hand of the enemy from completing the ruin he intended to inflict. Yet it is written of Rehoboam that, during the seventeen years of his life after this reverse, he did evil, because he prepared not his heart to seek the Lord.

The three years' reign of Abijah formed a notable episode in the history of the kings of Judah. He acknowledged that God was King, and executed a brilliant campaign against Jeroboam; yet he

walked in all the sins of Rehoboam, staining himself
with idolatry and personal immoralities.

Of Asa it is said, he "did that which was good
and right in the eyes of the Lord his God." His
piety and zeal were rewarded by success against
his enemies. He readily responded to the leader-
ship and teaching of Azariah the prophet, and put
away the abominations out of the land. His
prosperity attracted many from Israel when they
saw the Lord his God was with him. With a
renewal of covenant vows, an offering unto God,
and an earnest purpose to confirm his people in the
true worship, he aroused great enthusiasm in
Judah: and Jehovah gave him rest round about.

But the end was evil. Because of his reliance on
the king of Syria he incurred the rebuke of Hanani
the prophet. He crushed many of the people that
sympathized with the prophet, for which God
afflicted him with disease; and it is written against
him, that he sought not to the Lord, but to the
physicians. He died, mourned by his people, after
a long reign of forty-one years which were stained
by sanguinary wars, and closed his career with an
act of tyranny and injustice.

Jehosaphat, his successor, is conspicuous as one
of the best of Judah's kings. Signal blessings from
Jehovah encouraged his heart. He inaugurated a

revival of the teaching of the law in Judah and, as a result, the fear of the Lord fell upon all tne kingdoms of adjacent lands, and in his own kingdom peace prevailed. But his pacific intent toward Israel betrayed him into forming affinity with the house of Ahab, which brought about the marriage of his son to the notorious Athaliah, the daughter of Jezebel. In this alliance he incurred the scathing rebuke of Jehu the son of Hanani. "Shouldest thou help the ungodly, and love them that hate the Lord? Therefore is wrath upon thee from before the Lord." But the good things found in him were not forgotten. He met the formidable coalition of the Moabites and the Ammonites in the true spirit of a man of God. He set himself to seek the Lord, and proclaimed a fast throughout all Judah. His prayer at this crisis of his life is one of the beautiful things in the chronicle. In the wilderness of Tekoa, before the battle, he exhorts his soldiers with a prophet's fervor. "Hear me, O Judah, and ye inhabitants of Jerusalem:Believein theLord yourGod, so shall ye be established; believe his prophets, so shall ye prosper."

The best traditions of the house of David are recalled in his conduct and spirit in the victory that followed. But his last days were clouded by a commercial alliance with Ahaziah, the king of Israel, which was denounced by Eliezer the prophet. That

a king, in whose favor so much can be said, should
have formed such an alliance, only shows how deep-
rooted and inveterate was the evil that prevailed
in the kingdom of Judah. The alliance failed:
the combined fleet was shipwrecked at Ezion-geber.

Jehosaphat died; and, the scepter of Judah passing
into the hands of a prince of the character of Jehoram
with a daughter of Jezebel for his consort,the days
grew darker, and the cause of godliness more hopeless.

Whatever promise the great reign of Jehosaphat
might have awakened in the hearts of some, the
dark record of his son and successor, Jehoram, is
without a single redeeming feature. His wickedness
and moral subjection to the house of Ahab provoked a letter of scathing denunciation from the
prophet Elijah. All the energy of the eight years
of his reign is expressed in the inspired chronicle
— "He wrought that which was evil in the eyes
of the Lord." He died detested by his people, as
it is written of him: He "departed without being
desired." Nothing but the unconditional covenant
made with David prevented the dynasty from
extinction. *

*As a matter of fact his name and the name of his son and
the name of his grandson are blotted out altogether from the
genealogical record of the kings of Judah, recorded in the gospel
of Matthew, and this doubtless because of his marriage to the
apostate daughter of Ahab, God thereby visiting upon him his
sin unto the third generation.

"The Lord would not destroy the house of David because of the covenant that he had made with David, and as he promised to give a light to him and to his sons for ever." Even the wickedness of a Jehoram could not invalidate the covenant.

In the succeeding reign of Ahaziah the darkness deepens. He was the youngest son of Jehoram, all his brothers having been slain by a band of Arabians, some of the enemies whom God had stirred up against his father. He was therefore providentially the sole heir to the crown. His mother, the daughter of Ahab, the apostate king of Israel, was his evil counsellor, and Ahab himself seems to have been the king upon whom he modeled his government as well as his life. Ahaziah was involved in the awful vengeance inflicted by Jehu upon the house of Ahab as well as on the princes of Judah and on the nephews of the king.

The death of Ahaziah stirred up Athaliah, his mother, to murder all the seed royal of the house of Judah. But this act of impious extirpation of the royal line of Judah was arrested by Jehoshabeath, a sister of the dead king, who rescued one of the royal children, and concealed him and his nurse in a bed-chamber of the palace. This providential rescue was furthered by the fact that Jehosbabeath was the wife of the high priest Jehoiada, and she was therefore able to give this child — the sole hope of Judah — asylum in the temple during the six years that the murderess Athaliah reigned over the land. Upon that slender thread hung the continuity of the royal line of David! Nothing but the overshadowing power of the covenant preserved the young child's life.

Jehoiada headed a movement to rescue the throne from the hands of the usurping Athaliah. This influential man of God said to the congregation of Judah, "Behold, the king's son shall reign, as the Lord hath said of the sons of David." A covenant with the king was made in the house of God. Athaliah was executed and Joash was crowned king at Jerusalem at seven years of age. Jehoiada was his instructor and counsellor. The salutary influence of this aged statesman-priest guided the young king in the ways of righteousness. The chief work of his reign was the repairing of the house of God, which Athaliah, that wicked woman, had broken up. But his end was evil. Upon the death of the high priest, Joash, through the flattery of his courtiers, joined them in open sin by forsaking the house of Jehovah his God. His turpitude was shown in his refusal to hear the warnings of the prophets. His death was ignominious: he was murdered, while in bed, by his own servants.

4

The record gives another of those evidences that God does not forget to requite injustice in high places. Joash was stained with the guilt of tne murder of the son of his old adviser and friend Jehoiada. Such an act, so incredible in one whose early years gave promise of so much good, can be accounted for only by the fact that he had thrown off all fear of God. And this is the dark story of a king who reigned over Judah during a period of forty years.

The character of Amaziah, his successor, is given with the characteristic terseness of Scripture: "He did that which was right in the sight of the Lord, but not with a perfect heart." He inaugurated his reign by avenging the murder of his father. It is said in his favor that he did not slay the children of the servants of Joash, who were guilty of the crime of regicide, but did according to what was written in the law in the book of Moses, where the Lord commanded, saying, "The fathers shall not die for the children, neither shall the children die for the fathers, but every man shall die for his own sin."

The tendency to dangerous alliances with the kings of Israel was still manifested in him. Embarking upon enterprises before consulting God, and then, on reproof — though seeking to redress the error — suffering from self-will, is illustrated in his career. He had formed the deadly habit of doing things first; and then praying to be delivered from the consequences.

After a successful expedition against the Edomites he brought back to Jerusalem, with the characteristic perversity of his predecessor toward idolatry, the gods of the children of Seir, and set them up to be his gods, and bowed down himself before them, and burned incense unto them. The retribution of God followed him to the end of his reign. He was defeated in battle with the king of Israel, whom he had foolishly challenged. The house of God was spoiled, and the king fled to Lachish, and he was there captured and slain. He reigned over Judah twenty-nine years.

The prosperous and brilliant reign of Uzziah, the son and successor of Amaziah, continued many years. He came to the throne at the age of sixteen years, and an analogy with his father is intimated in Scripture. The early promise of his reign was not fulfilled at its close. The prophet Zachariah exerted a good influence upon the mind of the youthful king, and — as long as he sought the Lord — he was made to prosper. The glory of his military exploits, the strength of his kingdom at home, and his successful prosecution of the arts of peace — he loved husbandry — gave him a name and a fame which spread far beyond his own dominions. In the significant language of Scripture: "He was marvelously helped, till he was strong."

Like his royal predecessor, Saul, he transgressed the spirit of the Theocracy, and offended God by his intrusion into the priest's office. While in the act of offering incense in the temple the tokens of leprosy suddenly appeared on his forehead, and he remained a leper until the day of his death. For fifty-two years he was the king of Judah and during his reign the prophet Isaiah began his ministry. The opening words of the prophecy are an indictment against Judah, and an appalling description of her religious condition. She is described as a sinful nation, a seat of evil doers; her chief men are styled as rulers of Sodom: the hopelessness of her future is startlingly foretold in the words — "Ye will revolt more and more."

The impossibility of stemming the tide of iniquity in Judah is plainly indicated in the characterization of Jotham, the next king, who reigned sixteen years in Judah. He did that which was right in the sight of the Lord, according to all that his father Uzziah did: "Howbeit he entered not into the temple of the Lord. And the people did yet corruptly."

Apparently without any exception he is commended for his rectitude: yet the ungodliness, unrighteousness, hypocrisy, and corruption of his people continue without a check. The king himself with all his excellencies appears to have been unable to influence the moral condition of his time.

The hand of God in judgment began to move against Judah by stirring up an enemy who became formidable in the next reign. The cloud of "Rezin the king of Syria, and Pekah the son of Remaliah" was throwing its ominous shadow over the kingdom.

The multiplied transgressions of Ahaz, who succeeded Jotham, provoked the great anger of Jehovah his God to bring upon him correspondingly repeated and dire afflictions. The sacred historian seems as if he had reached the limit of words to describe his abominations when he writes: "This is that king Ahaz." He was a prince abandoned to superstition, cruelty, and immorality. With a madness induced by a sense of his own ruin "in the time of his distress did he trespass yet more against the Lord." The invasion from the north that menaced Jotham culminated now. Thousands were slain and multitudes more were carried captive into Samaria. Except for the intercession of Oded the prophet, and the indefeasible covenant, Judah would have suffered utter extermination.

The plea of the prophet and the promptness of Israel to respond in penitence for mercy forms the only bright page in connection with the reign of Ahaz.

This dark night of Judah, despoiled by enemies from without and weakened by impieties and follies of a king, is brightened by the light of a coming day. The covenant was in the mind of Jehovah. Isaiah gives us in chapter seven a deeply suggestive revelation of what was in progress beyond the knowledge of man. "It was told the house of David, saying, Syria is confederate with Ephraim." Then the Lord sent Isaiah to meet Ahaz and to tell him that the conspiracy should not stand.

The unstable king was warned: "If ye will not believe, surely ye shall not be established." Yet again the Lord spake, saying, "Ask thee a sign of the Lord thy God; ask it either in the depth, or in the height above." The faithless king declines. Then the voice of the prophet rings out: "Hear ye now, O house of David; A small thing for you to weary men, but will ye weary my God also? therefore the Lord himself shall give you a sign." And at once the bow of promise shines out through the storm: "Behold, a virgin shall conceive, and bear a son, and shall call his name Immanuel." This prophecy was not addressed to the faithless king, but to "the whole house of

David." It points onward so clearly and so precisely to Christ that any other application is inadmissible. The sign is followed by a prediction of impending invasion and deliverance.

The apostate Ahaz sacrificed to heathen gods and they were the ruin of him and of all Israel. After sixteen years of inglorious reign he died; but "they brought him not into the sepulchres of the kings of Israel."

Hezekiah succeeded Ahaz. The spirit of apostasy, so tedious and monotonous in its night-like uniformity, was checked during the twenty years of his great and good reign. He came to a kingdom upon which rested the wrath of the Lord, delivered to trouble, to astonishment, and to hissing. But he makes David his model and covets for Judah and Jerusalem the happier days of the great king.

The opening of his reign was blessed with a great revival. He opened the doors of the house of the Lord, which Ahaz had closed, and repaired the temple that had fallen into decay. The Levites rejoicingly responded to his appeal to put the sanctuary in order. Great joy on the part of the king and the people was expressed on the completion of the work: "for the thing was done suddenly."

The king proclaimed a solemn passover, and a great multitude, with many representatives of the tribes of Israel, assembled at Jerusalem. So great was the religious enthusiasm that the feast of gladness was continued another seven days. The fervor generated at the holy feast, the like of which had not been seen in Jerusalem since the day of Solomon, expressed itself in immediate reformation. Idols were banished from the kingdom and other necessary reforms quickly followed. Hezekiah himself is seen as the intrepid and inspiring leader. He "wrought that which was good and right and truth before the Lord his God. And in every work that he began in the service of the house of God, and in the law, and in the commandments, to seek his God, he did it with all his heart, and prospered" (II Chron. 31: 20, 21). In the fourteenth year of his reign, Sennacherib, king of Assyria, moved probably by the desire to emulate the victories of his father over Israel, invaded Judah.*

*Ten years before this date Samaria had endeavored to repel an attack of the Assyrians under Shalmaneser; but, after a siege of three years, the northern capital fell, and Israel was carried into captivity. We have not followed the fortunes of the kingdom of Israel. No one of the house of David ever ruled on that throne, and the history of the kingdom is therefore without immediate interest. However, the restoration of the ten tribes, and their incorporation with Judah and Benjamin into one kingdom, are demanded by the terms of the covenant.

The wisdom and piety of Hezekiah shine forth in this hour of need. The king and the prophet Isaiah pray for deliverance. An overwhelming judgment falls on the invading host, and the haughty Assyrian king is rebuked for his blasphemous words against the God of Jerusalem. The angel of the Lord went out, and smote in the camp of the Assyrians an hundred four-score and five thousand.

The sickness and recovery of Hezekiah, in answer to his own prayer and that of Isaiah, are recorded with some fulness. But Hezekiah was not able to keep his heart from pride, and the princes and the people with him appear to have erred by ingratitude: for it is written, "Hezekiah rendered not again according to the benefit done unto him; for his heart was lifted up: therefore there was wrath upon him, and upon Judah and Jerusalem." For his pride he was rebuked by Isaiah, who, whether with friend or foe, always stood for righteousness and for God. The shadow on the sun-dial of Ahaz may retreat ten degrees, but it cannot avert the Babylonian captivity.

And Hezekiah slept with his fathers, and they buried him — in contrast with the sepulture of his father — in the chiefest of the sepulchres of the sons of David: and all Judah and the inhabitants of Jerusalem did him honor at his death. And Manasseh his son reigned in his stead.

Manasseh came to the throne young and reigned long. His precipitancy in evil has made his name memorable for its infamy. He began at twelve years of age and continued in impiety for fifty-five years more. He outdid the heathen in iniquity. He set himself to destroy every reform accomplished by his father, utterly obdurate to the express word of the Lord to him; and his long record of crime is without a parallel among the wicked kings of Judah. The judgment of God brought him to a late repentance when he was a fettered king in a Babylonian prison. "When he was in affliction, he besought the Lord his God, and humbled himself greatly before the God of his fathers, and prayed unto him: and he was intreated of him, and heard his supplication, and brought him again to Jerusalem into his kingdom. Then Manasseh knew that the Lord he was God" (II Chron. 33 : 12, 13.).

Partial reforms were introduced by him on his return from Babylon, but they lacked thoroughness. The inspired epitaph is as melancholy as it is pathetic. He died and found a dishonored grave in his own garden.

Amon, the successor of Manasseh reigned for two

brief years. He continued the abominations of his father and was assassinated by his servants in the royal palace. This act of regicide was visited by the vengeance of the people of the land upon the conspirators.

The new king, Josiah the son of Amon, came to the throne as a boy of eight years and reigned in Jerusalem thirty-one years. The inspired chronicler would seem to indicate that there was a popular demand for something better than the iniquities and calamities of the past half century. Josiah was justly beloved and became a favorite with his people. While he was yet young, in the eighth year of his reign, he began to seek after the God of David his father. In the thirteenth year of his reign Jeremiah began his ministry. With him were Shaphan the scribe, Hilkiah the high priest, and Huldah the prophetess, forming a notable and God-fearing group, which abetted the young king in his reforms, and gave him a safe circle of advisers. Isaiah had died during the wicked reign of Manasseh.

The discovery of the book of the law in the house of God revealed to Josiah the desperate state of his kingdom. He prosecuted his reforms with great vigor. The greatest passover since the days of Samuel was solemnized. And yet, though the reformation was widespread, and a clean sweep was made of all the abominations that had accumulated during the previous reigns, it was for the most part external. The task of effecting a complete reformation of Judah was too great for him. The people were too far gone in iniquity. The spiritual condition of the nation was untouched; the heart was unreached by the efforts of this last of the reforming kings. The awful reality of the condition of the kingdom is described in the early prophecies of Jeremiah. Harvest was past, the Summer was ended, they were not saved. They were a doomed people. Jeremiah, in his grief over his country, cried: "Oh that my head were waters, and mine eyes a fountain of tears, that I might weep day and night for the slain of the daughter of my people!" Nor tears nor intercession could avail. The Lord said unto the prophet: "Though Moses and Samuel stood before me, yet my mind could not be toward this people: cast them out of my sight, and let them go forth."

The reign of the good king came to a mournful end. With too great precipitation he entered into a war with Necho, king of Egypt, to oppose his march through the kingdom. Disguised though he was, the archers found him; and mortally wounded he was hurried from the battlefield of Megiddo

to Jerusalem, where he breathed his last: and all
Judah and Jerusalem lamented for him. "The
breath of our nostrils, the anointed of Jehovah,
was taken in their pits, of whom we said, Under his
shadow we shall live among the nations."

With the death of Josiah, the throne of David
began to totter toward its overthrow

Brief record is made of the next king, Jehoahaz.
He came to the throne at the age of twenty-three
years. The three months during which he reigned
in Jerusalem were enough to earn for him a place
in that class of the kings of Judah who did evil
in the sight of the Lord, "According to all that his
fathers had done." He became a vassal of Pharaoh: and his kingdom was placed under heavy
tribute.

Eliakim, who succeeded this disgraced king,
was another son of Josiah. The abject state to
which the kings of the house of Judah were reduced
is exemplified by the fact that Pharaoh changed his
name to Jehoiakim. He reigned eleven years in
Jerusalem, and did evil in the sight of the Lord
his God. He was bound in fetters by Nebuchadnezzar and carried away into captivity. This
was the royal apostate, who contemptuously took
the writing of the prophet, and "cut it with a
penknife, and cast it into the fire that was on the

hearth." Jeremiah predicted his end, and that
of others like him, saying, "He shall be buried with
the burial of an ass, drawn and cast forth beyond
the gates of Jerusalem."

Jehoiachin, or Jeconiah, or Coniah, as he is
variously named, succeeded Jehoiakim his father.
His reign in Jerusalem ended in three months and
ten days. He shared the fate of his father, being
deported to Babylon, together with all the rest
of the inhabitants of Jerusalem, save the poorest
sort of the people.

Nebuchadnezzar left Mattaniah as tributary
king in Jerusalem, and changed his name to Zedekiah. He was brother of Jeconiah's father. While
the right of succession to the throne of David remained with the line of the deported king, attention
is given to Zedekiah in the chronicle. There is
nothing good to be said of him. He "stiffened his
neck" and "hardened his heart" from turning unto
the Lord God of Israel. Moreover, all the chief
of the priests, and the people, transgressed very
much after all the abominations of the heathen;
and polluted the house of the Lord.

Zedekiah was given repeated warnings. God had
compassion on His people, and on His dwelling
place: but they mocked the messengers of God,
and despised His words, until it is mournfully

said, "there was no remedy." The unalterable edict of judgment went out against the last of the kings of the house of David.

Of Jehoiachin it is written in the prophecy of Jeremiah: "As I live, saith the Lord, though Coniah the son of Jehoiakim, king of Judah, were the signet ring upon my right hand, yet would I pluck thee hence." The awful edict of wrath did not end there. It followed and rested upon his descendants. "O earth, earth, earth, hear the word of the Lord. Thus saith the Lord, Write ye this man childless, a man that shall not prosper in his days: for no man of his seed shall prosper, sitting upon the throne of David, and ruling any more in Judah."

Thus the direct line of David is put under the ban of divine proscription. Yet had God said to David: "Thine house and thy kingdom shall be established for ever before thee: thy throne shall be established for ever." That covenant unconditional, irreversible, unalterable, and irrevocable, stands as it was made. Though obstacles shall multiply, and impediments to its fulfilment increase through many centuries, until there is no memory or reminiscence in the earth of the ancient throne except the scattered and humbled people whose ancestors were once its subjects, still we are justified in looking confidently forward to its redemption in greater fulness of glory than when the great king received the promise.

The throne of David is in ruins. The direct line of accession to it is through Jeconiah smitten with a curse. The two kingdoms are still in world-wide dispersion. Jerusalem is still trodden down of the Gentiles. There is no hope save in God; and it is He who is concerned both with the promulgation of the covenant and with its triumphant fulfilment

CHAPTER V

LIGHT IN THE DARKNESS

DURING the decline and fall of the Jewish monarchy, and long after the wreck of it, all hope was centered in the Messiah that was to come.

All the prophets, whether addressing the northern kingdom of Israel or the southern kingdom of Judah, united in this proclamation. Their own undying faith in God inspired their undying testimonies to His faithfulness toward them. They looked forward to and proclaimed a Messiah that was to establish the house of David and upon David's throne rule over David's kingdom. No other construction of their messages would seem to be possible without the perversion of their meaning. It is the light of their testimony alone that illumines and interprets the history of Judah as her day darkens to its close.

When the black cloud of Assyria was casting its ominous shadow over the plains of the north, Isaiah saw the approaching storm; as in the preceding reign of Ahaz he had seen a similar storm approach from Syria and Samaria. If in the

5   51

approach of this latter calamity he had spoken of the virgin that was to conceive and bear a son and call his name Immanuel, he drops all mystery of speech as the Assyrian invasion comes near.

"Unto us," he says — and he is speaking to his own people the Jews — "Unto us a child is born, unto us a son is given: and the government shall be upon his shoulder: and his name shall be called Wonderful, Counsellor, The Mighty God, The Everlasting Father, The Prince of Peace. Of the increase of his government and peace there shall be no end, upon the throne of David, and upon his kingdom, to order it, and to establish it with judgment and with justice from henceforth even for ever."

In this glorious declaration all the light of sacred prophecy converges, and reveals that great and solitary Figure of human history, who is set forth as the one hope of Israel, and who is the one and only hope of the world.

The virgin's child, whose name was to be called Immanuel, is here seen distinctly as the King of David's line, upon whose shoulder the government was to be. But He is not only King of David's line, He is The Mighty God, The Everlasting Father, or, literally, The Father of Eternity, who shall bring eternity into being, and settle all things on everlasting foundations. No misapprehension of the language used by the prophet must be allowed to mar the matchless glory of Him who is not only Immanuel but also David's Son and David's Heir.

The whole of Isaiah's predictive prophecy is based on the promise that God made to David. In all the years of his ministry, until the time of his death during the reign of the wicked Manasseh, his faith in that promise remained unshaken.

In the far distant future he saw the Gentile hosts assemble for battle at Armageddon. His heart was undismayed. Over against that vision he places this: "There shall come forth a rod out of the stem of Jesse, and a Branch shall grow out of his roots." Before those gathered hosts of wickedness there stands alone in solitary grandeur The Son of David. Nor shall He be lacking in that great crisis. The Spirit in sevenfold power shall rest upon Him, and "righteousness shall be the girdle of his loins, and faithfulness the girdle of his reins." Once more the prophet's undying faith in God's covenant is proclaimed: "In that day there shall be a root of Jesse, which shall stand for an ensign of the people; to it shall the Gentiles seek: and his rest shall be glorious."

No day is dark when hope is sustained by an

issue so glorious.   No evil so inscrutable as not to
find its interpretation in this.   Beyond his own day
of evil the prophet saw that other day dawning over
the hills of time.   In that day — over against the
sorrow of his own — shall this song be sung in the
land of Judah: "We have a strong city; salvation
will God appoint for walls and bulwarks.   Open
ye the gates, that the righteous nation which keepeth
the truth may enter in.   Thou wilt keep him in
perfect   peace,   whose   mind   is   stayed   on   thee:
because he trusteth in thee.   Trust ye in the Lord
for ever: tor in the Lord JEHOVAH is everlasting
strength."

Across the cloud of Sennacherib's invasion this
same prophet throws another band of light: "Behold a king shall reign in righteousness, and princes
shall rule in judgment."   This is none other than
The Son of David, The Christ of God.

Looking to the more distant horizon, where even
thicker clouds were gathering, the prophet, still
trusting in God's covenant with David, says: "Look
upon Zion, the city of our solemnities: thine eyes
shall see Jerusalem a quiet habitation, a tabernacle
that shall not be taken down; not one of the stakes
thereof shall ever be removed, neither shall any
of the cords thereof be broken.   But there the glorious Lord will be unto us a place of broad rivers

and streams; wherein shall go no galley with oars, neither shall gallant ship pass thereby. For the Lord is our judge, the Lord is our lawgiver, the Lord is our king; he will save us."

There is much more of the same glorious optimism to be found in the utterances of this prophet. A coming deliverance through the Son of David is the sustaining note of his song. One of his last appeals is based on that hope: "Incline your ear, and come unto me: hear, and your soul shall live; and I will make an everlasting covenant with you, even the sure mercies of David."

Jeremiah, standing among the falling ruins of the kingdom, had the same unchangeable confidence in the covenant that God had made with David. Even though the house of David be carried into captivity, Jerusalem sacked, and the throne overturned, yet the promise of God was sure.

In the chapter that follows the one where the legal descent of David is smitten with a curse we read: "Behold, the days come, saith the Lord, that I will raise unto David a righteous Branch, and a king shall reign and prosper, and shall execute judgment and justice in the earth. In his days Judah shall be saved, and Israel shall dwell safely: and this is the name whereby he shall be called, THE LORD OUR RIGHTEOUSNESS."

In the crown of thorns, the rejected King, the
life taken from the earth, and all Israel more widely
dispersed than ever before, we shall find no answer
to this glorious promise. For the Son of David,
the Righteous Branch, the King of Glory, the
Lord Our Righteousness, the world still waits. And
He is worth waiting for. And it shall be said in
that day: "Lo, this is our God; we have waited
for him, and he will save us: this is the Lord; we
have waited for him, we will be glad and rejoice
in his salvation."

This hope alone sustained the heart of Jeremiah
as the swirling currents of apostasy swept the
southern kingdom onward to its ruin. His was no
easy mission. At the time of his call he had shrunk
from it. But God had set him over the nations
and over the kingdom "to root out, and to pull
down, and to destroy, and to throw down, to build
and to plant." He was more than the preacher
of impending calamity: he was the prophet of a
future glory to be ushered in at the last. He was
hated and persecuted for proclaiming the approaching judgment of God: he was given no credit for
heralding the glory that is yet to be. No prophet
of impending disaster is given a patient hearing:
he is often treated as if he were responsible for
the judgments he proclaims. So Jeremiah was

treated. But at whatever personal cost he rebuked and warned. It was all without avail. The stroke fell and the kingdom of David lay in ruins.

Even though one deny the fact of inspiration he might well wonder at the precision of Jeremiah's predictive prophecy. He began his ministry during the reign of king Josiah. The attempt on the part of this monarch to turn back the tide of iniquity was supported by the dauntless courage of Jeremiah. But it v. as impossible to turn back the tide. The reformation was superficial. Mournfully the prophet says: "Judah hath not turned unto me with her whole heart, but feignedly, saith the Lord."

Nothing but judgment remained. This the prophet announced. He foretold the coming Babylonian captivity: he predicted the seventy years of its duration: he declared that the people should return after the seventy years should expire: and then, with majestic sweep of vision, he foresaw the world-wide dispersion of the people, their final regathering and restoration to favor, and the kingdom of glory that should follow.

Jeremiah died in the early part of the captivity. Subsequent history bore witness to the truth of his testimony. After seventy years a remnant of the people returned under Ezra, Nehemiah, and Zerubbabel; the city was rebuilt, the temple was restored, and the national history resumed. This return and renationalization, though in precise fulfilment of the prophet's word, left untouched the great body of his prophecy. His prediction of final restoration includes both the northern kingdom of Israel and the southern kingdom of Judah. They were to come together once more. In anticipation of that coming day, the prophet says: "At that time they shall call Jerusalem the throne of the Lord; and all nations shall be gathered unto it, to the name of the Lord, to Jerusalem: neither shall they walk any more after the imagination of their evil heart. In those days the house of Judah shall walk with the house of Israel, and they shall come together out of the land of the north to the land that I have given for an inheritance unto your fathers." This final restoration should be accomplished after a time of unexampled trouble when Jehovah should raise "unto David a righteous Branch." The immutability of God's covenant with David was the only ground for national hope. The day of trouble to which the prophet refers has never yet darkened the horizon of human history. The counter assumption, if it could be maintained, would result in the collapse of the whole framework of prophecy.

"Alas! for that day is great, so that none is like it: it is even the time of Jacob's trouble, but he shall be saved out of it. For it shall come to pass in that day, saith the Lord of hosts, that I will break his yoke from off thy neck, and will burst thy bonds, and strangers shall no more serve themselves of him: but they shall serve the Lord their God, and David their king, whom I will raise up unto them. Therefore fear thou not, O my servant Jacob, saith the Lord; neither be dismayed, O Israel: for, lo, I will save thee from afar, and thy seed from the land of their captivity; and Jacob shall return, and shall be in rest, and be quiet, and none shall make him afraid."

The utter annihilation of the Jewish monarchy has challenged our faith in all this. The tedious procession of the centuries has added the weight of its testimony. We have tried to justify our belief by a process of reasoning reprobated by heart and conscience alike. Our labored attempts to force history into a justification of sacred prophecy have produced confusion of thought in the minds of the believer, and subjected our interpretations of Scripture to the contempt and ridicule of the ungodly.

The great prophecy found in the thirty-third chapter of Jeremiah is based on God's covenant

with David. "Behold, the days come, saith the
Lord, that I will perform that good thing which I
have promised unto the house of Israel and to the
house of Judah. In those days, and at that time,
will I cause the Branch of righteousness to grow
up unto David; and he shall execute judgment and
righteousness in the land. In those days shall
Judah be saved, and Jerusalem shall dwell safely:
and this is the name wherewith she shall be called,
The Lord our righteousness. For thus saith the
Lord; David shall never want a man to sit upon the
throne of the house of Israel."

Nothing from human history since the days of
the Babylonian captivity can be produced to prove
the fulfilment of this prophecy. We cannot claim
such fulfilment without impeaching the testimony
of both Isaiah and Jeremiah. Nor do these prophets
stand alone: they are sustained and authenticated
by the other prophets.

The message of Hosea is in reference to the dispersion and the restoration of the northern kingdom;
but the prophet's confidence in this rests on the
covenant that God made with David. This is
certain from the language he uses: "For the children of Israel shall abide many days without a
king, and without a prince, and without a sacrifice
and without an image, and without an ephod, and

without teraphim: afterward shall the children of Israel return, and seek the Lord their God, and David their king; and shall fear the Lord and his goodness in the latter days."

Joel, one of the earlier prophets of Judah, speaks with the same certainty of the future glory and blessing of Israel.

Amos, though a prophet of the northern kingdom, has a vision of the future of the whole house of Jacob. He predicted the dispersion of Israel, the overthrow of the monarchy, and its reconstruction under an heir of David. "In that day will I raise up the tabernacle of David that is fallen, and close up the breaches thereof; and I will raise up his ruins, and I will build it as in the days of old." The apostolic comment on this verse found in the fifteenth chapter of Acts should caution us against any attempt to seek for the fulfilment of this prophecy in the first advent of our Lord. The tabernacle of David has never been lifted from its ruins, and it never shall be until the Son of David, the Heir of the covenant, returns to accomplish it.

Micah was a contemporary of Isaiah. The burden of his prophecy centers in the future glory and kingdom of the Messiah. It was from this prophet that the chief priests and scribes gave answer to Herod when he demanded from them "where Christ should be born." Despite the smiting of the Judge of Israel, Micah saw the kingdom established in majesty and power. The Church does not answer to this kingdom nor was it ever intended that it should. Such identity, if it could be established, would abrogate the covenant that God made with David, and make all prophecy the inexplicable enigma it has become to such as hold that view.

Habakkuk, a contemporary of Jeremiah, was not so much concerned about the divine judgment impending over Judah. He sought rather the vindication of Jehovah's holiness in the permission of sin. The sublime answer given him foretells the captivity and dispersion. That would vindicate the divine holiness. But God is merciful and gracious; and, though Israel be judicially cast out of the land, "the earth shall be filled with the knowledge of the glory of the Lord, as the waters cover the sea." Divine judgment should not annul the covenants of God.

Zephaniah, another contemporary of Jeremiah, adds his testimony to that of the other prophets. He foretells the judgment of the nations, and the future kingdom-blessings of Israel. The least attention to his words should be enough to convince us that he does not refer to what took place at the first advent of Christ. It would be well for us if, like these prophets of old, our vision might leap over all intervening years and rest on the glory that is yet to be.

Ezekiel and Daniel were captives in Babylon. The book of Daniel is the connecting link between the Old and New Testament prophecies. Daniel and Revelation are complementary books and give us a vision of the consummation of all prophecy. Daniel covers the entire period from the captivity to the setting up of the Messianic kingdom: Revelation begins with the apostasy of the Christian Church and carries us on to the new heaven and the new earth wherein dwelleth righteousness.

In Ezekiel the predictions culminate in the wondrous blessing that should follow the restoration of the monarchy under Him who was to be Heir of the covenant that God had made with David. That Ezekiel's predictions were founded on this covenant is evident from the language in which they are expressed. In the name of Jehovah he foretells the restoration of the nation, and then adds: "Thus saith the Lord God: I will set up one shepherd over them, and he shall feed them, even my servant David; he shall feed them, and he shall be their shepherd. And I the Lord will be their God, and my servant David a prince among them; I the Lord have spoken it. And I will make with them a covenant of peace, and will cause the evil beasts to cease out of the land: and they shall dwell safely in the wilderness, and sleep in the woods. And I will make them and the places round about my hill a blessing; and I will cause the shower to come down in his season; there shall be showers of blessing." This promise is reiterated in a later message: "And David my servant shall be king over them; and they all shall have one shepherd: they shall also walk in my judgments, and observe my statutes, and do them. And they shall dwell in the land that I have given unto Jacob my servant, wherein your fathers have dwelt; and they shall dwell therein, even they, and their children, and their children's children for ever: and my servant David shall be their prince for ever. Moreover I will make a covenant of peace with them; it shall be an everlasting covenant with them: and I will place them, and multiply them, and will set my sanctuary in the midst of them for evermore."

Nothing like this has occurred since the Babylonian captivity. It would be folly to think so and at the same time hope to preserve the accuracy and authority of Scripture. In seeking to honor the prophets we should be careful lest we degrade them by a method of interpretation that makes their lan-

guage devoid of meaning. We do not commend
Scripture by wresting a text from its true meaning
in order to make it conform to some preconceived
opinion.

The post-exilic prophets, Haggai, Zechariah, and
Malachi, add their testimony to that of the prophets
gone before them. With unfaltering faith they
rest their hope on God's promise to David. That
hope is the hope of the nation and it is the only hope
of the world. For the Son of David, to whose
glory they gave witness, the world is unconsciously
waiting.

The Old Testament closes with the announcement
of the messenger that was to prepare the way before
Him: "Behold, I will send my messenger, and he
shall prepare the way before me: and the Lord,
whom ye seek, shall suddenly come to his temple,
even the messenger of the covenant, whom ye
delight in: behold, he shall come, saith the Lord
of hosts " (Mal. 3 : 1).

The first clause of this passage is quoted in application to John the Baptist (Matt. 11: 10); but
the Lord Jesus, who cites and applies the text,
significantly omits the last clause, which is nowhere
quoted in the New Testament. The reason for
this will be obvious to those that have learned to
distinguish between the first and second advents

of our Lord. Malachi, like the other Old Testament prophets, blends both advents into one prediction. The interval between the two advents
is a New Testament revelation announced after the
rejection of the King.

The kingdom proclaimed by the prophets was
to be established upon the earth by power under
the Messiah, the Son of David, and Heir of the
covenant. Though introduced by divine judgment
the power of the kingdom was to be characterized
by mercy and righteousness. It was to be a kingdom
of unbroken peace, with the knowledge and glory
of the Lord filling the earth, as the waters cover
the sea. Israel restored to divine favor under Christ
enthroned on mount Zion was to be the center of
refreshment and blessing to all the earth.

With this conception, and with no spiritual modi-
fication of it, John the Baptist appeared and announced the kingdom to be at hand.

CHAPTER VI

THE KING

INSPIRATION lapsed with Malachi, and no prophet's voice was heard in Israel for more than four hundred years, when the long silence was broken by the angel Gabriel, who appeared to Zacharias the priest while ministering in the temple, and predicted the birth of a son who was to be the "voice in the wilderness" foretold by Isaiah the prophet.

Six months later Gabriel appears again, but this time to Mary, a virgin of Nazareth, and he tells her that she is to have a son, and that his name is to be called Jesus.

The angel's announcement confirms the covenant that God made with David; for, concerning the Son to be born, he says, "He shall be great, and shall be called the Son of the Highest: and the Lord God shall give unto him the throne of his father David: and he shall reign over the house of Jacob for ever; and of his kingdom there shall be no end."

Dr. Schaff, the distinguished Church historian, says: "The idea of a spiritual Messiah who should crush the serpent's head and redeem Israel from the bondage of sin, was changed into the conception of a political deliverer who should reëstablish the throne of David in Jerusalem, and from that center rule over the Gentiles to the ends of the earth. The Jews of that time could not separate David's Son, as they called the Messiah, from David's sword, scepter and crown. Even the apostles were affected by this false notion."

This grave charge against the apostles applies with equal force to Gabriel and to the long line of prophets to whose voices we have listened. "The idea of a spiritual Messiah" was never entertained by them nor by any others until conceived by those who were too easily convinced by human history that the covenant was past redemption.

The rejection and death of the Messiah ended forever, in the minds of many in Israel, all expectation of the restoration of the throne of David. But it did not altogether extinguish the hope that had been cherished for centuries. The clouds that gathered round the disciples at the cross vanished in the light of the resurrection morning. Their own hope was revived and they believed, and proclaimed their belief, that the hope of Israel had not perished in the cross of Jesus. They found no difficulty in a literal construction of Gabriel's message, and there is no difficulty, except to those who are obsessed by the "false notion," that the second advent of Christ is coterminous with the end of the world. The fiction of a "spiritual Messiah," displacing the national hope of Israel, is extra-biblical and irreconcilable to sacred prophecy.

Gabriel's testimony is not to be set aside by any method of interpretation that permits history to interpret prophecy. Prophecy interprets history; and not the reverse: and all future history is governed bv prophecy yet to be fulnlled.

Gabriel's words are of unmistakable meaning, "The Lord God shall give unto him the throne of his father David; and he shall reign over the house of Jacob for ever; and of his kingdom there shall be no end." A literal acceptance of these words is without shock to faith or reason.

Matthew and Luke alone give an account of our Lord's coming into the world. They relate no incident in common. Each one confines himself to what is in harmony with the distinctive character of his Gospel.

In Matthew it is the birth of "The King of the Jews." That, surely, is in line with Gabriel and the prophets.

In Luke it is the birth of "a Saviour"; and yet — as if mindful of the covenant — the angel announces that "in the city of David" the Saviour is born.

Prophecy had marked out the place of his birth. "And thou, Bethlehem, [in the] land of Juda, art in no wise least among the princes of Juda; for out of thee shall come forth a Ruler who shall be a shepherd to my people Israel." So the chief priests and scribes quoted Micah the prophet in answer to the question of the Magi. Yet the words are not found in Micah exactly as they quote them. "Hebrew," says Grant, "was not any more the language of Israel as a whole; and it was quite the custom to paraphrase, rather than quote literally a Scripture appealed to. The Hebrew, besides smaller differences, does not give 'shepherd' in this passage, but simply 'Ruler'. The Greek of the Septuagint follows the Hebrew: so the variation is their own. And yet who can deny that the one word is God's thought as to the other? He who had sent Moses to the sheepfolds to learn how to guide his people in the wilderness — He who in the land had chosen David and 'taken him from

following the ewes great with young' (demanding
therefore, the tenderest care) to feed and guide
with no less tenderness the flock of his pasture —
He had indeed consecrated the 'shepherd' as the
picture of the Ruler whom He had appointed and
would raise up. There is but One who has outdone
this picture."

Mary is at Nazareth, but her child, in fulfilment
of promise, must be born in Bethlehem. To accomplish this, God sets the whole Roman world in
motion. Cæsar Augustus, in his palace on the Tiber,
though he be lord of the world, is troubled about
his revenue. He writes a decree that all the world
shall be taxed. He is but the unconscious instru-
ment of a higher power. His decree brings a
woman from Nazareth to Bethlehem: that accomplished, the whole scheme is abandoned, and
nothing more heard of it for some years afterward.
This measured conformity with prophecy, so repeatedly and so strikingly set before us in Matthew's
Gospel, should warn us against the spiritual
application to which so many, in order to
escape from presumed difficulties, have fled for
refuge.

Matthew gives us the Gospel of the kingdom.
Jesus is the Son of David, and Heir of the covenant
that God made with David. Matthew never

loses sight of this fact. The Gospel opens with "the genealogy of Jesus Christ," who as "son of David" is the King of Israel: as the "son of Abraham" He is not necessarily a King, but is Heir of the covenant that God made with Abraham.

As the Son of David he has legal title to the throne of Israel. The genealogical table of Matthew must be studied in connection with that of Luke in order to see how that title became his exclusive possession. In Matthew's table we have David's line through Solomon: the legal title to the throne of Israel being handed down from son to son until it is vested in Joseph, the last of the royal line before Jesus.

"The genealogy," says Grant, "shows the ruin hopeless but to God, in that Joseph, the last of the line here before Christ, is shown by it to be Jeconiah's son; and against Jeconiah prophecy had denounced that he should be (as to the throne) childless: for no man of his seed should prosper, sitting upon the throne of David, and ruling any more in Judah (Jer. 22: 30). The consequence was pressed, as far back as Irenæus, that here the direct line of descent is smitten with a curse, while yet it was not deprived of the legal title: it could hand on to another, therefore, that which could be of no advantage to itself." The empty title had been handed down from Jeconiah to Joseph. Promise and prophecy are here in a conflict that nothing short of divine wisdom can reconcile. How simply but how wonderfully divine wisdom effects this!

In the genealogy of Luke we have given to us the descent of David's line through Nathan. The genealogy in Matthew being that of Joseph through Solomon, the one in Luke must of necessity be that of Mary through Nathan. The coincidence of similar names in the two tables presents no serious difficulty: such a thing is of common occurrence in any long line of descent.

Jesus, being the Son of Mary, was of the house of David, and inherited whatever shadow of claim there may have been to the throne by virtue of the primogeniture right of Nathan. The marriage of Joseph and Mary made Jesus the adopted Son and legal Heir of Joseph. The title, unaffected by the curse pronounced upon Jeconiah, is thus conveyed to Jesus in whom there centers, through both Nathan and Solomon, exclusive right to the throne of Israel. "Who shall declare his generation?" asks the prophet, "for he was cut off out of the land of the living: for the transgression of my people was he stricken." Dying thus "without generation" He carried the title away with Him.*

But who shall venture to declare that title worthless? Its value must be determined by Scripture and by no preconception of our own. The throne of the Father upon which He is now seated is not the throne of David, and only by perversion and sophistry may a specious identity be established.

Joseph's hesitation in taking Mary is ended by

---

*David Baron, the distinguished Jew who was led by the Spirit through the unanswerable logic of Scripture to accept Jesus as the Messiah, is reported to have said in one of his addresses on prophecy that, if the claim of Jesus to the throne of David had not been known in Jerusalem to be absolutely without a flaw, the Jews would never have driven Him to the Cross. They would need only — on the day He entered Jerusalem and was received with royal acclamation as the son of David — to have denounced Him as an impostor and pretender, to silence forever any righteous claim He might make as leader or teacher; but neither on that day, nor on the day He put that solemn challenge to them as to the meaning of David calling Him Lord, was a voice raised to dispute His legal title. Mr. Baron is also reported to have said that, up to Christ's rejection as King, all genealogical records were preserved in the temple, and easily accessible to all the people; but, when Titus destroyed the city and the temple, these records were also destroyed and since that day the genealogical tables of Matthew and Luke alone remain to give the lineal descent from David. Whatever may be the traditional belief of a Jew as to his family and his tribe, no man can bring legal documentary proof that he is of the tribe of Judah and lineage of David and rightful heir to David's throne. Therefore, the *only living man* who to-day can bring forward an unbroken genealogy, directly and incontrovertibly from David, is Jesus of Nazareth, born King of the Jews, crucified King of the Jews, and to come again King of the Jews.

a dream in which the angel of the Lord appeared
unto him, saying, "Joseph, thou son of David,
fear not to take unto thee Mary thy wife: for that
which is conceived in her is of the Holy Ghost.
And she shall bring forth a son, and thou shalt
call his name JESUS: for he shall save his people
from their sins."

Joseph is addressed as "the son of David" and
is here — what the genealogy declares him to be
— the legal heir of David's line. And again we
are reminded of how all this was marked out by
prophecy. The superhuman birth and the name
given were in answer to what had been spoken of
the Lord by the prophet, saying, "Behold, a virgin
shall be with child, and shall bring forth a son,
and they shall call his name Emmanuel, which being
interpreted is, God with us." Thus Jesus —"Jehovah the Saviour"— is identical with Emmanuel —
"God with us." But Emmanuel, in prophecy, was
distinctively the King of David's line, upon whose
shoulder the government was to be. These closely
interwoven links cannot be broken without destroying the whole chain of sacred prophecy.

Thus, with clear title to the throne certified,
Jesus, the Son of David and Heir of the covenant,
is born unto the world. The magi, coming from
the East, own Him to be the King of the Jews, but

in recognition of His greater glory fall down and worship Him.

Herod, the Edomite usurper, who fills the throne, seeks the life of the new-born King. The flight into Egypt and the return to Nazareth are alike governed by prophecy. It is deeply significant that the voices of all the prophets unite in the testimony that he was to be called "a Nazarene."

"This," says Grant, "was a name actually given to the Lord, and generally in scorn, from the place to which in general His birth was accredited, and in which so large a portion of His life on earth was spent. Nazareth was, it seems, nowhere in very good repute, but especially among the Pharisees and traditionalists. It had no history, no memories, was consecrated by no great names; and its own name, which seems to have been but a feminine form of *netzer*, a 'sprout' or 'shoot,' may even refer to this. It was thus expressive of lowliness, if yet of life, and identical with the word in Isaiah 11 : 1, where Messiah is spoken of as the 'rod' or 'shoot out of the stem of Jesse'; and here His greatness and His lowliness are seen together. The stem has been cut down; it is better characterized as that of Jesse than of David, for royalty no more attaches to it: and thus the Son of David comes into no outward state or glory, but the opposite. And yet Jesse bears witness in his name also that 'Jehovah exists'; and He is God of resurrection. The Sprout, if lowly, has yet the energy of life in it. In Him the cut down tree is to revive, and to eclipse all its former glories. He is the 'righteous branch' of Jeremiah; and Zechariah's Branch, Jehovah's Servant, who is to build the temple of Jehovah, and bear the glory. His lowliness is but the stooping of strength in love and to service — even to death, because His work is resurrection. How great and wonderful is this lowliness, when once we penetrate its real character! how necessary, when once we have understood the need which He came to relieve! Here then is the key to His position; and it is manifestly the one in which we find Him throughout Matthew's Gospel. For this Branch is to reign, and be a Priest upon His throne."

Prophecy, so definite in its application to the birth and infancy of Jesus, was no less definite in its application to His later years. His whole public ministry was governed by it.

In John the Baptist the spirit of the Old Testament prophets became again incarnate. He announced the kingdom of heaven to be at hand. There was no misapprehension of the meaning of this expression on the part of those who flocked to hear him. They were looking for the restoration of David's kingdom with a son of David reigning on his throne; and their prophets without exception had by their testimony justified that expectation. That kingdom, and no other, was announced by John the Baptist to be at hand. No wonder the multitudes came into the wilderness to hear this strange prophet, with his raiment of camel's hair, and a leathern girdle about his loins! Was he a fanatic? There had been many such before. In answer to their question concerning him he declared himself to be a voice, long foretold in prophecy, crying in the wilderness. Would they listen to it — they who had been so deaf to the voices sounding in the ages past? They might reject him, and the King whose forerunner he was, but that could not affect the setting up of the kingdom: it might delay its setting up, it might affect the form it would take, it might open the way for the accomplishment of other purposes; it could do no more.

John, having announced the kingdom, completes his mission by the presentation of the King.

"Then cometh Jesus from Galilee to Jordan unto John, to be baptized of him. But John forbade him, saying, I have need to be baptized of thee, and comest thou to me? And Jesus answering said unto him, Suffer it to be so now: for thus it becometh us to fulfil all righteousness. Then

he suffered him. And Jesus, when he was baptized,
went up straightway out of the water: and, lo,
the heavens were opened unto him, and he saw
the Spirit of God descending like a dove, and light-
ing upon him: and lo a voice from heaven, saying,
This is my beloved Son, in whom I am well pleased."

"And John bare record, saying, I saw the Spirit
descending from heaven like a dove, and it abode
upon him. And I knew him not: but he that sent
me to baptize with water, the same said unto me,
Upon whom thou shalt see the Spirit descending,
and remaining on him, the same is he which bap-
tizeth with the Holy Ghost. And I saw, and bare
record that this is the Son of God."

The King of the Jews is the Son of God! This
amazing truth should have confirmed the faith
of them to whom He came. The voices of
their prophets had all united in proclaiming the
unique glory of His person. But the spirit of unbelief had sealed their eyes. The light shone in
the darkness; and the darkness comprehended it
not. There were individual exceptions as rare as
they were beautiful. Nathanael saw His glory
when he owned Him, saying, Rabbi, thou art the
Son of God; thou art the King of Israel. But
the mass of the nation remained stone blind. As
the Son of God He was condemned at the court of

Caiaphas: as the King of Israel He was rejected at the bar of Pontius Pilate.

"He came unto his own, and his own received him not. But as many as received him, to them gave he power to become the sons of God, even to them that believe on his name: which were born, not of blood, nor of the will of the flesh, nor of the will of man, but of God."

The King, having been anointed and proclaimed from heaven, was proved in the wilderness, and then presented Himself for acceptance to the nation. He declares Himself — nay, more, He proves Himself — to be The Son of God and The King of Israel; and as such, He is disowned, rejected and put to death.

After John was cast into prison Jesus departed into Galilee: and leaving Nazareth, he came and dwelt in Capernaum: prophecy directing Him in this, as in all else.

And from that time He began to preach, and to say, "Repent: for the kingdom of heaven is at hand." Jesus reiterates, but with greater emphasis and fulness, the message that had been proclaimed by John. The kingdom was at hand in the person of the King who had come to introduce it. There was no perplexity of thought in this announcement: the kingdom that was declared to be at hand was the kingdom predicted by the prophets of old. Had the nation received their King the kingdom would have been established in power and glory. In their blind unbelief they discrowned Him who alone could bring in the blessing for which they had so long waited. He furnished every possible proof to establish His identity. The Old Testament had prepared them to expect signs and wonders that would accredit Him. These credentials were offered. He healed all manner of disease, and all manner of sickness among the people. They brought unto Him all that were sick, holden with various diseases and torments, demoniacs and lunatics and paralytics, and He healed them all. He declared, in the sermon on the mount, the principles according to which His kingdom was to be governed. More signs followed: lepers were cleansed, the lame walked, the deaf heard, the dead were raised, all nature obeyed Him; and demons, quailing, owned Him to be the Son of God.

But by no evidence was He able to win their acceptance of His claims. Nevertheless He went on to His formal presentation at Jerusalem as their King. At Jericho He proclaimed His royalty in giving sight to the blind men that had appealed to Him as the Son of David. The so called "triumphal entry" into the city was a hollow mockery, and no ritualistic Palm-Sunday service, however elaborate, can wash the deadly stain from the pages of human history.

From the fountain of the human heart spring waters both sweet and bitter. The same voices that unite in the cry, "Hosanna to the Son of David," are easily persuaded by the priests at the bar of Pilate to cry, "Let him be crucified."

And they crucified Him, and parted His garments, casting lots: this even, as all else concerning His blessed person, being marked out by prophecy.

And sitting down they watched Him there! and Pilate wrote a title, and put it on the cross, and the writing was:

THIS IS JESUS OF NAZARETH THE KING OF THE JEWS

He had proved His title, but He could not take the throne.

The Church rising over the ruins of the House of David is not the kingdom: it is only the proof that the branches of Joseph have "run over the wall." The bow in the hands of the King still abides in strength. He shall yet be made strong by the hands of the mighty God of Jacob. From thence is the shepherd, the stone of Israel. Shiloh has come and the scepter is gone; but of Joseph

Jacob still may say: "The blessings of thy father have prevailed above the blessings of my progenitors unto the utmost bound of the everlasting hills: they shall be on the head of Joseph, and on the crown of the head of him that was separate from his brethren."

CHAPTER VII

SUFFERING AND GLORY

ABOVE the hills of Moab the streaks of dawn are in the sky. The giant shadow of the mount of Olives lies across the valley of Jehosaphat. On the hill beyond the city walls are the dim outlines of an empty cross.

Down through the centuries there had come a voice, like the sound of many waters, saying, Arise, shine; for thy light is come, and the glory of the Lord is risen upon thee. That empty cross where they had nailed their discrowned King was the nation's answer.

But the light that is rising over the hills of Moab is the light of the resurrection morning.

The disciples of the crucified King are under the burden of an inexpressible sorrow. In Him and in the kingdom He had come to establish their hopes had been centered. His death had left them with the shattered fragments of a broken covenant. Doubt and fear assailed them.

Two of these disciples, of whom we have no

previous knowledge and of whom we shall hear no more, were walking together to a village called Emmaus. They were talking to one another of the things that had taken place. A strange and amazing circumstance had been related to them by certain women who had gone early to the sepulchre, and not finding His body, they came saying that they had also seen a vision of angels, who said that He was alive. Others had gone to the sepulchre and found it empty, even as the women had said, but Him they saw not. As they reasoned together concerning these things, Jesus Himself drew near and went with them. But their eyes were holden that they did not know Him. In answer to His question they relate what had taken place, and they express their doubt and sorrow by saying, "We trusted that it had been he which should have redeemed Israel." Then Jesus, reproving them for their want of faith in what the prophets had long foretold, said unto them, "Ought not Christ to have suffered these things, and to enter into his glory? And beginning at Moses and all the prophets, he expounded unto them in all the Scriptures the things concerning himself."

With burning hearts they listened while He explained to them the meaning of the prophetic voices that had been sounding through the ages past. The covenant was neither profaned nor dishonored by aught that had taken place: the path of suffering led to glory: the King was on the way to the throne.

At the village the identity of the wondrous Stranger was revealed to them in the breaking of bread; and He vanished from them. Rising up that same hour, their hearts still burning within them, they returned to Jerusalem to join their testimony to that of the eleven — The Lord is Risen.

The light of that resurrection morning is the promise of a serene and endless day.

The peculiar prominence given to the word of God is the striking feature of our Lord's revelation of Himself to the sorrowful men on their walk to Emmaus: it is no less striking in His words to the eleven on the evening of the same day. He told them how of necessity all must needs be fulfilled that had been written in the law of Moses, and the prophets, and the Psalms, concerning Himself. And "he opened their mind to understand the Scriptures; and he said unto them, Thus it is written, and thus it was needful, that the Christ should suffer, and rise from among the dead the third day; and that repentance and remission of sins should be preached in his name unto all the nations, beginning at Jerusalem."

To the same Scripture we must appeal in order that we may know whether the rejection and death of the King was intended of God to modify in any way whatsoever the covenant He made with David. In reference to this the evidence is clear and convincing. The kingdom as announced by the prophets has never been established upon the earth: it is in vain to assert that Christianity answers to it: we know it does not.

In the eighty-ninth Psalm, which is the exposition and the confirmation of the covenant, we read how God, "willing more abundantly to shew unto the heirs of promise the immutability of his counsel, confirmed it by an oath," saying, "I have made a covenant with my chosen, I have sworn unto David my servant, Thy seed will I establish for ever, and build up thy throne to all generations." Again in this same Psalm God binds Himself to this obligation: "Once have I sworn by my holiness that I will not lie unto David. His seed shall endure for ever, and his throne as the sun before me. It shall be established for ever as the moon, and as a faithful witness in heaven."

All this is solemnly confirmed by another Scripture: "The word of the Lord came unto Jeremiah, saying, Thus saith the Lord, If ye can break my covenant of the day, and my covenant of the night, and that there should not be day and night in their season; then may also my covenant be broken with David my servant, that he should not have a son to reign upon his throne."

In the presence of such direct testimony constructive evidence is of no value. And the spiritual interpretation cannot be accredited by any assumption of infallibility.

A rejected and a reigning Messiah was in the foreview of the prophets, and they were themselves perplexed by this seeming contradiction, "searching what, or what manner of time the Spirit of Christ which was in them did signify, when it testified beforehand the sufferings of Christ, and the glory that should follow."

It is doubtful if any of the Old Testament prophets had any conception of the second advent of Christ: they certainly knew nothing of the Church as the body of Christ; for this is declared to be a New Testament revelation. (Eph. 3 : 3-6).

Had they known of the two advents it is difficult for us to understand how they could have been perplexed about "the suffering" and "the glory" that should follow.

We are relieved of this perplexity by the revelation of a second advent in which so many of their predictions are to find their application. They foretold both the suffering and the glory, but they blended these conceptions into one vision. Knowing of but one advent, they were led of the Spirit to utter what was beyond their intelligence. The Messiah was to suffer and die; yet upon His shoulder the government was to be, and as the Prince of Peace He was to fill the throne of David and reign over the house of Jacob forever. Such predictions were in apparent contradiction; and yet no one will deny that such was the burden of prophecy.

Listen to the exultant song of the prophet in the fifty-second chapter of Isaiah!

"How beautiful upon the mountains are the feet of him that bringeth good tidings, that publisheth peace; that bringeth good tidings of good, that publisheth salvation; that saith unto Zion, Thy God reigneth! Thy watchmen shall lift up the voice; with the voice together shall they sing: for they shall see eye to eye, when the Lord shall bring again Zion. Break forth into joy, sing together, ye waste places of Jerusalem: for the Lord hath comforted his people, he hath redeemed Jerusalem. The Lord hath made bare his holy arm in the eyes of all the nations; and all the ends of the earth shall see the salvation of our God."

Listen again to the contrasted cry in the fifty-third chapter!

"He is despised and rejected of men; a man of sorrows, and acquainted with grief: and we hid as it were our faces from him; he was despised, and we esteemed him not. Surely he hath borne our griefs, and carried our sorrows: yet we did esteem him stricken, smitten of God, and afflicted. But he was wounded for our transgressions, he was bruised for our iniquities: the chastisement of our peace was upon him; and with his stripes we are healed. All we like sheep have gone astray; we have turned every one to his own way; and the Lord hath laid on him the iniquity of us all. He was oppressed, and he was afflicted, yet he opened not his mouth: he is brought as a lamb to the slaughter, and as a sheep before her shearers is dumb, so he openeth not his mouth. He was taken from prison and from judgment: and who shall declare his generation? for he was cut off out of the land of the living: for the transgression of my people was he stricken."

It is easy for us, who know of the two advents, to identify these contrasting features; but it was not so easy to the Jews of old, who looked forward to a Messiah of whose second advent they knew nothing. Even the disciples, hearing Jesus say, "The Son of man must suffer many things, and be rejected of the elders and chief priests and scribes, and be killed, and the third day be raised up," found the saying "too hard" for them. In common with all Israel they were looking for a conquering Messiah. How then could He suffer and die?

This same perplexity is shown by the multitude that thronged to hear Him. When He said unto them, "And I, if I be lifted up from the earth, will draw all men unto me," they answered, "We have heard out of the law, that the Christ abideth forever: and how sayest thou that the Son of man must be lifted up?" Tney knew very well that this lifting up meant His death, but how could this be reconciled with the law that declared the Messiah was to abide forever? It was hard to reconcile what was so opposite. Messiah, in whom the national hope was centered, to be cut off and have nothing! It was an unwelcome truth.

Victory through defeat! Life through death! Glory through suffering! Who could imagine any such thing to be possible! Yet this was the burden of prophecy, perplexing, alike, the prophets, apostles, and people. They received and believed the predictions of glory: the predictions of suffering were unwelcome and rejected. Jesus reproved the two men on the way to Emmaus for being slow of heart to believe ALL that the prophets have spoken. But this was no easy thing. Faith is never easy.

And the minds of the apostles remained darkened until death and resurrection had taken place. Then Jesus said unto them: "These are the words which I spake unto you, while I was yet with you, that all things must be fulfilled, which were written in the law of Moses, and in the prophets, and in the Psalms, concerning me. Then opened he their understanding, that they might understand the Scriptures."

The prophecies of suffering have all been fulfilled according to the very letter of Scripture. Every circumstance was carefully marked out, from the virgin birth to the resurrection. There is not one variation from it.

Are these Scriptures so precise in their application to the Messiah of suffering to be considered less precise in their application to the Messiah of glory? The infallibility of the predictions of suffering should at least make us open to the conviction that the predictions of glory may be equally infallible. But is it possible to preserve this infallibility, this precise application of promise to fulfilment, if we confound Israel with the Church?

The Church has disinherited Israel and appropriated her promises. Is it any wonder that prophecy is so little understood?

The prophets predicted a Messiah who was to

be the Son of David and the King of Israel.   Every
prediction of glory was centered in this one conception.   No Jew misunderstood this: it was the thought
of suffering that confounded him.   It was not until
their understanding was opened that they understood that Messiah must suffer in order that He
might enter into His glory.   It was necessary for
Him to be the Sufferer before He could be the
Conqueror.   So their Scriptures had declared and
to this their eyes were opened.

The Conqueror was the ideal Messiah for whom
the nation waited: for whom they are waiting still.
They refused the Sufferer in their failure to identify
Him with the Conqueror.   This did not abrogate
the covenant that God made with David.   Nothing
could do that; for God had confirmed the promise
by an oath.   It delayed the setting up of the kingdom in the form predicted by the prophets.   Twenty
centuries have passed since then; and during all
these years Israel, governed in this as in all else
besides by prophecy, has been "without a king, and
without a prince, and without a sacrifice, and
without an image, and without an ephod, and without teraphim."

These generations of suffering are the heavy
toll for the rejection of Him in whom their hope is
still centered.   In pathetic sorrow they wail at

the walls of Jerusalem over their perished glory. But they are still waiting for their Messiah.

Zechariah, the prophet of glory, has given us a matchless picture of the coming day when their misery shall be ended.

His final prophecy, from the ninth chapter to the fourteenth inclusive, is a unity of inception and objective. Christ fills the whole scene. He is represented as the Messiah of suffering and as the Messiah of glory; but the two advents, after the manner of Old Testament prediction, blend in one vision.

We cannot wonder at the perplexity occasioned by this prediction when even yet, with the light of the first advent upon it, we find it so difficult to preserve the balance of truth.

First there is the formal presentation of the King to the nation. "Rejoice greatly, O daughter of Zion; shout, O daughter of Jerusalem: behold, thy King cometh unto thee: he is just, and having salvation; lowly, and riding upon an ass, and upon a colt the foal of an ass."

In recording the so-called triumphal entry into Jerusalem, Mark and Luke make no reference to this prophecy; but Matthew does, and in a manner of striking significance: he quotes the passage but omits the words "he is just, and having salvation."

Was he careless in his quotation? We dare not
affirm this. Then why did he leave out these
important words? Was it not because national
salvation could not then come? The King was on
his way to die.

The prophet's presentation of the King is followed by a vision of a world-wide kingdom, but
the dawning light goes out in the darkness. In
the place of the King we see the Shepherd of Israel.
He is represented as holding two staves: the one He
calls Beauty, and the other He calls Bands. He
is feeding the flock. But the sheep forsake Him and
they follow other shepherds. Then the staff called
Beauty is broken. Is this a parable? Yes! But
of what? Is there some subtle connection here
with the words of Isaiah — "He hath no form nor
comeliness: and when we shall see him, there is
no beauty that we should desire him"? At first
they wondered at the gracious words that proceeded
out of His mouth, but they soon turned to follow
other shepherds. So the staff called Beauty was
cut asunder. Then the voice of Israel's Shepherd
is heard saying, "If ye think good, give me my price;
and if not, forbear. So they weighed for my price
thirty pieces of silver." This is followed by the
breaking of the staff called Bands. Here the parable is interpreted and translated into plain speech.

The brotherhood between Judah and Israel was broken. For the price of a slave the Messiah was sold and the fatal blood money was applied to the purchase of a potter's field as a burial place for strangers. But they acquired more than this. It broke their national unity: it deprived them of the kingdom: it sent them forth to be in all lands strangers, and to find their graves in fields of blood.

The next picture, in the vision of the prophet, is that of a siege of Jerusalem. That city with its tragic history has never yet passed through what is here described. The besieging army is under the direction of one who is called the "idol shepherd." There was but one alternative to Him that came in His Father's name: that was one who should come in his own name. He is before us in this vision and has gathered the nations against Jerusalem to battle. But this time Jerusalem is to be saved. The inhabitants of the city are first strengthened: then follows the Lord's intervention. This is in remembrance of His covenant with David.

"The Lord also shall save the tents of Judah first, that the glory of the house of David and the glory of the inhabitants of Jerusalem do not magnify themselves against Judah. In that day shall the Lord defend the inhabitants of Jerusalem; and he

that is feeble among them at that day shall be as
David; and the house of David shall be as God,
as the angel of the Lord before them." The
Beast and his armies are driven back to the
battlefield of Armageddon. Then upon the house
of David and upon the inhabitants of Jerusalem
is poured "the spirit of grace and of supplications."
In the agony of that awful hour, while still pleading
for the Messiah of power, for whom they have so
long waited, heaven shall suddenly open, and they
shall look on Him "whom they have pierced."
Joseph and his brethren shall be face to face.

"In that day there shall be a fountain opened
to the house of David and to the inhabitants of
Jerusalem for sin and for uncleanness."

The King has come! This time, "Just and having salvation," and He goes on to take the crown.
When they shall say unto him, "What are these
wounds in thine hands? Then he shall answer,
Those with which I was wounded in the house of
my friends." But the sheep that were scattered
when the Shepherd was smitten are brought together once more. The Shepherd is now the King.
He stands upon the mount of Olives and views the
kingdom that has become His own.

"And it shall come to pass in that day, that the
light shall not be clear, nor dark; but it shall be

one day which shall be known to the Lord, not
day, nor night: but it shall come to pass. that at
evening time it shall be light."

All the prophets unite in similar testimony that
the Messiah must suffer in order that He might
enter into His glory.

The book of Revelation is the final prophecy
and the culmination of them all. In it we have
the broad flow of the river to which every rivulet
of prophecy has made its contribution. Here —
as everywhere else in Scripture — Christ in His
wondrous Person is the radiating center of glory.
In the fifth chapter, before the judgments that
inaugurate the kingdom begin, we have a description of the investiture of the Son of David with
kingdom authority. The apostle saw "in the right
hand of him that sat on the throne a book." The
book was sealed with seven seals. We know what
that book contained. We know this, because the
seals were broken, the parchment unrolled and
the contents spread before us. It contained the
record of the earth's judgment-salvation. But
authority to execute judgment has been given to
the Son of man. He Himself has so declared.
The Father judgeth no man, but hath committed
all judgment unto the Son. He alone has authority
to break the seals and to execute the judgments

therein written. When the angel proclaimed with a loud voice, Who is worthy to open the book, and to loose the seals thereof? there was no answer. Neither in heaven nor in earth nor under the earth could a man be found who was able to open the book or even to look thereon. The apostle wept much because no man was found worthy to open and to read the book, neither to look thereon. Then one of the elders came to him, saying, "Weep not: behold, the Lion of the tribe of Judah, the Root of David, hath prevailed to open the book, and to loose the seven seals thereof." John looked up that he might see this Lion of Judah, and, lo, in the midst of the throne and of the four living beings, and in the midst of the elders, stood a Lamb as it had been slain. The Lion of Judah is the Lamb that was slain. The Messiah of glory and the Messiah of suffering are One and the same.

"The Root of David" has become "the Branch of righteousness"; and He shall execute judgment and justice in the earth. "For thus saith the Lord; David shall never want a man to sit upon the throne of the house of Israel."

By the way of the Cross the King goes on to take the Crown.

8

CHAPTER VIII

ATTESTING THE OATH

CHRIST is risen! On that fact is founded the hope of the Church: the hope of Israel: the hope of the world.

The Cross was raised upon Golgotha: "the place of a skull" — the wreck of human wisdom. The Church is built upon an empty grave: "the destruction of death" — the reversal of sin's penalty.

O the depth of the riches both of the wisdom and knowledge of God! how unsearchable are his judgments, and his ways past finding out!

All of the four Evangelists record the resurrection of Jesus: Mark and Luke alone tell us of the ascension. The Spirit of God controls them in this as in all else.

Matthew has given us the Gospel of the kingdom and his Gospel closes with the appearance of Jesus on a mountain in Galilee. There Jesus meets his disciples and speaks to them about the kingdom, instructing them concerning it, and declaring that in Himself was vested all authority in heaven and on earth.

"Galilee of the nations" had been marked out by prophecy, as "the land of the shadow of death": where the light was first to shine, and it was so marked in immediate connection with the prediction of the child born, and the son given, upon whose shoulder the government was to be. Matthew, true to the purpose for which he writes, leaves us in the light shining upon Galilee.

Mark gives us the Gospel of the Servant of Jehovah. He goes further than Matthew, telling us that the Lord, having spoken to the disciples, "was received up into heaven, and sat on the right hand of God." We are not certain even from his account that the disciples were witnesses of this. This is likewise in keeping with his Gospel. The Servant, having finished His work, takes His seat "on the right hand of God."

Luke gives us the Gospel of the Humanity. He goes quite beyond Matthew and Mark. The Lord is seen still maintaining those human relationships so characteristic of this Gospel. "And he led them out as far as Bethany; and lifting up his hands" — the hands that had been nailed to the cross — "he blessed them. And it came to pass, as he blessed them, that he was separated from them and carried up into heaven."

"He ascends with his hands stretched out in

blessing, to take that place before God in which
He abides, the Representative of His people, the
Head of blessing for them. While Israel and the
earth wait for His return to find what the Old
Testament has pledged in their behalf, His place
in heaven is the sign of a new order of blessing which
the 'mysteries' of Christianity are to take up and
unfold to us."

It is this same Evangelist who, in the Acts of
the Apostles, gives us the connecting link between
the old dispensation about to pass away temporarily and the new dispensation in which the
"mysteries" of the kingdom are to find their
application.

The disciples are still clinging to their kingdom
hope; for, while at Bethany and just before the ascension, they say unto Him, "Lord, wilt thou at
this time restore again the kingdom to Israel?" He
does not rebuke them for this. He does not charge
them with holding a "false notion." He does not
even intimate that their conception was materialis-
tic and must be given up for a spiritual one. On the
contrary, He confirms their hope. How could He
do otherwise with His intense conviction of the
validity of Scripture? He tells them simply that
the time of Israel's restoration has not been revealed
by the Father. But they are to go forth, and, in the

power of the Holy Ghost, they are to be witnesses
for Him.

"And when he had spoken these things, while
they beheld, he was taken up; and a cloud received
him out of their sight."

Title to the throne and the power of the kingdom
are vested in Him, though He be thus taken from
them.

But did they not remember the parable that He
had spoken to them, when He was making His last
journey to Jerusalem, and because they thought
that the kingdom of God was to be manifested
forthwith?   He was a Nobleman — it is hard to see
how they could have missed the application of it —
who was going into a far country to receive for Himself a kingdom and TO RETURN. His absence
would give His servants opportunity to prove their
faithfulness which would be fully rewarded upon
His return, when upon His own citizens who had
sent a messenger after Him, saying, We will not
have this man to reign over us, He would execute
judgment.

Did they remember this when the cloud received
Him out of their sight? Perhaps so. If not, they
are immediately reminded of it: for "while they
looked steadfastly toward heaven as he went up,
behold, two men stood by them in white apparel,

which also said, Ye men of Galilee, why stand ye
gazing up into heaven? this same Jesus, which is
taken up from you into heaven, shall so come in
like manner as ye have seen him go into heaven."

This same Jesus who had journeyed from Bethlehem to Calvary; who had been with them in loving
and intimate converse during the years of His ministry; who had risen from the dead and shown Himself alive after His passion by many infallible proofs;
who had now ascended to fill the highest throne
in glory: this same Jesus would return to earth once
more.   So the hidden glory that was in Him breaks
through and fills their soul with gladness.

They returned to Jerusalem from the mount of
Olives and "were continually in the temple, praising
and blessing God."

The day of Pentecost, ten days later, finds them
together "with one accord in one place."   They
are all filled with the Holy Ghost, and they are
given the power to speak with other tongues, that
they may pursue with the gospel all men in all
places where sin had scattered them.

Peter becomes the public speaker and he links the
blessing, then being ministered from heaven to the
Jewish people, with Jesus of Nazareth ascended and
glorified.   He takes the prophecy of Joel as the text
for his sermon.   But the way in which he does this

is the striking feature of his sermon. He declares that Jesus of Nazareth, the Crucified One, who as Man in the midst of them has been approved of God by miracles and signs, is now in heaven; and that He is the God spoken of in the prophecy, who is now bestowing the promised Spirit. Moreover this same Jesus of Nazareth is also the Lord spoken of in that prophecy, in whom salvation is alone possible, and before whose coming day of judgment the sun shall be turned into darkness, and the moon into blood.

This Jesus of Nazareth they had taken, and with wicked hands had crucified and slain; but God had raised Him from the dead. This Peter declares, and then proceeds to what is of the utmost importance in our discussion. He says that God had raised Jesus from the dead because it was impossible "that he should be holden of it": and, for proof of this, Peter appeals to the sixteenth Psalm in which David the writer had said: "Thou wilt not leave my soul in hell, neither wilt thou suffer thine Holy One to see corruption." Peter calls their attention to the fact that David had been long dead and buried and that his sepulchre was still among them: then he flashes upon them — and upon us — the inspired interpretation of that Psalm.

"Therefore being a prophet, and knowing that

God had sworn with an oath to him, that of the fruit of his loins, according to the flesh, he would raise up Christ to sit on his throne; he seeing this before spake of the resurrection of Christ, that his soul was not left in hell, neither his flesh did see corruption. This Jesus hath God raised up, whereof we all are witnesses. Therefore being by the right hand of God exalted, and having received of the Father the promise of the Holy Ghost, he hath shed forth this, which ye now see and hear." Then with further corroboration from the one hundred and tenth Psalm he concludes his sermon, saying, "Therefore let all the house of Israel know assuredly, that God hath made that same Jesus, whom ye have crucified, both Lord and Christ."

If all this is not the attesting of God's covenant with David, then words must be given up as trustworthy vehicles for the conveyance of thought. Peter believed and taught that Jesus had been raised from the dead to be both Lord and Christ.

Christ meant for him, as it meant for every other Jew, the Messiah; and Messiah was to be the Son of David and was to reign on David's throne. For this purpose Jesus has been raised from the dead: for this purpose He is to return.

We are not trying to build up any preconceived opinion of our own. Of what worth would that be?

We are simply considering the testimony in reference to the covenant that God confirmed to David with an oath. It is here affirmed after the ascension that through Jesus the covenant is to be fulfilled. He has gone into the far country to receive a kingdom and to return. The form the kingdom is to take upon His return must be determined by the testimony of Scripture. If that be lacking in authority, the whole subject is without further interest: we may think whatever we choose.

The statement made by Peter on the day of Pentecost is not merely the expression of his personal opinion: it is Scripture *evidence* and we are bound to accept it as such. His conclusions rest upon citations to which he gives authoritative interpretation. Paul may withstand Peter in questions of *practice:* it would have been fatal to the New Testament had he withstood him in *doctrine*. Whoever withstands Peter in doctrine disqualifies himself as a teacher of prophecy.

What Peter affirms on the day of Pentecost he reaffirms a few days later. He is the first of the apostles to work a miracle, and that miracle is a sign attesting his word.

Mark, in the Gospel of service, tells us how the disciples went forth to serve, and how the Lord worked with them, "confirming the word with signs following." We are now to see the word confirmed in this way.

Peter and John are on the way to the temple. It is three o'clock in the afternoon, the hour of prayer, the time of the offering of the evening sacrifice. It was a memorable hour in the history of that people. At three o'clock in the afternoon God vindicated His glory in answer to the prayer of Elijah on mount Carmel. At that hour Gabriel appeared to Daniel and measured the cycle of Jehovah's dealing with Israel. At that hour Jesus, having accomplished redemption, offered Himself without spot unto God. His death was the substance of which the temple-sacrifice had been the shadow. The Jews, unconscious that the shadow had forever disappeared before the substance, were surging toward the temple at the hour of prayer. Peter and John join the crowd and move in the same direction. In that temple God had never given His honor to another than Himself. This fact is of the utmost importance in the consideration of what follows.

As the apostles are about to enter the temple their attention is claimed by a man who, lame from his birth, had been daily carried to the temple by his friends and left at the gate called beautiful, that his pitiable condition might appeal to the worshipers as they entered. This man, seeing Peter and

John approach, appealed to them for help. "Then Peter said, Silver and gold have I none, but such as I have give I thee: in the name of Jesus Christ of Nazareth rise up and walk. And he took him by the right hand, and lifted him up: and immediately his feet and ankle bones received strength. And he leaping up stood, and walked, and entered with them into the temple, walking, and leaping, and praising God."

This marvelous miracle filled the temple worshipers with wonder and amazement. They ran together to Solomon's porch where the lame man was voicing his praise to Peter and John. It was in Solomon's porch that Jesus had proclaimed His deity. (John 10 : 22-39). It was in this same place that many signs and wonders were wrought by the apostles. (Acts 5: 12). The massive ruins of Solomon's porch alone remained of the ancient temple from which the glory had so long departed. They had rejected Him in whom the glory had returned but they were to be given one chance more. Peter preaches to the crowd attracted by the miracle. This time he takes the lame man for his text. He disclaims any power or holiness in himself. On the contrary he says, "The God of Abraham, and of Isaac, and of Jacob, the God of our fathers, hath glorified his Son Jesus; whom ye delivered up, and denied him in the presence of Pilate, when he **was** determined to let him go ": and then the apostle continues, that in His name, and "through faith in his name hath made this man strong, whom ye see and know; yea, the faith which is by Him hath given him this perfect soundness in the presence of you all."

The glory that God had never before given to another is now given to Jesus of Nazareth. Him they had put to death while ignorant of the glory of His person; and yet, in so doing they had but fulfilled the prophecies concerning Him. Peter, therefore, urges them to repent, that their sins may be blotted out, and that so may come times of refreshing from the presence of the Lord, and that He may send back again Jesus Christ, "Whom the heaven must receive until the times of restitution of all things which God hath spoken by the mouth of all the holy prophets since the world began."

In other words, Peter proclaims that, upon their repentance, Jesus will return, and bring to pass the times of restoration of which the prophets had spoken. The restoration spoken of here — the word being used only here and in Acts, 1: 6 — is that restoration of which the prophets had spoken.

The prophets foretold the restoration of the nation to their land and the restoration of the throne of

David. They predicted no other restoration beside. But this was their constant theme. For this the nation had been waiting through the centuries: for this they are waiting still. That restoration would have been accomplished under the Messiah if they had accepted Him. But even the guilt of His rejection and death should be forgiven, if they should repent; and He would return from heaven and establish them in the kingdom so long foretold. Heaven must receive Him until the time of such restitution: and without Him no restitution should be possible.

Peter's message, ratified by the healing of the lame man, was not without effect: "for many of them which heard the word believed; and the number of the men was about five thousand."

But the representatives of the nation, and especially those of the Sadducees, who denied the possibility of resurrection, were "grieved" at the teaching, and they laid hold of the apostles, and put them in prison.

The following morning the whole Jewish council was assembled and the apostles were summoned. In answer to their question as to how the lame man had been healed, Peter, "filled with the Holy Ghost, said unto them, Ye rulers of the people, and elders of Israel, If we this day be examined of the good deed done to the impotent man, by what means he is made whole: be it known unto you all, and to all the people of Israel, that by the name of Jesus Christ of Nazareth, whom ye crucified, whom God raised from the dead, even by him doth this man stand here before you whole." He then declares that Jesus is the "stone," predicted in the one hundred and eighteenth Psalm, which, rejected though it had been by them, was nevertheless in the purpose of God to be the "headstone of the corner."

The council, amazed at the boldness of Peter and still more so with the healed man who was there in evidence, sent the apostles out of the court and went into executive session.

They acknowledged among themselves that a notable miracle had been done, and that there was no way in which this could be effectually denied: so they resolved to "threaten" the apostles, and to command them to preach no more "in this name."

The apostles were recalled to the council chamber and threatened, but with little effect, as Peter's bold answer shows. So when they had further threatened them, they let them go.

The apostles returned to their own company and reported what the chief priests and elders had said. In the prayer that followed they quoted the second Psalm, ascribing it to David, through whom God had spoken. That Psalm is God's answer to the nation's rejection of their King.

The kings of the earth had set themselves, and the rulers had taken counsel together. A most notable convention with its delegates of civil and ecclesiastical rulers! Surely wisdom will not be wanting with such as these. With conventional formality they pass a resolution and — adjourn. The resolution is marked with the finality that usually characterizes the deliverances of such assemblies. "Let us break their bands asunder, and cast away their cords from us." What gives extraordinary character to this resolution is the power against which it is directed. It is against the LORD, and against His anointed: against God and the foretold Messiah. To what insane folly does sin drive its infatuated victims! Are the decrees of God to be annulled by assembly deliverances? Hear the answer: "He that sitteth in the heavens shall laugh: the Lord shall have them in derision." Nothing but unparalleled iniquity could have evoked such a sentence from the lips of God. Did the rulers of this world, under the delusion of Satan, suppose they could set aside the covenant that God made with David (11 Samuel 7:8-17) and afterward confirmed with an oath (Psalm 89:34-37)?

Jehovah would have them in derision. Over

against their resolution of rebellion He places this: "Yet have I set my king upon my holy hill of Zion." That is God's purpose. Is He without power to accomplish it? Hear the answer in this same Psalm. It is the King that is speaking: "I will declare the decree: the Lord hath said unto me, Thou art my Son; this day have I begotten thee. Ask of me, and I shall give thee the heathen for thine inheritance, and the uttermost parts of the earth for thy possession. Thou shalt break them with a rod of iron; thou shalt dash them in pieces like a potter's vessel."

This King, as we are assured by the book of Acts and elsewhere, is Jesus of Nazareth, who is now seated upon the Father's throne, and who has but to ask, and the world shall be put in subjection to Him, that He may reign upon His own throne. This is not to be brought about by the gradual extension of Christianity as so many have vainly supposed: the rebellion of the world is to be broken by a rod of iron, and the rebels dashed in pieces like a potter's vessel.

Scripture everywhere confirms this. Jehovah's anger was seen in the destruction of Jerusalem, soon after the rejection of the King: it was further seen in the world-wide dispersion of the Jewish people that followed: it shall be seen in the great tribulation toward which the world is now hastening.

Then shall follow the advent of the King. He shall smite down all opposition. His advent shall be inaugurated by wonders in the heavens and in the earth, blood, and fire, and pillars of smoke. The sun and the moon shall be darkened, and the stars shall withdraw their shining. The Lord also shall roar out of Zion, and utter his voice from Jerusalem; and the heavens and the earth shall shake: but the Lord shall be the hope of his people, and the strength of the children of Israel.

And the kings of the earth, and the great men, and the rich men, and the chief captains, and the mighty men, and every bondman, and every free-man, shall hide themselves in the dens and in the rocks of the mountains; and shall say unto the mountains and rocks, Fall on us, and hide us from the face of him that sitteth on the throne, and from the wrath of the Lamb: and the mountains and the rocks shall stand in indignant protest, and shall refuse to cover these rebels in their last and futile revolt against God and His Christ.

So, and no otherwise, shall be ushered in the kingdom and the King.

CHAPTER IX

INDICTMENT OF THE NATION

THE refusal of grace leaves man with no door of escape from the consequences of his sin. The law was given by Moses, proving that, as to those under the law, there was none righteous, no, not one: for all had sinned and come short of the glory of God. That was the moral condition of the Jewish nation from Moses to Christ. It was in fact the condition of all men.

But grace and truth had come through Jesus Christ; and the refusal of this grace by the Jews led to the final indictment of the nation. Though judgment lingers, it comes at last with noiseless feet. The Jews rejected the testimony of Peter, though it was supported by that Scripture to whose authority they owned subjection. They refused the mercy so freely offered them; and judgment followed.

Stephen, a man full of faith and of the Holy Ghost, was chosen of God to bring in the nation's long bill of indictment. He had been doing great wonders and miracles among the people, which brought him

116

in conflict with certain members of the synagogue. They were not able to resist the wisdom and the spirit by which he spake: so men were suborned to testify against him, and he was arrested, and brought before the council.

It was the same relentless court that had condemned Jesus. Stephen was accused of blasphemy, and there was no hope for mercy from those grim judges, except he could prove himself innocent. The witnesses though perjurers made their solemn charge, and then the eyes of all that sat in the council were turned toward the prisoner.

Did they expect to see a man quaking with terror? That was the usual attitude of prisoners before this dreaded court. But here was a man of a different type. They looked steadfastly upon him and, instead of a face white with fear, they "saw his face as it had been the face of an angel."

Then said the high priest, Are these things so?

Not one sentence does Stephen utter in self-defense. Ignoring the charge made against him, he enters upon a slow and solemn recrimination. Not against his forsworn accusers, but against the whole nation in its awful history of unbroken rebellion against God.

He begins with Abraham, the acknowledged founder of the nation, to whom the God of glory

had appeared in the ages past. Briefly he sketches
the history until he comes to Joseph upon whom he
lingers, that he may flash into the minds of his judges
the foreshadowing of their history that they might
easily have read there. Did they think of Judas,
and the thirty pieces of silver, when he reminded
them of how Joseph was sold into Egypt?

Deliberately, Stephen goes on, showing how Joseph, despite all of his afflictions, was raised to the
place of supreme authority in Egypt, and how afterward he was made known to his brethren. Stephen
makes no application of all this: he passes it by,
as if it had no application to what had so recently
taken place among them; and then, with a brief
reference to the years of bondage in Egypt, he
dwells with the same deliberation upon the history
of Moses.

Will those stern judges, listening to this calm
voice interpreting the meaning of history long since
written, awaken to their own moral condition?

Moses? Did they accuse him of speaking against
Moses? He would summon Moses to testify against
them. Surely they were not ignorant of the personal history of that great prophet whose honor
and authority they were guarding with such sleep-
less vigilance. In those days of Egyptian bondage
he had seen one of his brethren wronged, and had

defended him, and had delivered him from the oppression, supposing that "his brethren would have understood how that God by his hand would deliver them: but they understood not." The next day he had attempted to effect a reconciliation between two of his contending brethren, and the one at fault had scornfully repudiated him, saying, "Who made thee a ruler and a judge over us?" And Moses had been compelled to flee into Midian where he continued for forty years. Then the Lord had appeared to him in the burning bush, and had commissioned him to return to Egypt. Stephen pauses here in his calm recital to make a stinging application of the truth.

"This Moses whom they refused, saying, Who made thee a ruler and a judge? the same did God send to be a ruler and a deliverer by the hand of the angel which appeared to him in the bush."

Was the council conscious that this history had been repeating itself? But Stephen goes on judicially summing up the case.

From the land of bondage the people had been delivered under Moses whose commission God had attested by signs and wonders. And this was that Moses, which said unto the children of Israel, "A prophet shall the Lord your God raise up unto you of your brethren, like unto me; him shall ye hear."

But to what extent did Jehovah's avouchment of Moses sustain him in authority over the people? Had they bowed in submission to him? Had they looked with any real earnestness for the appearing of that prophet which he had announced? Let their history answer.

Through that terrible wilderness they had been guided to mount Sinai and there, while the mountain was aflame with the glory of God, the oracles had been given to them. Did this display of the majesty of God move them? Nay! Even while Moses was in the mount with God the hearts of the people turned back again into Egypt, and they said unto Aaron, "Make us gods to go before us: for as for this Moses, which brought us out of the land of Egypt, we wot not what has become of him." And they made a calf in those days, and offered sacrifice unto the idol, and rejoiced in the works of their own hands. That was the reverence that their fathers had given Moses.

The apostasy that had begun at the holy mount had flowed in a channel ever wider and deeper. They had despised the ark of the covenant, and had taken up the tabernacle of Moloch, and the star of their god Remphan: and almost the only redeeming feature in those dark days was David's desire "to find a tabernacle for the God of Jacob." Then came the building of Solomon's temple in answer to this desire.

And what had been their history since those days? Did they look for any redemption of God's covenant with David after the monarchy had failed under Solomon? Did they patiently wait for that prophet under whose hand the throne of David was to be established forever?

Stephen does not follow the history beyond Solomon. It was not necessary. The moral unity of the whole nation had been established.

After this calm and dispassionate review of their history the final indictment, like an unexpected bolt from the blue, falls from the lips of Stephen: "Ye stiffnecked and uncircumcised in heart and ears, ye do always resist the Holy Ghost: as your father did, so do ye. Which of the prophets have not your fathers persecuted? and they have slain them which shewed before of the coming of the Just One; of whom ye have been now the betrayers and murderers: who have received the law by the disposition of angels, and have not kept it."

The word translated "resist" in this solemn charge of Stephen is found here, and nowhere else in the New Testament. It is a word of terrible significance, meaning "to run foul of." Ye do always run foul of the Holy Ghost.

It would be difficult to imagine the immediate effect of Stephen's charge. He had reversed the character of the court. Instead of a prisoner on trial for his life, he had become the judge, and had passed sentence upon the nation.

But power remained with the council. From these stern and now infuriated judges Stephen could expect no mercy and he received none. Yet by his message they were "cut to the heart." The sword of the Spirit had been used more effectively than on the day of Pentecost, when they had been but "pricked in their heart." But, if under Stephen's preaching there was conviction of sin, there was no repentance. They gnashed on him with their teeth. The cup of the nation's iniquity was full.

But Stephen is unmoved by their rage. He is engrossed in a vision of surpassing glory. He "looked up steadfastly into heaven, and saw the glory of God, and Jesus standing on the right hand of God."

Abstracted by this wondrous vision, and unconscious of any other presence, he said, "Behold, I see the heavens opened, and the Son of man standing on the right hand of God."

That was enough. They cried out with a loud voice, and stopped their ears, and ran upon him with one accord, and cast him out of the city.

Then they stoned him — with that light still upon his face — and Stephen, the first martyr of Jesus, went home to receive his crown. He was the messenger, sent after the departed Nobleman, and instructed to say, "We will not have this man to reign over us."

"He that sitteth in the heavens shall laugh: the Lord shall have them in derision.'

Following the murder of Stephen the sentence, so long held in abeyance, was executed upon Judah. Judgment had long before overtaken Israel. These two judgments, the one upon Israel the northern kingdom and the other upon Judah the southern kingdom, are recorded in the first chapter of Hosea; but the chapter closes with the promise of the restoration of both Israel and Judah. Only through such restoration is the hope of the nation to be realized and God's covenant with David to be fulfilled.

At the close of Mark's Gospel it is stated that Jesus "was received up into heaven, and sat on the right hand of God."

But Stephen says, "Behold, I see the heavens opened, and the Son of man standing on the right hand of God."

There must be some reason for calling our attention to these contrasted attitudes. Everything in Scripture is significant: its *manner* no less than its *matter*.

Did the Lord arise and stand to receive and welcome home this dying martyr? It would be like Jesus, in His compassion and grace to do that; but something more would seem to be implied.

The Lord, in His ministry to Israel, was "that prophet" of whom Moses had spoken. "A prophet shall the Lord your God raise up unto you of your brethren, like unto me; him shall ye hear." With the prophets of Israel there is an Old Testament expression of frequent occurrence. We hear it often from the lips of Elijah: "As the Lord of hosts liveth, before whom I stand."

This "before whom I stand" is the prophet's *attitude*, and it indicates an unfinished mission. It is evident, from Peter's sermon before the council, that our Lord's mission *as a prophet* to Israel did not terminate with His ascension to heaven. He, therefore, took the attitude of the prophet, and "stood on the right hand of God," awaiting the answer that should be given by the nation to Peter's appeal. That answer was given in the stoning of Stephen, who was sent into heaven, charged with the message, "We will not have this man to reign over us."

Until the stoning of Stephen, Jesus, in the characteristic attitude of the prophet, "stood on the right hand of God." It was in this attitude that Stephen saw Him. With Stephen's death His mission, as prophet to Israel, ended, and He "sat down on the right hand of God." He is now Israel's Priest, after the order of Melchisedek, a royal Priest. He is yet to be their King: a Priest upon His throne. This application, confined as it is to Israel, does not affect the blessed relation He sustains to His Church.

In that part of the epistle to the Hebrews where the Melchisedek priesthood of our Lord is presented we find a word of peculiarly beautiful significance. The writer tells us that Christ, by His atoning death upon the cross, having become the author of eternal salvation unto all them that obey Him, was "called of God an high priest after the order of Melchisedek" (Heb. 5 : 10).

The word translated "called" in this verse is found nowhere else in the New Testament. Its meaning must be determined from classic usage. That "called" does not express the meaning conveyed by the Greek word is absolutely certain. In ordinary usage the word meant "to name," "to salute by calling a name," "to greet."

"Named of God," as in the revision, is without

much significance. "Saluted of God" is justifiable and far better.

Appointment to office was in ancient times made by saluting the person by the title attached to the office. The word used on such occasions was the very word under consideration. When a person had been appointed to some position of great dignity he did not enter upon his official duties until the one who exercised the proper authority had "saluted" him by the title that was attached to the office to which he had been appointed. In this way his official position was publicly proclaimed and constituted. So Christ was "saluted" of God an high priest after the order of Melchisedek.

This interpretation explains the contrasted attitudes given by Mark and Stephen.

As "that prophet" to Israel, of whom Moses had spoken, Jesus, having accomplished redemption, ascended into heaven and "stood on the right hand of God." In that attitude He remained, as a sign of unfinished work for Israel, until the final verdict of the nation was rendered in the stoning of Stephen. Immediately thereafter God "saluted" Him as high priest after the order of Melchisedek, and "he sat down on the right hand of God."

The words of salutation are found in the one hundred and tenth Psalm. "Thou art a priest for ever after the order of Melchisedek." But that Psalm opens with the words: "The Lord said unto my Lord, Sit thou at my right hand, until I make thine enemies thy footstool." It is evident from this that the Lord did not take His seat until His enemies had finally declared themselves to be such. It is also evident that this final declaration was made in the stoning of Stephen.

At the stoning of Stephen, we are told, "the witnesses laid down their clothes at a young man's feet, whose name was Saul."

This "band of light" on that dark day may be more than an intimation of the impending dispensational change. In the gospel committed to Paul we shall find a glory hitherto unrevealed.

The declaration of the Melchisedek priesthood is confirmed by an oath. "The Lord hath sworn, and will not repent, Thou art a priest for ever after the order of Melchisedek" (Psalm 110 : 4).

In the prophecy of Zechariah (6 : 9-15) the crowning of Joshua, the high priest, constituting him a royal priest, is a veil transfigured by the glory shining through it. The judgment-salvation of the earth is followed by this vision of Christ in His kingdom and glory. The man whose name is

"THE BRANCH" is but the symbol of Christ in His Melchisedek priesthood. He shall build the temple of the Lord, and He "shall bear the glory, and shall sit and rule upon his throne."

Christ is now a Priest, and has been "saluted of God" as a "priest after the order of Melchisedek." By His own blood He has "entered in once into the holy place, having obtained eternal redemption." He is there seated upon the Father's throne.

The great day of Atonement is now in progress for Israel: for them — and for us also — He is "within the veil." "And unto them that look for him shall he appear the second time without sin unto salvation." He has already appeared once "to put away sin by the sacrifice of himself." He shall appear a second time without sin—that is, with no reference to sin—"unto salvation."

He is waiting until His enemies shall be made His footstool. Jehovah at His right hand "shall strike through kings in the day of his wrath." All opposing power shall be smitten with "the rod of his strength." All kings shall fall down before Him: all nations shall serve Him. He "shall have dominion also from sea to sea, and from the river unto the ends of the earth."

In fulfilment of the covenant made with David "his name shall endure for ever: his name shall be continued as long as the sun: and men shall be blessed in him: all nations shall call him blessed."

And the prayers of David the son of Jesse shall be "ended."

CHAPTER X

SENTENCED TO BLINDNESS

THE rejection of the King did not abrogate the covenant that God made with David. The kingdom, in the form announced by the prophets, must be established upon the earth or else the great volume of prophecy must be either spiritualized or given up as worthless.

The application of these prophecies to the Church, which has so long perplexed the study of prophecy, is justified neither by Scripture nor by reason. The Church and the kingdom are not the same and by no labored exegesis can such identity be established.

All the prophets unite in their predictions as to the form the kingdom was to take. The Messiah was to be of David's line and was to reign as King over all Israel. The throne was to be established in Zion from which the law of Jehovah was to go forth and His word from Jerusalem. Their King, thus enthroned, was to reign unto the ends of the earth. The kingdom, in this form, was announced by John the Baptist, proclaimed by the Lord, by the apostles and by the seventy. Instead of this we have the King crucified, the throne of David in ruins, Jerusalem trodden down of the Gentiles, and Israel scattered to the ends of the earth. In all this, sacred prophecy was fulfilled to the very letter, but only so far as it contemplated the rejection of Christ, the destruction of Jerusalem, and the dispersion of Israel. The much larger volume of prophecy is still to be fulfilled.

If we insist upon the identity of the Church with the kingdom, we must remain under the bondage of perplexity that such an assumption imposes. If, on the other hand, we keep these distinct and separate, we shall find that the voices of the prophets speak without confusion and blend into a glorious harmony.

Paul declares that to Israel "pertaineth the adoption, and the glory, and the covenants, and the giving of the law, and the service of God, and the promises" (Romans 9 : 4). To tell us that Paul is here speaking of a *spiritual* Israel is an assumption unwarranted by any authority from Scripture, and it is this, more than anything else, that has perplexed the interpretation of prophecy. That a spiritual Israel, or in other words the Church, is the kingdom contemplated by the prophets can be demonstrated neither by Scripture nor by logic.

10

The attempt to do this has strained the meaning of language beyond recognition and discredited prophecy altogether.

That there is a spiritual Israel, composed of those like Paul and others, who accepted Christ, and became members of the Church, and heirs of a glory unconceived by the Hebrew prophets, none will deny: but, apart from these, there is a literal Israel for whom Paul was so deeply concerned, and to whom pertain the covenants and the promises. This conception is alone worthy of Scripture and by no other can the coherence of prophecy be maintained.

It was to a literal Israel that the Messiah appealed: it was by a literal Israel He was rejected: it was a literal Israel contemplated in God's promise to David; and it is in and through a literal Israel that the promise is to be redeemed.

The national rejection of the King was finally ratified in the stoning of Stephen. Such an issue had been anticipated by prophecy, and Jesus had predicted it the day following the one when, in answer to Zechariah's prophecy, He had entered the city and formally presented Himself to the nation as their King. As He entered the city the multitude that went before Him and the multitude that followed, cried, saying "Hosanna to the Son of

David: Blessed is he that cometh in the name of the Lord; Hosanna in the highest." And in the temple, after its purification, the children cried, Hosanna to the Son of David! The heads of the nation objected to this acclamation, and Jesus leaving them returned to Bethany. The next day He returned to the temple and was questioned by them as to His authority. He answered; and then gave them the parable of the two sons, and followed this by the parable of the householder demanding fruit from his vineyard. In the latter He predicted His death and forced them to pronounce judgment upon themselves. (Matthew 21: 23-46).

"The vineyard of the Lord of hosts is the house of Israel, and the men of Judah his pleasant plant: and he looked for judgment, but behold oppression: for righteousness, but behold a cry."

So prophecy had declared, and the parable spoke to them in no strange tongue. The vineyard had been let out to husbandmen while the Owner was in a far country. When fruit was to be expected messengers had been sent to receive it. But what had been the result? Some of these servants had been beaten, others had been killed, and others had been stoned. Again other servants more than the first had been sent and had received like treat-

ment.   Last of all the Master of the vineyard had
sent his Son, saying, They will reverence my Son.
But when the husbandmen saw Him, they said
among themselves, This is the Heir.   They did
not mistake His identity.   The dignity of His
person and His position had been instantly recognized.   Did they reverence Him?   No!   But with
cold blooded deliberation they said, Let us kill Him!
"And they caught him, and cast him out of the
vineyard, and slew him."

So the Lord foretells, with omniscient wisdom, the
treatment He is about to receive at their hands.
But what shall be the consequences *for them* if
He in reality be the Son of God?   They are forced
to pronounce the doom that awaits them.   This
too He confirms from Scripture.   The "stone which
the builders rejected" was to become "the head
of the corner."   So their deed would be reversed.
And the result would be that the kingdom they
were refusing should be taken from them and be
given to another nation that would bring forth the
fruits thereof.

Prophecy, so abundantly clear as to all this,
should have kept us from confounding the "nation"
here spoken of with the Church.   It is a nation
of future Israelites to which the kingdom is
to be given.   Meantime, while the gift of the

kingdom is held in abeyance, the Church is being formed.

The chief priests and the Pharisees knew that He had beer speaking of them. The doom that overwhelmed them was more awful than that they had pronounced upon themselves.

The flames of persecution that leaped up after the death of Stephen scattered the disciples, excepting the apostles, in all directions, and their blood became "the seed of the Church." Antioch in Syria becomes the distributing center of *Church* truth: while Jerusalem, the center of *kingdom* truth, is given over to her desolation until a future Israel shall say, "Blessed is he that cometh in the name of the Lord."

With the exception of our Lord's prophecy upon the mount of Olives the New Testament makes little reference to the judgment that fell upon Jerusalem and the Jewish nation.

Upon the guilty city, stained with the blood of the prophets and desolated by the rejection of her glorious King, retribution fell swift and sure. In the siege, if Josephus is to be trusted, more than a million of the people were slain and nearly one hundred thousand captives followed Titus in his triumphal procession to Rome. The city was sacked and burned.

For unspeakable tragedy that city is without a

parallel in the annals of human history. The ruins of one city have fallen upon the ruins of another until the original foundations lie many feet below the wretched and filthy city of to-day. More than forty years after the burning of the city by the Romans there was another uprising by the almost unconquerable Jews. It was suppressed by the Roman emperor Trajan and a terrible punishment visited upon the insurrectionists. Twenty years later Hadrian rebuilt the city of Jerusalem, and called it Ælia Capitolina, forbidding all Jews a place of residence in it. A pagan god was installed upon the sacred summit of Zion. A cry of rage arose in every province where the Jews were scattered, and those in Palestine once more raised the standard of revolt. The fearful conflict lasted for four years. Hundreds of thousands of Jews were slain and when the revolt was finally suppressed the remainder of that unhappy race suffered either captivity or banishment. They were dispersed into every quarter of the known world and there they remain to this day. Banished from the presence of God also, they have like Cain, the first murderer, been wanderers upon the face of the earth, and like Cain with the mark of preservation upon them.

The earth stained with the blood of the Son of God has indeed cried for vengeance. Judicial blindness,

God's sentence of judgment upon them, has wrapped them in a mist from which there has been as yet no national escape. But this blinding of the nation was tempered with mercy. The apostle Paul declares that blindness "in part" is happened to Israel. This leaves the door open for the individual to accept Christ and be saved. Paul was a converted Jew. But the nation as such must remain blind until the Church, the body of Christ, has been formed.

The threat of their dispersion was of unbroken continuity from Moses to Christ. They resisted God until He gave them "the spirit of slumber, eyes that they should not see, and ears that they should not hear."

And that judgment had been long foretold. Twice before they had entered the land of promise, Moses had warned them of world-wide dispersion that would overtake them because of their sins. For two thousand years they have suffered as no other nation under heaven has suffered and in a way foretold by Moses when their national life began.

"Ye shall be plucked from off the land whither thou goest to possess it. And the Lord shall scatter thee among all people, from one end of the earth even unto the other; and there thou shalt serve other gods, which neither thou nor thy fathers have known, even wood and stone. And among these nations thou shalt find no ease, neither shall the sole of the foot have rest: but the Lord shall give thee there a trembling heart, and failing of eyes, and sorrow of mind: and thy life shall hang in doubt before thee; and thou shalt fear day and night, and shalt have none assurance of thy life: in the morning thou shalt say, Would God it were even! and at even thou shalt say, Would God it were morning! for the fear of thine heart wherewith thou shalt fear, and for the sight of thine eyes which thou shalt see."

With startling literality this heavy judgment has been borne by the nation in its long banishment from God.

It will help us to understand the prophecies about these unhappy people if we remember that the word "Israel" is sometimes used to denote the ten tribes that revolted from the house of David on the death of Solomon, and it is sometimes used to denote the entire nation. As a rule the context easily determines whether the whole nation is contemplated, or whether, in a more limited sense, only the ten tribes of the north are in view.

Israel, in the prophecy of Hosea, refers to the ten tribes, and in that prophecy seems so limited, because the word is used in contrast with "Judah"

which is used to indicate the southern kingdom constituted by the tribes of Judah and Benjamin, which
adhered to the family of David.   When, therefore,
Hosea declares that "the children of Israel shall
abide many days without a king, and without a
prince, and without a sacrifice, and without an
image, and without an ephod, and without teraphim"
— he refers to the dispersion of the northern kingdom, which took place after the king of Assyria
had besieged and captured the northern capital,
Samaria.   This dispersion took place long before
the Babylonian captivity of the southern kingdom.
From that dispersion of the northern kingdom of
Israel there has never been any national restoration.   There may have been individuals of the
northern kingdom that returned to Palestine with
Zerubbabel, Ezra and Nehemiah: but the northern
kingdom called "Israel" in the historical books
and by the prophets, and sometimes Ephraim by
the prophets, has remained in dispersion since the
time of the Assyrian captivity.

The Babylonian captivity was of the southern
kingdom only, and it was a remnant of this kingdom
that returned to Palestine after the Babylonian
captivity and started afresh the national history
that continued to the time of Christ.   "Israel,"
as a kingdom distinct from "Judah," had no part

in the rejection and crucifixion of the King, but the fact that God had long since given them up proves that they had become hopelessly apostate.

The refusal of the King by the house of David, represented by the tribes of Judah and Benjamin in the days of our Lord, demonstrated the moral unity of both kingdoms. The last revolt of these Jews took place during the reign of the emperor Hadrian who arrived in Jerusalem, A. D., 130, and rebuilt the city as a Roman colony, forbidding the Jews a place of residence in it. The revolt was soon suppressed, and the Jews that remained in Palestine were dispersed to every quarter of the known world. Thus the dispersion of the "whole house of Israel" was accomplished.

When Paul speaks of "blindness" judicially inflicted upon "Israel," he is undoubtedly referring to the entire nation. Both kingdoms, the north and the south, are now in the world-wide dispersion predicted by Moses. Together they constitute the "house of David" over which a King of David's line is to reign in fulfilment of the covenant. It is evident that no King, such as the covenant contemplated, ever occupied the throne up to the time of Christ, and it is equally evident that no such King has occupied the throne since. Christ alone had title to the throne, but His rights were denied

Him. He died with His royal title above the cross: He rose from the dead with that title still in His possession: He ascended to heaven taking that title with Him: He is coming again to make it good.

Habakkuk, who seems to have prophesied just before the Babylonian captivity, tells us that, while the vision of future glory awaits fulfilment, "the just shall live by his faith." This was the great sentence that was flashed into the mind of Martin Luther when he climbed the sacred stairs at Rome, and it became the watchword of the Reformation.

The same sentence is used by Paul in the epistle to the Romans as having application to Jew and Gentile alike. It is applied to the Gentiles in Galatians 3 : 11-14, and to the Jews in Hebrews 10 : 38. It proclaims a gospel of eternal salvation through faith to Jew and Gentile alike; whereas the gospel of the kingdom, as proclaimed by Johr the Baptist, was a proclamation to the Jews alone. This latter gospel of the kingdom has not been proclaimed since the days of Peter, and will be no more proclaimed until it goes forth once more as "the everlasting gospel" during the time of Israel's tribulation now so near at hand. When this "gospel of the kingdom shall be preached in all the world for a witness unto all nations": then "shall the end come."

Meanwhile the other gospel of salvation through faith is being sounded forth. It is offered to Jews and Gentiles alike. It is preached while Israel is dispersed among the nations. It makes possible the salvation of the individual Jew while the nation, as such, is in blindness and unbelief, with neither priesthood nor temple, and unable therefore to keep the ordinances of the law. While the nation is under sentence of judicial blindness and cast out of their land, the individual Jew may exercise the faith of Abraham and be saved. Such is the mercy of God! But this does not set aside the covenant that God made with David. This too must be fulfilled.

It is for the want of distinctions such as these that there has been so much of confusion in the study of prophecy. For two thousand years Israel has suffered under the hand of God, and we know not when the "kingdom shall be restored." It is not for us "to know the times or the seasons, which the Father hath put in his own power." But in the meantime we are to be "witnesses" of a crucified, risen, ascended and coming Saviour: "both in Jerusalem, and in all Judea, and in Samaria, and unto the uttermost part of the earth."

The solemn pages of history bear witness to what has been accomplished.

We must remember that Israel's banishment was self-inflicted; and, if it yet be considered as God's judgment, it is not without mercy. The gracious "whosoever" of the gospel is reaching out after all alike.

Jacob, on the night of his banishment from the land, had his vision at Bethel; and the nation, in the person of Nathanael, had its vision before the final dispersion took place.

Hereafter they "shall see heaven open, and the angels of God ascending and descending upon the Son of man."

CHAPTER XI

THE MYSTERIES OF THE KINGDOM

THE kingdom of heaven, announced by John the Baptist to be at hand, was unquestionably the kingdom predicted by the prophets of old. It was called "the kingdom of heaven" because it was to be subject to the authority of the Son of God.

Such a kingdom was not established. The King uncrowned was cast out of the kingdom; and there is no possibility of such a kingdom ever being inaugurated, except the King return to the earth to receive His crown and reign.

During the King's absence the world has been subject to every conceivable form of government, and men have drearily demonstrated their utter incapacity to rule themselves in righteousness.

Israel as a nation has been given up and shall not be restored until the time comes for the constitution of the kingdom. The judgment upon Israel is one of the many mysteries revealed in the New Testament. Paul says, "For I would not, brethren, that ye should be ignorant of this mystery, lest ye should be wise in your own conceits; that blindness in part is happened to Israel, until the fulness of the Gentiles be come in" (Romans 11 : 25).

Other mysteries in connection with the kingdom are revealed in the seven parables of the thirteenth chapter of Matthew. On reading the first of these, we find that "the vineyard," so constantly used to represent Israel, is given up, and a "sower" goes forth to sow. The unwearied Worker in behalf of men goes forth to labor in a field beyond the limits contemplated by the prophets. The seed, sown in the broad field of the world, is declared to be "the word of the kingdom," and the "wheat" produced constitutes "the children of the kingdom."

It is thus seen that the thought of the kingdom is not given up even though the kingdom was not set up in the form predicted by the prophets. It shall be so set up when the King returns. In the meanwhile God has been gathering together a people who, sharing with Christ His present rejection, shall also reign with Him. This is the first mystery of the kingdom represented by the Sower going forth to sow.

Other "mysteries of the kingdom" are unfolded in the parables that follow. The exposition of these parables has been so contradictory that we shall have to examine them with care.

The first two, by the Lord's interpretation, are beyond the pale of dispute. Any interpretation of the others that does not accord with that of the first two is thereby convicted of error.

The field in which the seed is sown is "the world": it is therefore the scene also of Satan's activity and opposition.

In the first parable the "seed" is declared to be the "word of the kingdom," and is "sown in the heart." The seed is good; but it is the character of "the soil" upon which the seed falls, that gives to the parable its deeply solemn significance.

Some seed fell by the wayside — the hard beaten path—and were instantly devoured by the birds that followed the Sower. Some hearts are like that, unexercised and unresponsive, hardened by the world's traffic. The truth falling into such a heart is neither welcomed nor understood. And this is Satan's opportunity. He is the god of this age and he has the power to blind the minds of those that believe not. He catches away the seed that is sown in the heart that refuses to accept it. Some seed fell in rocky places. This is not merely "stony ground"; but, as Grant says, "bed-rock, with a slight layer of earth over it, in which the seed grows rapidly but superficially, the very cause of its destruction in a little while, operating at first to produce hot-house growth; but, there being no depth of earth, it is without root, and so withers away."

"Here then is that 'heart of stone' of which the prophet speaks. In such a heart the word may be received with joy, but there is no deep conviction, no true repentance: the sentiments are engaged, but not the conscience; and such an one may be warm and enthusiastic, and make rapid progress in the learning of truth; but he has not counted the cost: when affliction or persecution ariseth because of the world, immediately he is stumbled."

Some seed fell among thorns. The thorn is the sign of the curse come into the world through sin. The heart overgrown with these is altogether in the power of the world; and the "care of the world and the deceitfulness of riches choke the word, and he becometh unfruitful."

The seed falling upon the good ground is but partially successful, some bearing an hundredfold, some sixty, and some thirty.

In this first parable, says Grant, we see the beginning of the kingdom to be in the sowing of the word of the kingdom. The kingdom is, ideally at least, a kingdom of the truth. The subjects are disciples. How far the kingdom being in the hands of men may affect this we have yet to see; but even as we find it already we find in it unreal disciples

11

as well as true; and this the after parables confirm. The sphere of the kingdom is profession, a profession which shall be in due time tested by the fruit it bears. There is no undue haste to realize this: the picture is that of a field of growing wheat, as to which the harvest alone can properly decide what the fruit may be; and the harvest itself is not yet spoken of. Manifestly it is a kingdom introduced in a very different way, not merely from any Jewish conception, but from anything that the prophets had announced. Thus it is of the "mysteries" of the kingdom that the Lord is speaking.

A mystery is something that is kept secret for a time, to be afterward revealed. The form that the kingdom was to assume in consequence of the rejection of the King was kept a secret until revealed by the Lord Jesus who, surpassing beyond expression the glory of Joseph, became the true "Revealer of Secrets" and "The Saviour of the World."

The coming of the kingdom in a fashion so different from that foretold was a revelation of the riches of God's grace "according to counsels hidden from generations past, but now to make known to principalities and powers by means of the church the manifold wisdom of God" (Eph. 3 : 10).

The kingdom, as announced by the prophets,

has not been given up.   The time of its setting up has been delayed until these secret counsels of God have been accomplished.   For the time being, Israel is set aside, and the kingdom comes after the manner told out in these parables.   It shall finally come in power and glory: the wheat-harvest of the first parable indicating those who are to be co-heirs with Christ when He comes to reign.

In the second parable Satan is shown to be in relentless opposition to Christ.   His antagonism is not open but secret and of devilish ingenuity. The field sown with wheat is oversown with tares. It is "while men slept" that Satan does this, indicating a state of spiritual decline, and reminding us of the fact that when the Bridegroom comes He shall find all the ten virgins fast asleep.

The tares, or darnel, sown by Satan is said to be "a poisonous kind of rye, which among the Jews was credited with being a degenerate wheat: its grain is black and bitter."   Wherever the wheat is sown there also the darnel is sown, and they both are allowed to grow together until the time of the harvest, when the true and the false are separated: the darnel to be bound in bundles for burning: the wheat to be gathered into the barn.

The kingdom, instead of being established upon

the earth in power and glory, as the prophets declared it should be, resembles a field in which wheat and tares are growing together: it is a form the kingdom assumes under the administration of men during the absence of the King.

That such a condition has obtained since the days of Christ none will deny. Although truth and error are alike in it, it is nevertheless His kingdom, to be purged when the time of the harvest shall come. The separation of the false and the true is not to take place until then. The eradication of the tares is not to be effected by the preaching of the gospel as so many have idly dreamed. Though the kingdom of Christ be a "kingdom of truth," it has been oversown with error, and the good and the bad must continue on together until "the completion of the age." Unpalatable as this may be, it is what Jesus teaches in this parable, and what two thousand years of history has abundantly confirmed.

The sowing of the darnel is undoubtedly the "mystery of iniquity" of which the apostle speaks (II Thess. 2 : 7), which, however much it might be hindered, would continue to work until it should manifest "that wicked one," whom the Lord "shall consume with the spirit of his mouth, and shall destroy with the brightness of his coming."

The separation of the wheat and the tares has

never taken place, nor does the Lord's interpretation of the parable allow us to think that it ever shall take place until the end of the age. The Church has no commission to purge "the kingdom of heaven." It has a commission to "preach the gospel to every creature"; and, wherever the good seed is sown, the devil will see to it that the darnel is sown also. The Church is to purge evil out of her own assemblies; but that is another matter: the Church and the kingdom are not the same.

But we must look at the interpretation of this parable given by the Lord, not as of the first one to the multitude, but to the disciples privately.

The harvest is the completion of the age, and the reapers are the angels. The Son of man shall send his angels, and they shall gather out of his kingdom all things that offend, and those committing lawlessness, and shall cast them into the furnace of fire; there shall be weeping and gnashing of teeth. Then shall the righteous shine forth as the sun in the kingdom of their Father. He that hath ears let him hear.

Here, then, we have the separation of the wheat from the tares, and the destiny of both. Those who have received and believed the truth are the wheat: those who have received and believed a lie are the tares. It is unspeakably solemn that there should be such as these last; but Scripture decisively declares that such there shall be. Men and women who will not receive the love of the truth, that they may be saved. "And for this cause God shall send them strong delusion, that they should believe the lie: that they all might be damned who believed not the truth, but had pleasure in unrighteousness" (II Thess. 2 : 11, 12).

The heirs of a doom so terrible resist it; they hate those who proclaim it, and they do not hesitate to be at issue with Christ Himself. It is a fearful thing to realize that those who refuse to believe God's truth shall be forced to believe the devil's lie.

But there is another destiny to which God in patient mercy has ever sought to win us. The Son of man shall send his angels, and they shall purge "his kingdom": and "then shall the righteous shine forth as the sun in the kingdom of their Father."

They *shine* "in the kingdom of the Father": they shall *reign* "in the kingdom of the Son."

In the closing chapter of the Old Testament, God speaks through the prophet, saying, "Unto you that fear my name shall the Sun of righteousness arise with healing in his wings." In the glory of that "sun-rise" the righteous shall shine when they come with the King to reign.

The "mysteries" of the kingdom do not end until the kingdom is finally established in power.

In the parables that follow we are without the help given us by the Lord in the first two, and the result has been a singular unanimity of error, which is the more difficult to overthrow because of the support given to it by the traditional authority of many otherwise trustworthy commentators. The Church, which is undoubtedly one of the "mysteries" of the kingdom, has loomed so big before the eyes of many, that it has blotted out every other feature. The Church is one thing: the inheritance of Israel nationally is quite another matter; and the confusion of these is responsible for so little intelligence in the understanding of these parables. There are other features besides these, and we must give consideration to every one of them if we are to preserve the balance of truth. The "wheat" is one feature; the "darnel" is another; the growth of the mustard tree another; the woman leavening the meal another; the "treasure" another; the purchase of the field, the hiding of the treasure, the purchase of the pearl, and the casting of the drag-net are still other features: and the failure to distinguish these produces nothing but hopeless confusion. They are all of them distinct and separate mysteries of the kingdom of heaven.

The kingdom is here upon the earth under the administration of the servants of the King, who is now in heaven. These servants, equipped by the King to occupy until He comes, are but men; and, like men in general, who have violated every trust that God ever reposed in them, they sleep at their post: and the administration of the kingdom is further vexed by the active opposition of Satan. Under such conditions the kingdom assumes a form very different from that predicted by the prophets, and one foreign to the mind of the King. It continues in this form until the King returns and purges it of evil.

The parables under consideration give us the various features which combine to represent the kingdom in its present administration. In them we have the foretelling of history by One alone competent to give it. We must not allow one feature to obliterate another and so obscure what He has given us. The history of past centuries has fully demonstrated what the first two parables have represented.

In the parable of the mustard seed we have a picture of the external growth of the kingdom. We must be prepared to find evil in this; as we have already found it in the two preceding parables.

The kingdom of heaven is like a grain of mustard

seed, which a man took and sowed in his field; which indeed is less than all seeds, but, when it is grown, it is greater than herbs, and becometh a tree, so that the birds of heaven come and lodge in its branches.

"A tree" says Edersheim, "whose wide-spreading branches afforded lodgment to the birds of heaven, was a familiar Old Testament figure for a mighty kingdom that gave shelter to the nations.   Indeed it is specifically used as an illustration of the Messianic kingdom."

In the thirty-first chapter of Ezekiel, and in the fourth chapter of Daniel, the Assyrian and Babylonian kingdoms are respectively represented in this way.

In the seventeenth chapter of Ezekiel the Messianic kingdom is represented by a "goodly cedar"; under the shadows of whose branches shall dwell "all fowl of every wing."   But this represents the kingdom of Christ to be established in power and glory in a future day.   It is, in fact, the resurrection of the house and throne of David, and therefore does not represent the present "mystery" form of the kingdom.

A "mustard seed" springing up into abnormal growth and becoming a tree, in the branches of which the birds of heaven find shelter, is used to represent the kingdom in one of its present "mystery" forms.

Whoever heard — apart from this parable — of a mustard tree? The mustard seed, in its normal growth, produces a garden plant; but in the East, under favorable conditions, it may become a shrub seven or eight feet in height: but that could scarcely be considered a tree of sufficient proportion to give shelter to the birds of heaven. It is the anomalous growth that gives the parable its significance. A tree, as we have already seen, represents an earthly kingdom: here a tree of unnatural growth represents a mystery of the kingdom of heaven. It is a form the kingdom assumes during the absence of the King. Prophecy determines the course of human history, and history, in turn, demonstrates and confirms prophecy.

After the death of Stephen, Paul assumes a commanding position among the apostles, and he declares himself and his fellow-laborers to be "the servants of Christ, and stewards of the mysteries of God" (I Cor. 4 : 1).

He gloried only in the cross on which the world had crucified his Saviour, and by which he had been crucified to the world. He called upon men everywhere to separate themselves absolutely from the world, to accept Jesus as their Saviour, to suffer with Him in His present rejection: that they might reign with Him when He came in glory. Such believers, constituting the Church, the body of Christ, were to be pilgrims and strangers on the earth. God would deliver them from the kingdom of darkness, and translate them "into the kingdom of his dear Son" (Col. 1:13).

The Church is *in* the kingdom, but the kingdom itself is like the anomalous tree that shelters in its branches the birds of the air. The "birds of the air" are the same that carried away the seed in the first parable. So Babylon, the painted harlot of Revelation, claiming to be the bride of Christ, becomes the cage of every "unclean and hateful bird."

"If we remember" as another has said "that this seed and its development give the kingdom as a whole, and that the previous parable has shown us a mixed condition — the result of the enemy's work — then the anomalous tree becomes perfectly intelligible. The state of the whole has been affected by this mixture of diverse elements." The result of this has been what is commonly regarded as the Church.

But we have long since learned to distinguish the *visible* Church, or what professes to be christian in the world, from the *invisible* Church, or the body of true believers. Almost immediately after the so called conversion of Constantine, "the simplicity of the Gospel was corrupted; pompous rites and ceremonies were introduced; worldly honors and emoluments were conferred on the teachers of Christianity, and the kingdom of Christ in a great measure converted into a kingdom of this world." It is none the less the kingdom of heaven, in its present "mystery" form; and the birds of the air, which have so long been the burden of its reproach, shall be driven from it when the King returns in glory.

"Wherefore come out from among them, and be ye separate, saith the Lord, and touch not the unclean thing; and I will receive you, and will be a father unto you, and ye shall be my sons and daughters, saith the Lord Almighty" (II Cor. 6 : 17, 18).

"Another parable spake he unto them, The kingdom of heaven is like unto leaven, which a woman took and hid in three measures of meal, till the whole was leavened."

Of this parable also contradictory interpretations have been given. We shall present both, and then subject them alike to the testing of Scripture.

Lange, representing a large number who may differ among themselves only in slight and unimportant variations, interprets the parable as follows:

"The woman is an apt figure of the Church. Leaven, a substance kindred, yet quite opposed, to meal — having the power of transforming and preserving it, and converting it into bread, thus representing the divine in its relation to, and influence upon, our natural life. One of the main points of the parable is the 'hiding,' or mixing the leaven in the three measures of meal. This refers to the great visible Church, in which the living gospel seems, as it were, hidden and lost. It appears as if the gospel were engulfed in the world; but under the regenerating power of Christianity it will at last be seen that the whole world shall be included in the Church."

Grant, representing a much smaller number who, however, agree substantially in almost every detail, declares that the leaven represents an "evil principle" introduced into the three measures of meal, or meat offering, "which," he says, "speaks, as these offerings in general do, of Christ as the food of His people, of which they partake in communion with God. God insists upon the feast being kept to Him with *un*leavened bread: all mixture with leaven is adulteration; and if the Church, as Trench with Lange and others rightly says, is intended by the woman, then the professing Church is here seen as adulterating the pure doctrine of Christ, the bread of life,

with impure admixture." He further says: "Christ,
the bread of life, is what the professing Church has
had entrusted to her for her own sustenance and
for the blessing of others. The doctrine of Christ
is her most precious deposit, and the maintaining
this in purity her great responsibility. Alas, she
has adulterated it with leaven: the Lord's own explanation of this as 'the leaven of the Pharisees and
of the Sadducees' and the 'leaven of Herod,' remains
still for us in Christian times as wherewith to interpret His parable of the kingdom. Formalism,
ritualism, rationalism, the corrupting tendencies
of world-pandering Herodianism, have all had their
share in perverting the precious doctrine of Christ.
The leaven is leavening the whole lump. No doubt,
there is a present hindrance to this in the power of
the Spirit working, and as long as the present purpose of God is not complete, the lump as a whole
cannot be leavened. God will preserve His truth,
which never has been as a whole allowed to be in
the woman's hands to be leavened. Once let the
true Church be removed, the truth of God shall be
removed with it, and the leaven of falsehood do
its fatal work on all that is left."

Between such conflicting interpretations Scripture is alone competent to decide the truth. On
this evidence our conclusion should rest and on no

other.   But is Scripture decisive as to the meaning of the figures used in this parable?

All seem to agree that the "woman" represents the Church, and our acceptance of this is warranted by Scripture.

Our right understanding of the parable depends on the meaning of "leaven," and of the "three measures of meal."

It is beyond dispute that leaven is everywhere used in Scripture as a symbol of evil.   If, in this parable, it be the symbol of good, the usage is so exceptional, that we must demand the most positive proof that it does mean good.   Mere individual opinion is of no value.   If we turn to Scripture for proof that leaven is a symbol of good, we find none: on the contrary we find objections that are absolutely fatal to such a view.   It does violence to the meaning fixed to the word by the Lord Himself (Matt. 16 : 6-12.   Mark 8 : 15).   Its implication, that the world is to be converted by the gospel — till the whole was leavened — is explicitly denied by the Lord in His declaration that the "tares" are to be left until they are separated from the wheat by "the angels" at the end of the age.   More than this, symbols in Scripture have a meaning fixed by inspired usage, and in all other places where the word is found it is used as the symbol of evil.

In reference to the "three measures of meal" it may be said, that meal was used in one of the offerings, which, being typical of Christ, was eaten by the priests: a shadow of the true bread that came down from heaven. The doctrine of Christ is that bread and it is the food of His people. Leaven, the doctrine of the Pharisees, the Sadducees and the Herodians, is therefore the symbol of formalism, scepticism and worldliness. That the doctrine of Christ has been adulterated with all these is attested by many a page of Church history.

Paul has declared that "the mystery of iniquity," already at work in his day, would continue to work, until the present hindrance should be taken away, and then there should follow a falling away into a fearful and final apostasy.

The woman, "bedecked with gold and precious stones and pearls, having a golden cup in her hand full of abominations and filthiness of her fornication," riding the scarlet colored beast of world-empire, is the apostate church of Christendom, after the deadly leaven has done its work.

The development of professing Christianity into "Mystery, Babylon" is one of the strange and fearful "mysteries" of the kingdom of heaven.

CHAPTER XII

THE TREASURE AND THE PEARL

THE parables of the treasure, the pearl, and the drag-net also represent "mysteries of the kingdom of heaven"; but, unlike the four that precede them, they are addressed to the disciples alone and not to the multitude. Such esoteric teaching was not unusual with Jesus. It implies the possession of a spiritual discernment by the disciples that would be lacking in the general public.

The first four parables give the outward aspect of the kingdom; the form it was to assume in the sight of all men.

The last three are very different: they give us "the things of the Spirit of God," which the natural man receiveth not: neither can he know them because they are spiritually discerned. This may account for the very different interpretations that have been given: "but he that is spiritual judgeth all things."

"The kingdom of heaven is like unto treasure hid in the field, which a man having found, hath

12

hid, and for joy thereof goeth and selleth all that he hath, and buyeth that field."

The commonly accepted interpretation is, in its main features, that of Luther, who says: "The hidden treasure is the gospel, which bestows upon us all the riches of free grace, without any merit of our own. Hence also the joy when it is found, and which consists in a good and happy conscience, that cannot be obtained by works."

This interpretation is so counter to the general tenor of Scripture that it passes the subtlest power of the imagination to conceive how it came to gain such currency. It is singular that Luther, who so stoutly resisted the sale of indulgences and who so fearlessly proclaimed salvation by faith alone, could have tolerated the thought of "buying" the riches of free grace. His interpretation involves this, and much else besides, when you consider the purchase of the field; if here, as in the first parable, "the field" should be "the world."

Lange, who accepts Luther's interpretation, gives an extraordinary solution of the difficulty in the thought of the sinner's purchase of the field. "If," he says, "the field refers to external worldly ecclesiasticism, the expression might mean that we were not to carry the treasure out of the visible Church, as if we were stealing it away, but that we should purchase the field in order to have full title to the possession hid in it. Accordingly it would apply against sectarianism." Of such oracular wisdom we are able to make nothing. Such a *reductio ad absurdum* is enough to discredit any method of interpretation that is driven to an extreme like this in order to be consistent. The interpretation is unscriptural and therefore impossible.

We must remember that the parable represents one of the "mysteries" of the kingdom; and the kingdom, stripped of all mystery, is the one offered to Israel in fulfilment of God's covenant with David. So much, at least, is positively clear. Furthermore, Israel's rejection of the kingdom did not nullify the promise: nothing could do that, for the promise was sovereign and unconditional. The kingdom must be set up according to the terms of the covenant. Israel's refusal of the King has delayed this; and, during the time of the suspension of the promises made to Israel, the kingdom takes the form represented by these parables. It would be strange indeed if these parables revealed nothing of Israel's national inheritance. If, in the parable of the treasure, God's thought of Israel be allowed, then an interpretation consistent throughout is possible; and this should, at the least, commend its consideration.

At the very beginning of their national history the Lord called unto Moses out of the mountain, saying, "Thus shalt thou say to the house of Jacob, and tell the children of Israel: Ye have seen what I did unto the Egyptians, and how I bare you on eagles' wings, and brought you unto myself. Now therefore, if ye will obey my voice indeed, and keep my covenant, then ye shall be a peculiar treasure unto me above all people: for all the earth is mine: and ye shall be unto me a kingdom of priests, and an holy nation" (Ex.19 : 3-6).

Peter's application of these words to the Church, in the ninth verse of the second chapter of his second epistle, does not disinherit Israel. It means that the conditional blessings of the law are freely bestowed by grace.

Israel is yet to be "a peculiar treasure," a "kingdom of priests, and an holy nation": when, under the new covenant, the law "shall be written in their hearts." God has not given up His thought concerning Israel, and the Psalmist but reminds us of this when he says: "The Lord hath chosen Jacob unto himself, and Israel for his peculiar treasure."

The blessing which they forfeited under the law was offered to them in grace, but, refusing this, they were set aside until the fulness of the Gentiles be come in. Meanwhile the treasure is hidden until the time for its display has come. The parable under consideration is in every part consistent with such a thought.

When the Lord came into the world, Israel was the first object of His search. To the woman of Canaan He declared, "I am not sent but unto the lost sheep of the house of Israel" (Matt. 15 : 24). When He commissioned the twelve, He charged them, saying, "Go not into the way of the Gentiles, and into any city of the Samaritans enter ye not: but go rather to the lost sheep of the house of Israel" (Matt. 10 : 5, 6).

He discovered the treasure "hid in the field" of the world; and, unable to take immediate possession of it, He hideth it again: and for joy thereof goeth and selleth all that He hath, and buyeth that field.

The field must be purchased at the cross before He could take title to the hidden treasure. Unconscious of the wondrous depth of its meaning the Sadducean high priest must prophesy, "that one man should die for the nation" (John 11 : 51). In no other way could Israel's blessing be secured. The field must be purchased; and with Israel's blessing, the blessing of the world is inseparably bound. The note of joy that rings out in the parable is the echo of the jubilant song sung by the prophet.

"Break forth into joy, sing together, ye waste places of Jerusalem: for the Lord hath comforted his people, he hath redeemed Jerusalem. The Lord hath made bare his holy arm in the eyes of all the nations; and all the ends of the earth shall see the salvation of our God" (Is. 52 : 9,10).

"And the Gentiles shall see thy righteousness, and all kings thy glory: and thou shalt be called by a new name, which the mouth of the Lord shall name. Thou shalt also be a crown of glory in the hand of the Lord, and a royal diadem in the hand of thy God" (Is. 62 : 2,3).

The parable ends with the purchase of the field: it does not carry us on to the time when the treasure shall be unearthed; for this belongs not to the " mysteries," but to the kingdom in its manifestation and glory.

This interpretation removes every difficulty and is both scriptural and consistent. It is the only parable of the seven in which Israel's inheritance may be recognized, and we must not deny them their place in the kingdom promised to David. The blindness of Israel is named by Paul as a "mystery," and it is here given its place among "the mysteries of the kingdom."

The parable of the pearl is not — as some would have it — a mere repetition of the other; but another and distinct "mystery" of the kingdom whose application is apart from Israel altogether.

"The kingdom of heaven is like unto a merchant-man, seeking goodly pearls; and when he had found one pearl of great price, he went and sold all that he had, and bought it."

The interpretation that makes "the pearl of great price" represent Christ, for which the sinner sells all that he has in order to acquire it, is open to so many objections that it is impossible of acceptance.

It is difficult to rid ourselves of preconceptions or to part with some thought that has become precious to us; but absolute truth is of far more value than imagined truth, however much the latter may appeal to us.

In the chapter that pledges to Israel the everlasting covenant, "even the sure mercies of David," we also read, "Seek ye the Lord while he may be found, call ye upon him while he is near: let the wicked forsake his way, and the unrighteous man his thoughts: and let him return unto the Lord, and he will have mercy upon him; and to our God, for he will abundantly pardon" (Is. 55 : 6, 7).

The sinner is urged to seek the Lord, and to

turn from his wicked way, that he may obtain forgiveness: but the same chapter begins with this: "He that hath no money; come ye, buy, and eat; yea, come, buy wine and milk without money and without price."

We understand such language, and, instead of its confirming the common thought about the purchase of the pearl, it is opposed to it: for one does ot sell "all that he has" in order to buy that which in reality is bought "without money and without price."

The objections to the sinner's purchase of the field apply with equal force to his purchase of the pearl.

Looking at the two parables together, we are convinced that the finder in the one is the seeker in the other. This is true whichever method of interpretation be adopted. The Lord Jesus, who is the Finder of the treasure, is also the Seeker of the pearl. But what is the pearl upon which He places so great a value? The difference in figure implies a difference of object before Him. The treasure and the pearl are not identical. They are alike in being the object of pursuit, and the purchase price of the one is equal to that of the other, but this does not prove their identity.

"The lost sheep" of the house of Israel were His

treasure, and in finding them, He had found what He had lost: for they were His, the sheep of His pasture and the flock of His hand, over which He was to exercise the shepherd-rule, to which He was ordained in God's covenant with David. He had come with Jehovah's warrant to do this. Prophecy had proclaimed Him:

"I will set up one shepherd over them, and he shall feed them, even my servant David; he shall feed them, and he shall be their shepherd: and I the Lord will be their God, and my servant David a prince among them; I the Lord have spoken it" (Ezek. 34 : 23,24).

David was long dead when this prophecy was uttered, and it could only refer to Him who was to be of David's line, the Messiah, whom they were taught to expect. And he had come at the time definitely predicted by Daniel, was born at Bethlehem, was of David's line; displaying the signs that bore witness to the unique glory of His character and mission, He had come to the Jewish fold, and was calling out His sheep.

But a wider mission than this had brought Him from heaven to earth. "Other sheep," He says, "I have, which are not of this fold; them also must I bring; and they shall hear my voice, and shall become one flock, one shepherd." The far away

Gentiles were to be brought near, and were to hear
His voice; and the fold that was Jewish and legal
was to be given up, and there was to be one flock —
with all national distinction gone — and He the
Shepherd of them all. So the Church comes into view.

Is it not antecedently probable that, if the treasure represent Israel, the pearl may represent the
Church?

There are those who claim that both treasure
and pearl represent the Church, and who would
justify the thought by saying, "The parable of
the hidden treasure did not sufficiently convey
what the saints are to Christ. For the treasure
might consist of a hundred thousand pieces of gold
and silver. And how would this mark the blessedness and beauty of the Church? The merchantman
finds 'one pearl of great price.' The Lord does
not see merely the preciousness of the saints, but
the unity and heavenly beauty of the assembly.
Every saint is precious to Christ; but He 'loved
the Church' and gave Himself for it."

But if this were the only distinction, two parables
were not necessary: that of the pearl would have
been enough. Both Israel and the Church are
"mysteries" of the kingdom, and it is at least
reasonable to suppose that both should be represented in these parables. That the pearl is the

Church would seem to be evident to any one who has discernment of the truth these parables were intended to convey.

A pearl is said to be the "result of injury done to the animal that produces it. Its material is *nacre*, as it is called, or mother of pearl, which lines the interior of the shell, and which is renewed by it as often as injured or worn away. A particle of sand getting between the animal and the shell, the irritation causes a deposit of nacre upon it, which goes on being deposited, layer after layer, till a pearl is formed. But completely spherical pearls — and these are the valuable ones — can be formed loose in the muscle or soft parts of the animal. The Chinese obtain them artificially by introducing into the living mussel foreign substances, such as pieces of mother of pearl fixed to wires, which thus become coated with a more brilliant material. The pearl is thus, as we may say, an answer to an injury; and it is the *offending object* that becomes, through the work of the injured one, a precious and a beauteous gem. It is clothed with a comeliness put upon it, as the objects of divine grace are, with the beauty and glory of Him we crucified! Between a common pearl and one of great price, the difference is only one of degree. The size and brilliancy depend, not upon the grain of sand that may be inwrapped, but upon the number of layers of nacre which inwrap it. The greatness of the grace bestowed is the distinguishable feature in what is here. Different bestowals of grace there are, and Scripture asserts this in the fullest way. The calling of Israel is not that of the Church, which is Christ's body": and in confusing these we confuse the purpose and destiny of each.

"In the treasure we find Israel preserved for blessing, but reserved, they having in the meanwhile rejected the only possible way in which it could be theirs. In the pearl we have that in which, during this reservation the purpose of God as to the Church comes out."

In holding to these distinctions we escape from the mist in which so many are bewildered.

The unauthorized summaries, which have been placed at the head of the chapters in so many of our Bibles, should be ruthlessly eliminated: they are intolerable for many reasons, but especially for their persistent and unvarying failure to distinguish between Israel and the Church.

Israel and the Church, though distinct from each other, are each related to the kingdom in its "mystery" form: the form it assumes during the absence of the King.

The field, which is the world, has been purchased neither with gold nor with silver, but with the precious blood of Jesus; and in that field of the world Israel remains the hidden treasure until the kingdom, according to the terms of the covenant made with David, shall be established. In that day Israel "shall blossom and bud, and fill the face of the earth with fruit" (Is. 27 : 6)

Meanwhile the Church, the pearl of great price, is being formed. This also is a "mystery" of the kingdom. It is not territorial, as are other kingdoms of the world, but a kingdom of truth, established by no act of divine power, but by the sowing of "the word of the kingdom" in the hearts of men.

In the kingdom, as the other parables assure us, there is mingled the false and the true: it is a sphere of discipleship in which profession may be either nominal or real, but in this kingdom, the Church, the body of Christ, is to be found: so that we cannot even say that the limits of the kingdom and the Church are the same. The purchase of the field implies world-wide possession, and Christ is more than the King of Israel: He is at His manifestation declared to be the King of kings and Lord of lords. The kingdoms of this world are all to become His kingdom. Everything is forced to contribute to this all-glorious consummation.

The stream of human history flows on and on until it empties itself into the open sea of apostasy and revolt from God. But this brings the King. The true David shall come forth, the Christ in divine glory, the apocalyptic Rider of the white horse, and on the ruins of the constitution of the kingdoms of this world the kingdom of the Son of David shall rise. And then, like Moses and Elijah on the mount, Israel and the Church shall be transfigured with His glory. Israel shall become an holy nation: the Church, the bride of Christ, shall reign with Him. But these are no longer "mysteries" of the kingdom.

The sowing of the seed, the oversowing of the darnel, the abnormal growth of the tree, the subtle working of the leaven, the purchase of the field, the hiding of the treasure, the forming of the pearl: these are the "mysteries" of the kingdom, that are to issue at last in the manifestation of the Kingdom and the King.

The last parable of the series is related neither to Israel nor the Church nor to anything else that has yet been before us. It has reference to the proclamation of the kingdom, that is to be made immediately after the removal of the Church from the earth.

"Again, the kingdom of heaven is like unto a

draw-net, cast into the sea, and gathering of every kind: which when it was filled, they drew to shore and sat down and gathered the good into vessels and cast the worthless away. So shall it be at the completion of the age: the angels shall go forth, and separate the wicked from among the righteous, and shall cast them into the furnace of fire; there shall be weeping and gnashing of teeth."

This is a new gathering, apart from Israel and the Church, and is the result of God's grace to the Gentiles after the Church has been formed.

Nothing so far has been inclosed in this net, for it is not let down into the sea [of the nations] until the completion of the age: it does not therefore apply to the present time, and the putting of the fish "into denominational vessels" — as some have maintained — is out of the question.

In His prophecy on the mount of Olives, Jesus says, "This gospel of the kingdom shall be preached in all the world for a witness unto all nations; and then shall the end come."

He is speaking of a proclamation that is to be sounded forth immediately before His advent in glory. It is "the gospel of the kingdom": and it differs from the gospel committed to Paul for proclamation during the present dispensation. It is true that the kingdom has its place in present

evangelical preaching, but not in the sense it was
understood by the prophets, and announced by
John the Baptist. Neither the prophets nor John
knew of the Church as the body of Christ: this was
a revelation of a later date, as is declared in the third
chapter of the epistle to the Ephesians, and was
therefore of necessity hidden from the Old Testament saints. Types and figures of the Church
there are in abundance in the Old Testament, but
we must go to the New Testament revelation for
enlightenment as to these.

The gospel proclaimed by the prophets was the
gospel of the kingdom, and it contemplated the
setting up of David's throne, according to the
covenant that God had made with him. This was
to be accomplished — so the burden of prophecy
runs — by the King in person, who would inaugurate the kingdom by thoroughly purging His
threshing-floor, gathering the wheat into the garner,
and burning up the chaff with unquenchable fire.
This meant the severing of the wicked from among
the just; that the earth might be prepared for the
King. So John the Baptist preached, and so had
preached his long line of predecessors: it was a gospel
of judgment, and not one of eternal salvation
through faith in the Crucified One. In the fourteenth
chapter of Revelation there is mention of this

same gospel, and it is there said to be proclaimed in immediate prospect of the coming of the King.

There is in it an element which it would be impossible for us to preach now.

"And I saw another angel fly in the midst of heaven, having the everlasting gospel to preach unto them that dwell on the earth, and to every nation, and kindred, and tongue, and people, saying with a loud voice, Fear God, and give glory to him; for the hour of his judgment is come: and worship him that made heaven, and earth, and the sea, and the fountains of waters."

In the gospel that is now being preached we cannot say: "The hour of his *judgment* is come." Not, at least, in the sense in which it is used in Revelation: for there it is an exhortation to the nations, after the Church has been removed from the earth, as its place in Revelation shows, and in view of the establishment of the kingdom in power and glory.

This "gospel of the kingdom" is the testimony of God's mercy to the Gentiles left here upon the earth when the Church has been taken from it.

It is represented by the "net" cast into the sea, which gathers of every kind, and is then drawn to the shore, and the angels separate the wicked from among the righteous.

This is done at the "end of the age" and im-
13

mediately before the inauguration of the kingdom. It is therefore coincident with, but different from, the harvesting of the wheat-field.

The harvesting of the wheat-field is the removal of the Church from the earth to meet the Lord when He comes. Immediately thereafter the gospel of the kingdom goes out to all nations that are left upon the earth: and then comes the end. There is a judicial separation of the wicked from the righteous, as of the goats from the sheep in the twenty-fifth chapter of Matthew; the wicked departing into everlasting fire, and the righteous remaining for blessing in the kingdom, under the Shepherd rule of the Son of David.

This judicial separation is what comes before us in the net drawn to the shore. The net is cast into the sea [of the nations] immediately after the Church has been removed. Those that have refused grace in the day of grace are given up to strong delusion that they may believe the lie: and with the beast and the false prophet they go on to their doom. Then those who have never had the truth before them — and the Church failing in her testimony shall leave many such — shall hear the "everlasting gospel," and shall then find their opportunity of salvation. Just and equal are the ways of God.

This brings to an end the parables of the "mysteries of the kingdom of heaven." They characterize the spiritual features, whether for good or for evil, of this present dispensation, which fills in and measures the time between the first and second advent of our Lord.

While in these parables the essential and distinctive features of Christianity are to be found, they represent much more besides. The field, which is the world, has been purchased: in it Satan for a time is permitted to work in hostility to Christ; but his activity is limited by the restraining power of the Holy Spirit, and he shall ere long be bound and cast into the pit of the abyss: then the world shall be filled with unimagined glory under the righteous rule of her glorious King the Son of David.

The Church shall reign with the King in glory; and Israel shall constitute that "holy nation," and become the channel of blessing to all the other nations of the earth.

The "mysteries of the kingdom" are the forces which, during the absence of the King are moving steadily on under the hand of God to bring in this infinitely glorious consummation.

CHAPTER XIII

TIMES OF RESTITUTION

CONCERNING "the times of restitution of all things which God hath spoken by the mouth of all the holy prophets since the world began," the testimony of the Scripture is so voluminous, so general, so consistent and so clear that any misunderstanding must be due either to prejudice or to ignorance.

The restitution of which the prophets speak is not of *all things* without exception, as some false teachers have declared, but is limited to the things "which God hath spoken by the mouth of all the holy prophets since the world began."

The holy prophets speak of the restitution of the land long alienated from Israel; they speak of the restitution of the twelve tribes long since dispersed on account of their disobedience; they speak of the restitution of David's throne and of David's kingdom: of such restitution the prophets speak and of no other.

Scripture is Scripture, and facts are facts, and there is no argument against them. Specious reasoning can neither annihilate hell nor in any way whatsoever modify the terms of the covenants that God has made with His ancient people. Let us beware lest being blind we be led of blind guides and together with them fall into the ditch.

Israel did not take possession of the land of promise under the covenant that God made with Abraham, nor was Israel established there under the covenant that God made with David: Israel entered the land under the covenant that God made with them at Horeb and conditioned on the plains of Moab; they shall be established in the land under the new covenant that God shall yet make with them.

Except a proper distinction be observed between these different covenants there can be no clear conception of the question under consideration.

The covenant that God made with Abraham guaranteed to him and to his seed the perpetual inheritance of the land; and there never was a right or title to any inheritance or possession so inviolable, attested by the oath of the Lord God of all the earth, as that title to the land of Canaan, conveyed to Abraham and to his seed by the Lord God, and confirmed to them by covenant and oath as an everlasting possession. In that deed of conveyance there was no clause of reversion, no restriction, no condition, no reservation of any kind whatsoever. It assigned and secured to Abraham and his heirs for an everlasting possession a tract of land the ample extent of which is little realized by the average Bible reader.*

The limits of the land, its area and geographical boundaries were clearly defined by the Lord God who made the grant, and it is important to observe that these boundaries, defining the land decreed to the twelve tribes of Israel for an everlasting possession, were explicitly stated long after the ten tribes had been swept away by the Assyrians, and while Judah and Benjamin were captive in Babylon.

Moses and Ezekiel, the one before the twelve tribes entered the land, and the other after they had been cast out of it, record the boundaries that define the limits of the land given by the Lord God to Abraham by covenant and oath renewed and ratified to Isaac and to Jacob and to their heirs forever.

The description given by Ezekiel in the forty-

---

*For the full and scholarly discussion of the extent of the land promised to Abraham the reader is referred to the book entitled, "The Land of Israel," by Alexander Keith, D. D., published by Harper Bros., 1844. This book was given to the writer by a lady in Toronto, and grateful appreciation for the information obtained from it is hereby expressed.

seventh chapter of his prophecy is conclusive in testimony to the inviolability of the covenant, and defines the extent of the territory granted by Jehovah to the twelve tribes of Israel. To determine the area included within the boundaries given by Ezekiel may be the work of an antiquarian, but it is of vital interest to the Christian believer, whose hope is inseparably bound with the original covenant according to the ter. s of which that grant of land was made.

In reference to the extent of the land we are not content to accept the opinions of men whose conclusions are reached through the study of Jewish history past and present and without any attention being paid to divine revelation.

God has Himself drawn the boundaries, and these landmarks are as fixed as the covenant by which they have been established.

We may not be able to identify all these landmarks, nor is it of special importance that we should be able to do this: the outstanding features of the delineation are so distinct that we cannot fail to see the great importance and wide extent of the inheritance granted to Israel by the oath of Jehovah.

God, who set the bounds of the people according to the number of the children of Israel, at the time when He divided among the nations their inheritance

and separated the sons of Adam, established such
borders to Israel's inheritance as befitted the gift
of an everlasting possession; and, though these
landmarks may now be questioned through their
having been displaced in the ages past, they shall
yet be known to all men when the covenant shall
be fulfilled, and when the whole earth shall be
filled with God's glory.

According to the fixed borders, as specified by
Ezekiel, the land of promise extends from the Nile
to the Euphrates and from the Mediterranean Sea
to the Persian Gulf.

It is too late, as another has said, to tell us that
the east sea is the Dead Sea, because it lies to the
east of Jerusalem. If this were true, the breadth
of the land, instead of being one thousand, would
be restricted at the utmost to sixty miles; and scep-
tics might with justice scoff at the diminutive
inheritance. But in the record regarding the
borders of the land, as anciently possessed, the
Dead Sea is unquestionably mentioned under its
proper scriptural name of the Salt Sea; and, though
on its northern extremity it did lie to the east of
Jerusalem, it is nowhere in Scripture denominated
as the east sea. Even at the time when it formed,
on the extreme south, the southern border of Judah,
instead of being an east border, two and a half

tribes of Israel had their portions eastward of *it* and of the Jordan, which flowed into it from the north. And whatever was its relative positon to Jerusalem, it never had a name from hence; and if it had, yet from the Hauran, and the land of Israel by Jordan, which, even in ancient days, reached of right to the Euphrates, the Dead Sea lay to the west and not to the east.

From the Hauran, and Damascus, and from Gilead, and the land of Israel beyond Jordan, all the land, according to the covenant, pertained to Israel on that side of the Euphrates. And, according to the prophetic definition given by Ezekiel of the east side in all its length, from the border — the north border of which he had immediately before specified — to the east sea, the east side and the south side thus terminated in the same sea, the Persian Gulf, which is worthy of the name, for where the Euphrates enters it it is far wider than the Red Sea.

The peculiar and strategic character of the inheritance thus defined has often been mentioned. The Mediterranean, the Red Sea, and the Persian Gulf form, on the west, the south, and the east, borders of the land, which, but for these *inland* seas, would be wholly encircled by Asia, Africa, and Europe, and shut out from all direct communi-

cation with the Pacific and Atlantic, and the lesser
oceans of the globe.

The River of Egypt to the Mediterranean, and
that Sea from the mouth of the Nile to the estuary
of the Orontes, and the Euphrates from the foot
of Amanus to the Persian Gulf, leave not the smallest
portion of the west side or of the east side that is
not actually or virtually a navigable coast to the
extent on both sides of two thousand miles; while
on the north the intermediate barrier of Amanus,
at a breadth of less than one hundred, renders the
land a garden enclosed. The hand of the Lord,
who hath laid the foundations of the earth, and
made the sea, and the dry land, is in all this; and
here, though not here alone, He has magnified His
Word above all His name.

The first glance at the borders of Israel,
when they are looked at in the latitude assigned
them by a divine and irrepealable decree, may show
that they were set in subserviency to the final end,
as declared, from the beginning, to be accomplished
by the Lord, for which Israel was set apart from the
nations, and not numbered among them, so that,
as assuredly as their covenanted land shall be their
everlasting possession, all the families of the earth
shall be blessed in the seed of Jacob.

The land so given by covenant and oath to

Israel is said to exceed, in the aggregate amount of square miles, the territories of ten kingdoms of Europe: Prussia, Belgium, the Netherlands, Bavaria, Saxony, Hanover, Wirtenberg, Denmark, Sardinia, and Greece; and its relative proportion to Great Britain and Ireland is three hundred to one hundred and eighteen, or more than two and a half to one. Were the average breadth to be reckoned at five hundred instead of the medium six hundred miles, which from the inequality of the sides may be nearer the truth, the superficial extent of the promised land alone would still exceed that of the largest kingdom of Europe.

The same writer has declared that while the perpetuity of the covenant concerning the land has been disregarded, the extent of the inheritance has shriveled into mean dimensions. As if the kingdom were never to be restored to Israel, and the perpetual covenant had ceased forever, many critics and commentators, in dealing with the Word that abideth forever, have set themselves to a merely antiquarian task, and have sought rather to fix the borders of the promised land by the limited region which the Israelites occupied of old than to measure the guaranteed inheritance itself by the borders which the Lord of the whole earth assigned it. The borders, as prescribed, can alone rightfully determine what the extent of the land is which they bound and comprehend. They alone fix what the everlasting possession shall be. But they are not to be drawn from their true stations and transported from them, in order to form an imaginary boundary around a temporary and partial possession, which in reality never reached them. The borders must determine the promised land, and not the land, as actually possessed, the borders.

The land as thus defined, in the full extent of it, has been promised to Abraham and to his seed. They have never yet received it as an everlasting possession, and it must therefore be given to them or else the covenant be made void.

As before stated, Israel did not enter the land under the covenant that God made with Abraham, but under the covenant that God made with them at Horeb and conditioned on the plains of Moab. These two covenants are absolutely distinct and must not be confused if we expect to gain any clear conception of their purpose and meaning.

The covenant with Abraham was without condition of any kind: the other had conditions annexed to it, the breach of which on the part of Israel would bring the curse of the covenant upon them. The first gave to Abraham and to his seed the land for

an everlasting possession without reserve or condition of any kind whatsoever: the second conveyed
title to the land on condition of obedience, and
threatened dispersion and a blasted heritage if
they did not obey.

The legal covenant that God made with Israel
when He brought them up out of Egypt consisted
of the law, the judgments and the ordinances.
The law gave expression to the righteous will of
God; the judgments were to regulate the social
and the civic life of Israel; the ordinances were to
direct and govern their religious observances.
Differing from the unconditional covenant that
God made with Abraham, the covenant that He
made and repeatedly renewed with Israel under the
law was coupled with express conditions, on the
breach of which fearful judgments were denounced,
and both the blessings and the curses attached to
the covenant, according as they obeyed or dis-
obeyed, were announced to them by Moses before
they entered the land, and again from the summits
of Gerizim and Ebal after they had entered the
land.

Paul distinguishes between these covenants and
declares, in the epistle to the Galatians, that the
legal covenant could affect in no wise the unconditional covenant that God had made with Abraham.

This same distinction is made by the prophets. In the history of the Israelites, however fearful the judgment upon them for their violation of the legal covenant, the immutability of the promise that God made to Abraham was repeatedly affirmed. No disobedience, however protracted, should ever cause God to abrogate the covenant He made with Abraham, and the certainty of its fulfilment was repeatedly affirmed however distant the time might be when this should be accomplished.

Heaven and earth were called to witness against the children of Israel that, if they did evil in the sight of Jehovah, they should utterly perish from off the land which He had given them, and that they should be scattered among all nations from one end of the heaven even unto the other.

But however much they might by their sins provoke His anger and deprive themselves of the promised blessing, however great the degree of their iniquity or however long the duration of their misery, however fearful the punishments Jehovah might mete out to them until His anger should be turned away; yet He pledged Himself that He would neither abhor them nor utterly destroy them out of His sight; and that no sin of theirs, however inveterate, should ever be allowed to annul the covenant that He had made with their fathers and for the completion of which He had lifted up His hand in oath. They might forget this covenant, but the Lord should remember it forever. Even as the promise was given to Abraham before the law: so, when long after the breach of the legal covenant should bring its curses upon them, God would still remember Abraham and keep the everlasting covenant to the performance of which He had obligated Himself by oath.

Before they entered the promised land they were warned of the consequences that would follow their breaking the legal covenant: yet God declared that, if at any time thereafter, they should confess their iniquity, and accept His punishment, He would remember His covenant with Abraham and remember the land.

"When all these things are come upon thee," He says through Moses, "even in the latter days, if thou turn to the Lord thy God, and shalt be obedient unto his voice: (For the Lord thy God is a merciful God); he will not forsake thee, neither destroy thee, nor forget the covenant of thy fathers which he sware unto them" (Deut. 4 : 30-31).

"And it shall come to pass, when all these things are come upon thee, the blessing and the curse, which I have set before thee, and thou shalt call them to mind among all the nations, whither the

Lord thy God hath driven thee, and shalt return unto the Lord thy God, and shalt obey his voice according to all that I command thee this day, thou and thy children, with all thine heart, and with all thy soul; that then the Lord thy God will turn thy captivity, and have compassion upon thee, and will return and gather thee from all the nations, whither the Lord thy God hath scattered thee. If any of thine be driven out unto the utmost parts of heaven, from thence will the Lord thy God gather thee, and from thence will he fetch thee: and the Lord thy God will bring thee into the land which thy fathers possessed, and thou shalt possess it; and he will do thee good, and multiply thee above thy fathers. And the Lord thy God will circumcise thine heart, and the heart of thy seed, to love the Lord thy God with all thine heart, and with all thy soul, that thou mayest live. And the Lord thy God will put all these curses upon thine enemies, and on them that hate thee, which persecuted thee. And thou shalt return and obey the voice of the Lord, and do all his commandments which I command thee this day. And the Lord thy God will make thee plenteous in every work of thine hand, in the fruit of thy body, and in the fruit of thy cattle, and in the fruit of thy land, for good: for the Lord will again rejoice over thee

for good, as he rejoiced over thy fathers: If thou
shalt hearken unto the voice of the Lord thy God,
to keep his commandments and his statutes which
are written in this book of the law, and if thou
turn unto the Lord thy God with all thine heart,
and with all thy soul" (Deut. 30 : 1-10).

"I call heaven and earth to record this day
against you, that I have set before you life and
death, blessing and cursing: therefore choose life,
that both thou and thy seed may live: that thou
mayest love the Lord thy God, and that thou
mayest obey his voice, and that thou mayest cleave
unto him: for he is thy life, and the length
of thy days: that thou mayest dwell in the land
which the Lord sware unto thy fathers, to
Abraham, to Isaac, and to Jacob, to give them"
(Deut. 30 : 19, 20).

Scripture such as this, and this is supported and
confirmed by the whole burden of prophecy, shows
conclusively, except the Word of the Lord God be
denied, that there is to be a restoration of the
twelve tribes of Israel. The oath sworn to Abraham
insures their return.

They have wandered long and far from God.
They have indeed "sung the requiem of nations"
and held "the death-watch over departing dynas
ties"; they have "outlived the pyramids and the
14

catacombs": but they will never "renounce the miracle of their preservation," nor "hand over their spiritual assets to any syndicate of modern liberalists": for their destiny is in higher hands than their own.

Zionism might justly be thought of as an "utopian dream" if its accomplishment be left to the hands of emancipated Jews who seek in it relief for their oppressed brethren. The orthodox Jew will have none of it: for he waits and prays for the coming of the Messiah who shall accomplish this without the help of man. In this he is right: for the hand that scattered them is alone competent to regather them.

Under the legal covenant Israel entered the land of promise; under it the Canaanites were never driven from before them; under it the extremities of their borders never reached from the river of Egypt to the Euphrates; under it the ten tribes of the north were swept away into the Assyrian captivity; under it Judah and Benjamin were carried away captives into Babylon; under it, though not forever, the tabernacle and the throne of David fell; under it the tribal rod of Judah continued until Shiloh came; under it the Messiah was rejected, Jerusalem sacked and burned, and the Jews dispersed throughout every country under heaven.

The breach of the legal covenant, which has brought such untold misery upon this unhappy people, has not made void the unconditional covenant that God made with Abraham; nor has it in any way affected the unconditional covenant that God made with David many years afterward.

David feared no infringement of the covenant that God had made with him: he speaks like a king with whom and with whose house the eternal God had made an everlasting covenant: he uses language that expresses his faith in the endless duration of his own dynasty, when he calls on the sons of Jacob to be always mindful of the covenant which the Lord had commanded to a thousand generations, that the land of Canaan should be the lot of their inheritance. I will sing, he says, of the mercies of the Lord forever: with my mouth will I make known thy faithfulness to all generations. For I have said, Mercy shall be built up forever: thy faithfulness shalt thou establish in the very heavens. I have made a covenant with my chosen, I have sworn unto David my servant, Thy seed will I establish forever, and build up thy throne to all generations.

According to the terms of this covenant and the one sworn to Abraham, the throne and kingdom of David must be reëstablished, and the twelve tribes be brought back into the land.

Gentile believers, claiming "the sure mercies of David" as their own, have left nothing but the curses to be borne by Israel, and have appropriated for themselves the blessings, under the conviction that Israel is no longer the inheritor of the promises that God made to Abraham and to David.

Such an opinion, it is declared, derives sanction from the high attributes with which it clothes the everlasting covenant of grace and mercy by our Redeemer, and forbids the overshadowing of the glory of the latter days by any merely territorial allotment to any peculiar people, when the same great salvation in all the fulness of the gospel extends alike to all

But such an opinion was entertained neither by prophets nor apostles. The prayer of the remnant of Israel, recorded in the sixty-third chapter of Isaiah — "O Lord, why hast thou made us to err from thy ways, and hardened our heart from thy fear? Return for thy servants' sake, the tribes of thine inheritance" — is followed in the sixty-fourth chapter by the glorious avowal — "Since the beginning of the world men have not heard, nor perceived by the ear, neither hath the eye seen, O God, beside thee, what he hath prepared for him that waiteth for him."

The introduction of the gospel dispensation, and

the calling out of the Church, and the Jews left in their dispersion and seeming excision forever, have caused us to forget the concurrent testimony of the prophets and of the apostles, that God hath not cast away Israel, that they are beloved for the father's sake, and that the gifts and calling of God are without repentance.

The restoration of the house of David to the land, and the building of David's throne, are to be accomplished under the new and everlasting covenant that the Lord God will make in the latter days with the house of Israel and with the house of Judah.

The terms of this new covenant were announced by Jeremiah after the southern kingdom had been carried away into Babylon.

The thirty-first chapter of his prophecy opens with the promise of a restoration which comprehends more than the return of Judah from Babylon: for it is addressed to all the families of Israel.

"Again I will build thee, and thou shalt be built, O virgin of Israel: thou shalt again be adorned with thy tabrets, and shalt go forth in the dances of them that make merry. Thou shalt yet plant vines upon the mountains of Samaria: the planters shall plant, and shall eat them as common things. For there shall be a day, that the watchmen upon the mount Ephraim shall cry, Arise ye, and let us go up to Zion unto the Lord our God. For thus saith the Lord; Sing with gladness for Jacob, and shout among the chief of the nations: publish ye, praise ye, and say, O Lord, save thy people, the remnant of Israel. Behold, I will bring them from the north country, and gather them from the coasts of the earth, and with them the blind and the lame, the woman with child and her that travaileth with child together: a great company shall return thither. They shall come with weeping, and with supplications will I lead them: I will cause them to walk by the rivers of waters in a straight way, wherein they shall not stumble: for I am a father to Israel, and Ephraim is my first-born" (Jeremiah 31: 4-9).

Then, beginning with the thirty-first verse, we have given to us the terms of the new covenant:

"Behold, the days come, saith the Lord, that I will make a new covenant with the house of Israel, and with the house of Judah: not according to the covenant that I made with their fathers in the day that I took them by the hand to bring them out of the land of Egypt; which my covenant they brake, although I was an husband unto them, saith the Lord: but this shall be the covenant that I will make with the house of Israel: After those days, saith the Lord, I will put my law in their inward parts, and write it in their hearts; and will be their God, and they shall be my people. And they shall teach no more every man his neighbour, and every man his brother, saying, Know the Lord: for they shall all know me, from the least of them unto the greatest of them, saith the Lord: for I will forgive their iniquity, and I will remember their sin no more" (Jeremiah 31 : 31-34).

It is presumed that no one will deny the precise application of this prophecy to "the house of Israel" and to "the house of Judah."

In the epistle to the Hebrews — and we must remember that the epistle is addressed to Hebrews — such precise application is not denied, but is rather confirmed. Christ is declared to be the Mediator of this "better covenant" which is established upon "better promises."

The new covenant is not morally better but efficaciously better: it is established upon better promises because the promises of the legal covenant were conditioned on obedience, whereas the promises of the new covenant are absolutely unconditional: human responsibility was annexed to the first, but in the second responsibility of any kind whatsoever is neither expected nor required of man.

The whole house of Israel is to be regenerated. A nation shall be born in a day. The laws of God shall be put into their minds, and shall be written in their hearts; and it shall be just as natural and easy for them to do right, as it has been natural and easy for them to do wrong.

When this new and everlasting covenant shall be forever established with the house of Israel and with the house of Judah, the testimony of the prophets shall be cleared of the obscurity occasioned by the spiritualizing of the promises made through them. We shall perhaps be surprised to find that God meant exactly what He said when He declared:

"Behold, the days come, saith the Lord, that I will perform that good thing which I have promised unto the house of Israel and to the house of Judah. In those days, and at that time, will I cause the Branch of righteousness to grow up unto David; and he shall execute judgment and righteousness in the land. In those days shall Judah be saved, and Jerusalem shall dwell safely: and this is the name wherewith she shall be called, The Lord our righteousness. For thus saith the Lord; David shall never want a man to sit upon the throne of the house of Israel" (Jeremiah 33: 14-17).

"Behold, the days come, saith the Lord, that they shall no more say, The Lord liveth, which brought up the children of Israel out of the land of Egypt; but, The Lord liveth, which brought up and which led the seed of the house of Israel out of the north country, and from all countries whither I had driven them; and they shall dwell in their own land" (Jeremiah 23 : 7, 8).

To do all this, God has obligated Himself by covenant and oath; and for the completion of this covenant we must look forward to the day when, according to the orginal terms of the promise, the seed of Abraham shall be put in possession of the land "from the river of Egypt unto the great river, the river Euphrates" (Gen. 15 : 18).

CHAPTER XIV

THE REMOVAL OF THE CHURCH

The Church, the body of Christ, is the pearl of great price for which the heavenly Merchantman sold all that He had; and it is formed during the time that Israel is set aside. Distinct in the plan and purpose of God the Church does not inherit the promises that God made to Israel, but has a preëminence of glory in which Israel as a nation has no part.

The Church is composed of those who shall sing the new song unto Him that was slain, and who have been redeemed to God by His blood out of every kindred, and tongue, and people, and nation.

When the question was first raised about the admission of Gentiles into the Church the whole matter was referred to the apostles and the elders for consideration.

The decision having been reached, James, before announcing it says: "Men and brethren, hearken unto me: Simeon hath declared how God at the first did visit the Gentiles, to take out of them a people for his name. And to this agree the words of the prophets; as it is written, After this I will return, and will build again the tabernacle of David, which is fallen down; and I will build again the ruins thereof, and I will set it up: that the residue of men might seek after the Lord, and all the Gentiles, upon whom my name is called, saith the Lord, who doeth all these things" (Acts 15:13-17).

James quotes the eleventh and twelfth verses of the ninth chapter of the prophecy of Amos.

If we turn to that prophecy we shall find that the words quoted are followed by a promise of the restoration of Israel from their captivity and their reëstablishment in the land.

It is perfectly plain, from the way in which James interprets the prophecy, that the tabernacle of David is not to be built up until God has taken out from the Gentiles "a people for His name." In other words, the covenant that God made with David is under suspension until the Church is formed. This being accomplished, Israel shall be restored, and God's covenant with David shall be fulfilled.   It is during the time of Israel's national unbelief that the Church is formed.

The Church is to be glorified and enthroned in heaven before the judgments that issue in the restoration of Israel are poured out upon the earth.

The four and twenty elders, referred to in the fourth chapter of Revelation, are enthroned and clothed in white garments and crowned with golden crowns before the earth-judgment begins.

If these elders, proclaimed by robes and crowns a royal priesthood, be not the Church, it will be difficult to identify them.

Elders are mentioned both in the Old and the New Testaments. In the Old Testament they appear as the representatives of the people and are so identified with the people that the words elders and people frequently have an equivalent meaning. After the disruption of the kingdom they are spoken of as national representatives — elders of Israel or elders of Judah. They sometimes filled the office of local magistrates in the provincial towns and sat at the gate to administer justice. They retained their position throughout all the political changes in the Jewish commonwealth. They were prominent in the period of the Judges, in the time of Saul and the later kings, during the captivity, after the return, and during the period of the Maccabees.

During the time of our Lord they were recognized as a body distinct from the Sanhedrim, but they are usually connected with it as a class from which the members of the Sanhedrim were chosen. They were always actively associated with the dominant classes; sometimes with the chief priests; sometimes with the chief priests and scribes; sometimes with the council: and they always took part in the management of public affairs.

There is in the New Testament no account of the origin of the office of the eldership in the Church. The office comes, with no reference to its origin, from the old dispensation into the new, and is given recognition in the Church. The elders were the rulers and teachers of the people, and the exposition of Scripture was the special function of their office. They were simply the representatives of the people, who through experience acquired by age, were qualified to oversee and direct the affairs of the Church.

The Church is a royal priesthood, and the elders, representing the Church in Revelation, proclaim themselves to be such in their ascription of praise: "To him that loveth us, and hath washed us from our sins in his [own] blood, and hath made us a kingdom. priests to his God and Father; to him be the glory and might unto the ages of ages. Amen."

Grant says that this "reminds us at once of what was conditionally offered to Israel, that if they would obey God's voice and keep His covenant,

they should be to Him a kingdom of priests and
a holy nation. They must be, first of all, a holy
nation, in order to be in this way priests to God.
The white linen garment of the priest was the testimony of the character required of one who came
before God in this way, and in this Israel had
signally failed. They had chosen a covenant of
law, instead of the grace that had taken them up
and brought them out of Egypt, and the law for
them, as for all others, was a law working wrath."

Under the law they did not and could not abide.
They were "without strength" to become, through
obedience of the law, a holy nation. The priesthood of Aaron and his sons — merciful provision
as it might be in view of their circumstances — only
bore witness to the utter ruin of the people and
their failure as a nation to become a holy priesthood.

The Church by divine grace is unconditionally
constituted a royal priesthood to offer up spiritual
sacrifices, acceptable to God by Jesus Christ, and
to show forth the virtues of Him who hath called
them out of darkness into His marvelous light.

The elders, spoken of in Revelation, robed in
priestly garments, and seated upon thrones, are
undoubtedly the representatives of the Church
glorified, and they are seen in their exalted position

before the beginning of the judgments through which are accomplished the restitution of all things.

The exaltation of the Church to this high place in glory awaits future fulfilment. Like all other unfulfilled prophecy this requires time and place for its accomplishment. Scripture has defined both time and place; and all the predictions that await future fulfilment must find their application in the time and place so assigned.

The Bible speaks of "ages past," "the present age," "the ages to come," "the ages of ages"; and these expressions denote periods of time, rounded off from all other time, and are distinct in plan and purpose.

With the "ages past" we are not now concerned, except with the "Jewish age," which began when God made an unconditional covenant with Abraham, and shall be brought to a close by the coming of the Son of man in the clouds of heaven.

The present Christian dispensation, or Church age, is absolutely distinct from the Jewish age, having no connection whatever with it except as an interjected, parenthetical period that divides the Jewish age into two periods of unequal duration. In other words, the Jewish age has been temporarily suspended until the Church be formed: after which it, that is, the Jewish age, shall be resumed and finished. The Church period, or present age, is thus interjected into but forms no part of the Jewish age. The failure to observe this distinction has produced much of the confusion in prophetic interpretation.

Daniel was one of the Babylonian captives. From the prophecy of Jeremiah he had obtained positive information respecting the definite period of the exile. The seventy years of exile proclaimed by Jeremiah were coming to an end, and Daniel saw no sign of liberty or of a return of his people to Judea. He therefore set his face toward the Lord God in prayer and supplication. While thus engaged in prayer, Gabriel, whom he had before seen in a vision, approached him at about the time of the evening oblation. He had come from God with a special communication that concerned the prophetic future of the Jews.

"Seventy weeks are decreed upon thy people and upon thy holy city, to finish transgression, and to make an end of sins, and to make reconciliation for iniquity, and to bring in everlasting righteousness, and to seal up vision and prophecy, and to anoint the most holy. Know therefore and discern, that from the going forth of the commandment to restore and to build Jerusalem unto the anointed one, the prince, shall be seven weeks:

and threescore and two weeks, it shall be built again, with street and moat, even in troublous times. And after the threescore and two weeks shall the anointed one be cut off, and shall have nothing: and the people of the prince that shall come shall destroy the city and the sanctuary; and his end shall be with a flood, and even unto the end shall be war; desolations are determined. And he shall make a firm covenant with many for one week: and for half of the week he shall cause the sacrifice and the oblation to cease; and upon the wing of abominations shall come one that maketh desolate; and even unto the consummation, and that determined, shall wrath be poured out upon the desolator" (Daniel 9 : 24-27. R.V.).

"Seventy weeks"— the word for weeks in Hebrew is *heptades* — "are decreed upon thy people."

The word "heptades" is a participial form and means "computed by sevens." The expression should read, literally, "Seventy periods of seven are decreed upon thy people."

Stuart says: "The Jews had three kinds of heptades in respect to time: First, that of days, seven of which make a week; secondly, that of years, seven of which make a sabbatical year. (Leviticus 25 : 27); thirdly, that of the seven periods of years before the Jubilee year — for this last comprises

15

seven times seven years, or forty-nine years — after which comes the Jubilee year (Leviticus 25 : 8)."

The vast majority of commentators are agreed that Gabriel speaks of *heptades* of years. The adoption of any other meaning leads either to inconsistency or absurdity. Daniel had been thinking about the seventy literal years of exile. Gabriel tells him that the Messiah would come, and that Jerusalem should be restored: but for the accomplishment of this there must be not merely seventy literal years of exile, but seventy times seven years of trouble and trial. In other words, during four hundred and ninety years various things should come to pass and bring to an issue the consummation of the hopes of the Jewish nation. Gabriel further informs Daniel that these seventy prophetic weeks were to be divided into three distinct periods; namely, into seven, sixty-two, and one. Each of these periods was to be marked by specific peculiarities and occurrences. It is with the last of these weeks, or the final seven years of the prophecy, that we are now concerned.

We must bear in mind that this prophecy has to do with Daniel's people, the Jews. It contemplates their prophetic future and the circumstances that shall accomplish for them the realization of their hopes. The four hundred and ninety years were decreed upon them "to finish [their] transgression, and to make an end to [their] sins, and to make reconciliation for [their] iniquity, and to bring in everlasting righteousness, and to seal up vision and prophecy"; that is, to give them their full accomplishment, "and to anoint the most holy." This, therefore, is the complete cycle of Jewish prophetic history. At the end of the four hundred and ninety years Israel should be restored.

We need not confuse our minds in the effort to discover the chronological point of time when these four hundred and ninety years begin. That question has no bearing upon what is now before us. We need only to bear in mind that four hundred and ninety years were to measure the time intervening between the return from the Babylonian captivity and the time of Israel's restoration to the full and final favor of God.

According to the terms of the prophecy, Messiah, the Prince, would appear and be "cut off" at the end of the sixty-ninth week; that is, at the expiration of four hundred and eighty-three years. We shall not pause to discuss this; for it would needlessly confuse a somewhat more difficult proposition. Let us assume, for the present, that four hundred and eighty-three years of the prophecy expired when our Lord was crucified. Seven years would yet be necessary to complete the prophecy, and to bring the Jewish people into the full favor of God. Here is where confusion and perplexity prevail among interpreters.

It is at least perfectly clear that, if the seven years required to complete the prophecy follow immediately after the death of our Lord, then the prophecy is made void; because Israel was not reinstated into divine favor at the expiration of the seven years beyond the cross.

It must be equally clear that, if these seven years have run their course at any time since the crucifixion of our Lord, then it follows that the prophecy has been made void; for the Jewish nation has never yet, since the rejection of Christ, been restored to divine favor.

There is but one way to preserve the integrity of the prophecy. The seven years are yet future. There is no alternative for this. Either these years have run their course or they have not. If they have, the prophecy is worthless. If they have not, then in some future period of seven years Israel is to be restored to divine favor, and all the predicted blessings are to be brought in. There is no reason to stumble over this statement. In no other way can the concurrent testimony of the prophets be brought into harmony.

Before considering the occurrences in this last week of the prophecy, let us fortify the position by Paul's argument in the eleventh chapter of the epistle to the Romans.

The rejection of Israel, because of their refusal of Christ, was not final, but only temporary.

"God," says the apostle, "hath not cast away his people which he foreknew." The foreknowledge of God embraced their entire history. It was foreknown and foretold. They would reject the Christ sent unto them; and, on account of that rejection, they should be judicially blinded and scattered among the nations. Then the grace of God was to go out to the Gentiles; and, afterward, God would return to the Jews and take up their broken history and finish it. This is the sum of the apostle's argument. The Scripture to which James appeals in the fifteenth chapter of the Acts confirms this. It is as clear as daylight. Israel, as a nation, was judicially given up when Christ was rejected. This was followed by a period of grace going out to the Gentiles. That time of grace is still running its course; but, when it comes to an end, Israel shall be taken up once more and brought into that full and final favor predicted by all the prophets. In other words, there is a break in Israel's history. The Church period is interjected and fills up the gap in time between the dispersion of Israel and their final restoration. This gap in time, now extending over two millenniums, separates the sixty-nine weeks of Daniel's prophecy from the seventieth week, and shows us that the seventieth week, or final seven years of Jewish history, are yet future. During those final seven years Israel shall be restored.

Instead of restoration and blessing following the crucifixion of Christ, disaster and ruin fell upon Israel. The prophecy in Daniel preannounced this. The people of the prince that was to come should destroy the city and the sanctuary; and that part of the prophecy, in the sack and ruin of Jerusalem by the Roman army under Titus, has been long since accomplished. The destruction of the city by the Romans took place about forty years after the crucifixion. Up to that time there was neither restoration of Israel nor blessing to the earth such as the prophets predict. On the contrary, Israel received a stroke of divine judgment that denationalized her from that time until now. The Roman people destroyed the city and the sanctuary. So much, at least, is clear. The remainder of the prophecy concerns a certain prince of that people; that is, the Roman people, and his connection with the Jewish nation. This prince, whoever he may be, is not named, but is spoken of simply as a prince of the Roman people. The prophecy declares that "His end shall be with a flood, and even unto the end shall be war, desolations are determined."

There was to be a time of indefinite sorrow that was to go on to what is here declared to be "the end." At "the end" of this long period of trouble and desolation the blessing should come. But how is the blessing to be introduced? It is brought in, according to the seventh chapter of Daniel, *by the coming of the Son of man from heaven.* He comes at the end of the final seven years. These seven years, therefore, mark the period of Israel's restoration to divine favor; and they begin their course seven years before the second advent of our Lord.

The prophecy declares that the prince "shall confirm a covenant"— not *the* covenant as in the common version —" with many for one week." If it were the definite article before the word covenant, then this might refer to that divine covenant with Israel, the maker of which could be none other than Christ Himself. But this interpretation, as is abundantly proved by those who have undertaken to defend it, leads into the most hopeless confusion. Whoever the maker of the covenant may be, it is at least clear that the covenant is made with the Jewish people, and that it is made for the final seven years, or the seventieth week, of Gabriel's prophecy. We have already seen that the maker of this covenant is not Christ, but rather a Roman prince — a prince of that people who came and destroyed the city and the sanctuary. This prince, according to the prophecy, "shall make a firm covenant with many for one week: and for half of the week he shall cause the sacrifice and the oblation to cease; and upon the wing of abominations shall come one that maketh desolate; and even unto the consummation, and that determined, shall wrath be poured out upon the desolator."

This week, for which the covenant is confirmed, is without question the last week of the predicted seventy. The maker of the covenant is a Roman prince, and the people with whom he makes it are Daniel's people. "In the midst of the week" the prince violates the covenant by causing the sacrifice and the oblation to cease. No one will question that these are the Jewish sacrifice and oblation. The prophecy contemplates the sanctuary as still in existence, and the violation of the covenant is seen in taking away of the daily offering. In the place of that daily offering, "the abomination that maketh desolate" is set up; and this "overspreading of abomination" constitutes the desolation that lasts until the consummation.

The consummation is at the end of the seven years. These seven years are thus seen to be divided into two equal parts. This division of the seven years into two equal parts of three and one half years each will account for the expressions so frequently found in connection with this very period: "A time, times, and a half a time"; that is, a year, two years, and a half a year: forty-two months; that is, according to the Jewish reckoning of thirty days to the month, three and one half years: twelve hundred and sixty days; that is, forty-two months, or three and one half years.

The one that causes the sacrifice and oblation to cease is the same one that sets up the abomination, on account of which desolation comes. The desolation continues for three years and a half, and is terminated by the coming of the Son of man in the clouds of heaven. Israel is thereupon brought into divine favor and the blessing of the earth follows. The details are thus intelligible and can be understood in no other way.

In the book of Revelation the reckoning of time is in exact harmony with Gabriel's prophecy. The holy city is trodden under foot of the Gentiles forty and two months — the half week. The two witnesses, clothed in sackcloth, prophesy a thousand two hundred and threescore days — the half week.

After they have finished their testimony, the Beast makes war with them, and overcomes them, and kills them. This Beast is none other than the prince spoken of in Gabriel's prophecy.

This interpretation, which is in fact the only logical one, clears up for us the entire field of prophecy, and gives both time and place for its fulfilment. In the seven years that are yet necessary to complete Jewish prophecy, and that do not begin to run their course until the Church is formed and taken from the earth, Israel's history, broken at the cross because of their rejection of Christ, is taken up again and carried on to the close. Their transgressions are finished. Their sins are ended. Reconciliation is made for iniquity. Everlasting righteousness is brought in. Vision and prophecy are all accomplished. The holy place is anointed; and Jerusalem, with Israel restored to divine favor, becomes the center of blessing for the whole earth.

The seven years of unfulfilled Jewish history constitute an interval between the appearing of Jesus and His return to the world in power and great glory. It measures the time between the appearing of the "morning star" and the rising of the "sun of righteousness."

At the beginning of this interval, the dead in Christ shall be raised, and the living in Christ shall be changed and, with glorified bodies, they shall with the resurrected dead be together caught up to meet the Lord in the air: and so shall they ever be with the Lord.

Such is the teaching of Paul in the first epistle to the Thessalonians. In the Greek text the definite article before the word "clouds" is wanting. Whether sleeping in Jesus, or living when He comes, all believers shall be caught up not in *the* clouds but in clouds to meet the Lord in the air. Caught up in clouds! Clouds from Europe, clouds from Asia, clouds from Africa, clouds from America, clouds from whatever place the dead or the living in Christ shall be, rising in glorious ascension to meet and to be forever with the Lord.

In the fifteenth chapter of first Corinthians we have the same inspired and soul stirring revelation.

We shall not all sleep, but we shall all be changed, in a moment, in the twinkling of an eye, at the last trump: for the trumpet shall sound, and the dead shall be raised incorruptible, and we shall be changed. For this corruptible — he is speaking of the dead — must put on incorruption, and this mortal — he is speaking of the living — must put on immortality. So when this corruptible shall have put on incorruption, and this mortal shall have put on immortality, then shall be brought to pass the saying that is written, Death is swallowed up in victory.

So shall the Church forever freed from trial and conflict be caught up into the ineffable glory to meet her Lord. And so shall she ever be with Him.

CHAPTER XV

THE JEWISH PROBLEM

THE removal of the Church is followed by that period of seven years which in accordance with Gabriel's prophecy is required for the completion of Israel's prophetic history.

At the end of the seven years the twelve tribes of Israel shall be reestablished in the land under the new covenant, and God's promise to Abraham concerning the land, and His promise to David concerning the kingdom shall be fulfilled.

These seven years are divided prophetically into two equal periods of three and a half years each. The last three years and a half measure the duration of a period, called in Scripture, "Jacob's trouble" (Jer. 30 : 7); "a time of trouble" (Daniel 12 : 1); "great tribulation" (Mat. 24 : 21): all these expressions referring to that period and characterizing it.

At that time the Jewish problem, which has vexed and baffled the wisdom of twenty centuries, shall be solved; and any prior solution of it shall be subject to revision by the King of kings.

The destiny of the united tribes of Israel is not to be determined apart from sacred prophecy.

The ten tribes, so long ago carried away into the Assyrian captivity, have been ever since lost to human history, and all search for them has been foredoomed to failure. Never has a hidden treasure been so industriously sought after as these lost tribes. Enthusiastic seekers, going in different directions, have "positively identified" them with almost every nation under heaven. English, Irish, Spanish, Huns, Franks, Greeks, Romans, Mexicans, Aztecs, Peruvians, Japanese, the Kareens of Burmah, American Indians, north and south, Papuans, and others, have all been heralded as "the lost ten tribes"; and laborious arguments have been offered to establish their various claims to recognition.

It is vain to search for what the Lord hath hidden. It is enough to know that Israel and Judah must be together restored.

Whether the prevailing type of Jew represents all of the twelve tribes of Israel, or the southern kingdom only, is a matter of speculation. The people themselves, whatever theory we may hold as to their racial purity and national unity, have offered a Jewish problem that no one seems able to solve.

Some writers are "at a loss" to account for the world-wide distribution of the Jews, but this is because no serious attention has been given to the Word of God. Moses told them that, if they were disobedient, God would pluck them from off the land and scatter them among all people, from the one end of the earth to the other: and we shall seek in vain for any other explanation of their world-wide dispersion.

It has been thought equally difficult to account for the "singular preservation" of the Jews among the nations whither they have been scattered; but Moses also told these people that, when they should return unto the Lord their God, He would turn their captivity, and have compassion upon them, and bring them oack; and, though they might be driven out unto the utmost parts of the heaven, from thence the Lord their God would gather them, and put them into possession of the land promised to their fathers.

The ability of the whale to swallow Jonah is no more wonderful than its inability to assimilate him. If God be not reckoned with, neither the one nor the other can be explained.

The present number of Jews is in round numbers estimated at 12,000,000, and they are said to be distributed as follows:

Europe.....................9,000,000 or 74.87 per cent.
America....................2,110,000 or 17.66 "

Asia	500,000	or	4.16	per cent.
Africa	380,000	or	3.17	"
Australasia	17,000	or	0.14	"

According to the same authority,* Russia has the largest number of Jews, the last census returning a population of 5,110,548, of whom 3,578,229 live in the "Pale of Settlement." This "consists mainly of provinces which Russia has annexed within the last two hundred years, and where Jews have lived for centuries before that annexation. The fifteen provinces of western and southwestern Russia, embracing White, Little, and New Russia, as well as the ten provinces which make up the part of Poland which Russia has sliced off for itself during the division of that country, are the 'Pale.' Outside of these provinces, in the interior of Russia and Siberia, only some special privileged classes of Jews may live, such as merchants of the first guild, who pay about 1,000 roubles annually for a license; Jews who have graduated from the higher educational institutions; and some artisans. That very few of these can avail themselves of these privileges is seen from the fact that only six per cent. of all the Jews in that country live outside of the Pale. A peculiar feature of these

*Dr. M. Fishberg, "The Jews," page 10. Published by Chas. Scribner's Sons, 1911.

restrictions of habitation is the fact that no Jew may live in Siberia unless convicted for a serious crime. But, after the term of his banishment has ended, he may not remain in Siberia, unless he commits another crime."

In Poland there are 1,321,100 Jews; and 202,000 are scattered throughout the remainder of European Russia.

During the last fifteen years probably a million Jews have been received into the United States by immigration; there being now in Greater New York not less than 1,200,000, or one out of every ten Jews under heaven.

The peculiar distribution of the Jews is thought by Fishberg to be due to the repressive legislation which has compelled them to segregate in cities. He says that "while in western Europe these laws have already been abolished, more than one half of all the Jews in the world are not yet free to choose their abode in the country of their allegiance."

Just as in the Middle Ages when the Jews were compelled to live in *Judengassen, Ghettoes, and Jewries,* so at the present time in Russia and Roumania they are compelled to live in the cities, and in some of these cities they are restricted to certain quarters called *Mellahs.*

For centuries the great majority of the Jews have

been obliged to endure such disabilities. They cannot possess themselves of land; they cannot become agriculturists; they cannot live in the rural districts; and they are rigorously excluded from nearly all industrial occupations. Fishberg declares that "less than one half of the number of contemporary Jews enjoy the civic and political rights of the non-Jewish inhabitants of the countries in which they live. Only England, France, Italy, Germany, Austria-Hungary, Holland, Belgium, Switzerland, Scandinavia, Servia, and Bulgaria, as well as America and Australasia, consider the Jews citizens more or less on an equal basis with the Christian population. We find that of the twelve million Jews in the world only five millions, a little over forty per cent. can be considered in that category. The rest, sixty per cent. of all the Jews, are to-day being treated by the nations among which they live as aliens, and, in some countries, as even beyond the law."

Even when emancipated it is next to impossible to divert them from urban settlements: so that, in all the ages of their wandering, whether by coercion or by choice, they have blindly followed in the path of Abraham, who "looked for a city which hath foundations. whose builder and maker is God" (Heb. 11: 10).

Under the limitation of social, political, and

economic disabilities the Jews, at least a great majority of them, are living in appalling poverty.

Jacobs says, "If we choose to regard them as a nation, it is probable that they are the poorest of all that can claim to be civilized; and if we were to capitalize their wealth and distribute it among the 12,000,000 of Jews, they would dispute with any poor nation for the lowest place in the scale of wealth."

The misery existing in the Russian Pale is said to exceed in destitution and starvation the conditions found in India during a famine.

When freed from restriction they quickly win for themselves commercial, intellectual and political distinction.

Socially they have never attained to freedom in countries where they are in other respects emancipated. Fishberg says: "This ostracism brings many more Jews to the Church than mediæval massacres or the Russian pogroms of the twentieth century. The position of the emancipated Jew is most singular. He succeeded, through two to four generations of freedom, in acquiring wealth; from a small trader who peddled his wares on the highroads, or sold second-hand clothing in the dingy streets of the Ghetto, or lent small sums of money on high interest, he became a great merchant, a manufacturer, a banker, a stock-jobber. Only one hundred years ago he was not permitted to pass the threshold of a university as a pupil, and within that short space of time he succeeded in becoming a scholar, a scientist, a painter, a sculptor, musician, actor, and the like; but he is repulsed when he attempts to break into the drawing-room of modern Society; repulsed when he attempts to enter a social club or college fraternity; or when he desires to teach in a university the science to which he has devoted the best years of his life. In the Ghetto he did not invite social intercourse with the non-Jews around him. In fact, his separate religion precluded social intimacy with those who had not a Jewish table; he could not eat with his Christian or Mohammedan neighbor, nor could he share with him his joys and sorrows. The reputation of the pride and aloofness of the Jew has its origin in these separate tenets of his religion, which he followed implicitly. But with the emancipation not only were the portals of the Ghetto opened to him, but he also began to discard most of those tenets of his creed which made an unsocial being of him in former times. He eats now at any table, he does not rest on the Sabbath but on Sunday, he is even not averse to marry out of his faith. Under the circumstances, he desires, and often

craves, social intercourse with the people of other
faiths. When rebuffed he feels it more keenly
than he felt the blows given him during the massacres of Mediæval Europe or the frequent expulsions
to which he was subjected; indeed, Jews are more
sensitive about social discrimination than about
political and civil discrimination."

The emancipated Jews are quite willing to give
up their ancient faith that is alone supposed to keep
them "insoluble" among the nations, and they
demand assimilation by the people among whom
they live. But it is impossible to assimilate them
or to destroy their identity by casting them into
the "melting pot" of western civilization.

In Russia the restrictions are of such a character
that assimilation is not to be thought of even. The
Jews there are not permitted to learn the Russian
language; they are rigorously segregated within the
"Pale"; they have no opportunity, even if they
wished it, to adopt the habits, language and cus-
toms of the people of other faith. Their singular
and long continued isolation; their persistence as
a type; their national unity and racial purity,
despite all claim to the contrary; their ubiquity
and resistance of assimilation, present a problem
that cannot be solved apart from Revelation.

Lazarus says: "There is no more a Jewish nationality; there is absolutely not a Jew who has a Jewish spirit or mind. They necessarily draw for this reason from the national minds of peoples among which they live, of which they became an integral part, and on whom they react. Even in their religion, which is their only distinctive characteristic, they differ according to the country in which they live. This is evident from the way in which they designate their co-religionists, saying, 'This one is a Pole,' 'that one is a Russian,' 'that one is a German.' By this they do not mean to imply the geographical home of the particular Jew, but refer to his character, the disposition and sentiment, even to his mode of study of the Talmud. Even the difference in the ritual and liturgy of the synagogue is designated, as can be seen on the title-pages of the prayer-books, as nationally French, Spanish, German, Polish, Moravian, Bohemian, etc. Owing to this differentiation of the national traits of the Jews in various countries, they can energetically participate in the culture of their non-Jewish neighbors, and contribute their own share to the civilization of the nation. Philo wrote in Greek, Maimonides in Arabic, Spinoza in Latin, Munk and Derenbourg in French, Mendelssohn in German.''

Despite this wholesale disclaimer, we are all

conscious of the fact that there is a Jewish race,
as indestructible as Gibraltar, with a destiny defined and secured to them by the oath of the Lord
their God, and we agree with the one who has said
that, notwithstanding all the vicissitudes which
he was subject to for four thousand years, the type
of the ancient Hebrew survives to-day in the modern
Jew, whether we meet him peddling his wares on
the high road, working in a sweat shop, or specula-
ting in the stock exchange or the bourse. But
Israel Zangwill says the depth of his degradation is
to be found in this: "If you want to compliment
a Jew, tell him that he does not look like
one."

Such Jews are not looking forward to the advent
of the Messiah who shall accomplish their renationalization, and establish them as a kingdom in the
land given by covenant and oath by the Lord God
to their forefathers. Such renegade Jews are in
reality exceptional.

Thoughtful and earnest Jews, though still under
sentence of judicial blindness, are seriously trying
to solve the problem that has been forced upon the
attention of all nations. Some of these are
nationalists who believe that the only way to solve
the problem of their people is to segregate them in
a land of their own, whether it be Palestine or some

other country, and give to them an autonomous government. In order to accomplish this they are doing what they can to preserve the national consciousness and to prevent as far as possible the assimilation of their race with the other races of mankind.

Others who are without national pride and care nothing about the disintegration of Judaism insist that the only solution of the Jewish problem is their world-wide emancipation and absorption into the national life of the people with whom they have lived. It is insisted that "denationalization, has gone too far to admit repatriation of the Jews, and the solution of the perennial Jewish problem can be, and is being, accomplished in the countries in which they are living at present."

On the other hand it is maintained that many of these have given up the struggle against social ostracism and are returning in heart to the great hope that has been the consolation of their countrymen during the long ages of their persecution.

"They again begin to dream of the Jewish kingdom or republic in Palestine, their own home, where they will not be exposed to political and civil disabilities, to massacres or to social discriminations at the hands of those who believe differently. They look forward to a revival of the national consciousness of the Jews, and do their best to assert themselves as Jews at every opportunity. These are the Zionists, Territorialists, and other nationally conscious Jews who have been ardently advocating their cause within the last twenty years."

It is interesting to notice the reasons "not of an academic kind" offered against repatriation. We are positively assured that it is utterly impossible to nationalize the Jews in Palestine because that country is not large enough to accommodate them.

Leroy Beaulieu says: "The whole of Syria could shelter only a small minority of Jews now in the world. Must we, to make room for them, expel the Christians and the Moslems? Shall we confide the care of the Holy Sepulchre to the synagogue? What Christians would propose or tolerate such a thing?" "Supposing," he says, "we were to relinquish to Israel all the unoccupied tracts of Syria including the desert as far as the Euphrates, not a third, nor even a quarter of the European Jews could find subsistence there. The ancient country of Canaan and the neighboring regions are certainly not able to accommodate more than a few hundred thousand."

Zangwill, so ardent an advocate of renationalization, says that "not only is mount Zion private property politically, it is a holy mountain for Mohammedanism and Christianity as well as for Judaism, and this makes it rather like a volcano, very dangerous for those who dwell on its slopes."

Another tells us — with calm assurance of authority—that "Palestine is not a large country." That "according to the English Palestine Exploration Fund Survey, the region west of the Jordan is about 6,040 square miles; the district east of the Jordan is much smaller, hardly exceeding 4,000 square miles. Altogether it is somewhat smaller than Belgium. The fertility of the land varies greatly in quality. On the whole it is not of a superior quality. The fact is it has never been a very fertile place. The reference to 'a land flowing with milk and honey' does not allude to the fertility of the soil, but to a country with great pasturage for cattle, the land probably not being cultivated in antiquity at all. It is deficient in water in that the arable land has not a quantity sufficient for its productive capacity. If sufficient rain does not fall in time, many of the springs dry up, and the land cannot be properly cultivated; the crops wither, there is no harvest, and a general scarcity of grain results, so that the price of bread is closely connected with the rainfall. Irrigation, to be sure, might be effective in improving the soil, but it is problematical whether it would pay to bring thousands of people, as well as a great capital, for the purpose."

The same writer says that "Palestine was never a fertile land, and centuries of neglect have made the greater part of that region practically a desert. The means of transportation are primitive, the mileage of railroads insignificant, the high-roads are bad, and there are no navigable rivers or canals and no first-class harbor. Speedy industrial and commercial development cannot be expected in this kind of land. It will take many years, with even the indefatigable energies of pioneers, which are lacking among the Jews, to bring Palestine to a degree of development adequate to support a population of the size of that of Belgium. Even then it will hardly provide accommodation for half the number of Jews in the world. Meanwhile, not many over one million people can find profitable employment and subsistence there. Considering that there are about 600,000 Moslems and Christians there, it is evident that, even if the Zionists brought over the same number of Jews, the country would be overcrowded for the time being. This would by no means contribute anything to the solution of that vexing Jewish problem. No perfect autonomy or Jewish theocracy could be expected in a country in which half the population is non-Jewish. In-

deed there are many Jewish cities in Russia and
Galicia in which the population is more than fifty
per cent. Jewish.   But what is of more importance,
it would not at all help the Jews in Russia and
Roumania.   In these countries there are about
6,000,000 Jews, and the removal of 600,000, leaving
5,400,000, would not by any means convince the
Anti-Semites that they have been relieved of the
Jews.   More than double that number have emi-
grated from those countries within the last twenty-
five years, and conditions have aggravated, if
changed at all.   The Zionists have realized all this,
and they speak of establishing their Jewish government not alone in Palestine, but also in the neighboring countries, such as Syria, Mesopotamia, and
other parts of Asia Minor.   But disregarding the
fact that they have less claims on the greater parts of
these countries than on the lands in which they live
at present, and also the fact that Turkey will never
cede that region to anybody for the establishment
of an autonomous government, it must be recalled
that there are living there about 15,000,000 Moslems
and Christians.   They cannot be driven out to make
place for Jews.   Now, the establishment of a Jewish
government in which the majority of the population
is non-Jewish — granting that all the 12,000,000
Jews in the world go thither — will not be satis-

factory to those enthusiasts who see salvation for
the Jew only in isolation from foreign influences."*

Zangwill declares that after "twelve years of
Zionism the Jew is still forbidden to enter Palestine
(his stay is limited to three months). Even under
the Turkish Constitution, of the four members
returned to Parliament not one is a Jew. Nor
have the Jews numerically a right to a Jewish
representative, since out of every seven inhabitants
of Palestine only one is a Jew. Of a population of
600,000 only 86,000 are Jews. Nor are these the
sort of people who can assert themselves even as
a minority and form the nucleus of a larger growth.
They do indeed constitute a two thirds majority
in Jerusalem; but as few possess Turkish citizenship,
even the member for Jerusalem is not a Jew. If
the Jews are such a small fraction of the population
in Palestine, still smaller is their holding of land.
Despite all the Jewish colonies established by Baron
E. Rothschild, and by so many societies in Europe,
the Jews hold only two per cent. of the land in Palestine. The constitution of Turkey appears to have
altogether dissipated the idea that Palestine will
grant autonomy to the Jews."

All these are curious and uninteresting opinions
of men who are without confidence in God's covenant

---

* "The Jews," by Dr. M. Fishberg, page 496.

and oath. They speak and write as if they were ignorant of God's promise or else diligently intend to ignore it.

The land given by oath to Abraham is ample enough to accommodate all the Jews in the world and millions more besides. Its fertility shall also be seen when the curse now resting upon it has been repealed. The twelve tribes are going back in God's time and in God's way. The seven years during which their restoration is to be accomplished are especially characterized by the great tribulation that is to bring this period to a close. This great tribulation involves the whole habitable world and yet it is spoken of in Scripture as distinctively the time of "Jacob's trouble." Though the whole world shall be under affliction, Jerusalem and the Holy Land shall be the storm center in those days of sorrow. In blindness and in unbelief the Jews are to be taken back to Palestine under a covenant made with them by the "beast out of the sea" (Rev. 13:1). After three years and a half he shall violate this covenant, under the terms of which the Jews have had restored to them their temple worship, and then this same beast, the anti-Christ, shall show himself in the temple and demand of the Jews that he be worshiped as God. (Matt. 24:15; II Thess. 2:4).

This shall usher in the great apotheosis toward which the boasted wisdom of this world is so steadily moving. This man shall be exalted to a rank among the gods and as such he shall be worshiped. Little indeed shall his dupes realize that they are in fact worshiping Satan by whom he is instigated. There is to be "given him a mouth speaking great things and blasphemies"; and he shall be given "authority to practise forty and two months." The "forty and two months" define the limit of, and are identical with, the time of the great tribulation.

The blasphemy of the beast is directed against God and His tabernacle, and against them who, safe beyond the reach of his malice, are already tabernacled in heaven.

His authority is world-wide, extending over "every tribe and people and tongue and nation; and all the dwellers upon the earth shall worship him, whose names are not written from the foundation of the world in the book of life of the Lamb slain."

Solemnly, as in the letters to the seven churches, the admonition is given, "If any one hath an ear, let him hear." It is the warning of God against the deification and worship of man to which the sure word of prophecy points and toward which the world is so recklessly moving.

Israel is warned against meeting the beast in armed resistance. Through that awful tribulation she is to wait in patience for deliverance that can come only through the Messiah. And that deliverance shall come, for: "Immediately after the tribulation of those days shall the sun be darkened, and the moon shall not give her light, and the stars shall fall from heaven, and the powers of the heavens shall be shaken: and then shall appear the sign of the Son of man in heaven: and then shall all the tribes of the earth mourn, and they shall see the Son of man coming in the clouds of heaven with power and great glory" (Matt. 24:29, 30).

"In that day there shall be a fountain opened to the house of David and to the inhabitants of Jerusalem for sin and for uncleanness" (Zech. 13:1).

"And the Lord shall be king over all the earth: in that day shall there be one Lord, and his name one. All the land shall be turned as a plain from Geba to Rimmon south of Jerusalem: and it shall be lifted up, and inhabited in her place, from Benjamin's gate unto the place of the first gate, unto the corner gate, and from the tower of Hananeel unto the king's wine-presses. And men shall dwell in it, and there shall be no more utter destruction; but Jerusalem shall be safely inhabited" (Zech. 14:9-11).

"In that day shall there be upon the bells of the horses, HOLINESS UNTO THE LORD; and the pots in the Lord's house shall be like the bowls before the altar. Yea, every pot in Jerusalem and in Judah shall be holiness unto the Lord of hosts: and all they that sacrifice shall come and take of them, and seethe therein: and in that day there shall be no more the Canaanite in the house of the Lord of hosts" (Zech. 14 : 20, 21).

CHAPTER XVI

THE RETURN OF THE KING

THE Hebrew prophets did not contemplate two advents of the Messiah: one in humiliation, and the other in power; but they combined these features in the portrayal of a single advent. A Messiah was to come who was to suffer and who was to reign; that was their concurrent testimony: beyond that they did not go.

The necessity of two advents for the completion of prophecy is a New Testament revelation. This truth was implicit in the prophecies but not explicit until after the resurrection of Jesus.

The two men on their way to Emmaus were the first to receive this revelation, and on the evening of the same day it was given to all the disciples.

Their minds were opened that they might understand the Scripture.

The New Testament revelation enables us to discern and discriminate these two features in the message of the prophets, and so escape the perplexity occasioned by the testimony of the Spirit to the sufferings of Christ and the glory that should follow.

He came the first time to bear the sins of many: unto them that look for Him shall He appear the second time, without sin — without reference to sin — unto salvation.

At the beginning of the seven years which in accordance with Gabriel's prophecy are necessary for the fulfilment of promises made to Israel, He appears; and the Church is caught up in clouds to meet Him: at the end of the seven years, He shall come for the salvation of Israel, in the clouds of heaven with power and great glory.

All the prophecies that testify to the sufferings of Christ refer to His first advent; those that testify to the glory of Christ refer to His second advent.

The momentous events appurtenant to the second advent of our Lord are, in their various features, set before us in sacred prophecy.

The book of Revelation, from the first verse of the fourth chapter to the tenth verse of the nineteenth chapter, gives an account of what is to take place upon the earth from the time the Church is taken away until the Lord returns in glory. The duration of this time is exactly seven years: the last half of this period being the time of Jacob's trouble. The Jews, during this time of unutterable sorrow, are still under sentence of judicial blindness.

But among them are those who cling to the one hope that has sustained the heart of the orthodox Jew in all generations. Under the pressure of an affliction, greater than anything they have yet known in the years of their banishment from God, they shall plead for the coming of the Messiah in whom alone their hope of deliverance is centered. They shall not plead in vain. Suddenly the everlasting doors shall be rolled back; and the King — their King — of glory shall come. He is to be followed by the armies of heaven: for He is the Warrior King come for the deliverance of His people.

He is called Faithful and True: because the testimony of Jesus is the spirit of prophecy; and He has now come to perform God's oath, and to keep the covenant that God made with David.

His eyes are "as a flame of fire": as they were when He stood in the midst of the seven golden lampstands and viewed the wreck of the apostate Church. Here He is to view and to judge the wreck of empires as they fall before Him.

On His head are *many* crowns — or diadems — proclaiming His sovereignty over dominions beyond His inheritance as the Son of David. This and what follows may be figurative language; but we must remember that it is figurative of facts, and beyond Scripture we cannot go to determine what the facts may be.

He hath a name written that no man knoweth but He Himself. It may be that wondrous name that is to be written upon him that overcometh, and who shall become a pillar in the temple of God to go no more out forever.

He is clothed with a vesture dipped in blood: and we shall know Him, not by the print of the nails in His hands, but by the blood-red vesture that shall so unmistakably distinguish Him from the white-robed company of the redeemed.

His name is called The Word of God: the full and final expression of the mind of God. All of God's thought and all of God's counsel are told out in Him. How marvelous the Person worthy of such a name! His name shall be called Wonderful. Here the interpreter must of need become the abstracted worshiper.

And the armies which are in heaven follow Him, clothed in fine linen, white and clean. The Church is in reality not militant until she becomes triumphant. How great her glory! She is the queen in gold of Ophir. She shall reign with the King.

And out of His mouth goeth a sharp sword, that with it He should smite the nations: and He shall rule them with a rod of iron.

He is come to fulfil the prophecy of the second Psalm; and He finds the world in armed resistance. In the fifth chapter of Revelation the whole government of God, as related to the earth, is seen to be in action to put Jesus in possession of His purchased inheritance. Stroke upon stroke of judgment falls until the King appears and brings to an end the world's rebellion. His kingdom is not to be established by the proclamation of the gospel.

He treadeth the winepress of the fierceness and wrath of almighty God. This does not look like the gradual evolution of a spiritual kingdom upon the earth. It is not until the judgments of the Lord are in the earth that the inhabitants thereof shall learn righteousness.

He hath on His vesture and on His thigh a name written, King of kings and Lord of lords. This title is of wider significance than the one nailed on the Cross.

As the Son of David He is not merely the King of the Jews: He is the King of *Israel*.

As the Son of man He is the heir of the world, as the eighth Psalm declares Him to be; and as

such He is proclaimed by the title written on His
vesture and on His thigh:

KING OF KINGS AND LORD OF LORDS.

And the Lord shall be King over all the earth:
in that day there shall be one Lord, and His name
one.

Just prior to His coming, an angel is seen, "standing in the sun; and he cried with a loud voice, saying
to all the fowls that fly in the midst of heaven, Come
and gather yourselves together unto the supper of
the great God; that ye may eat the flesh of kings,
and the flesh of captains, and the flesh of mighty
men, and the flesh of horses, and of them that sit
on them, and the flesh of all men, both free and bond,
both small and great."

This is another figure of a fearful fact.   It is but
the echo of the prophecies of the past.   I will also
gather all nations, saith the Lord, and will bring
them down into the valley of Jehoshaphat. and will
plead with them there for my people and for my
heritage Israel, whom they have scattered among
the nations, and parted my land.

I will gather all nations against Jerusalem to
battle; and the city shall be taken, and the houses
rifled, and the women ravished: and half of the city

shall go forth into captivity, and the residue of the people shall not be cut off from the city.

So shall the beast and his armies be gathered together to make war against Christ and against His army. And this is what shall happen to them that shall be found under the banner of the beast:

"Their flesh shall consume away while they stand upon their feet, and their eyes shall consume away in their holes, and their tongue shall consume away in their mouth" (Zech. 14:12).

No wonder that the kings of the earth, and the great men, and the rich men, and the chief captains, and the mighty men, and every bondman, and every freeman, hide themselves in the dens and in the rocks of the mountains; and call on the mountains and the rocks to fall on them, and hide them from the face of Him that sitteth on the throne, and from the wrath of the Lamb! Once more we hear the echoes of other prophecies in the ages past.

Behold, I will make Jerusalem a cup of trembling unto all the people round about, when they shall be in the siege both against Judah and against Jerusalem. In that day, saith the Lord, will I make Jerusalem a burdensome stone for all people: all that burden themselves with it shall be cut in pieces, though all the people of the earth be gathered together against it. In that day, saith the Lord,

I will smite every horse with astonishment, and his rider with madness: and I will open mine eyes upon the house of Judah, and will smite every horse of the people with blindness. Then shall the Lord go forth and fight against those nations, as when He fought in the day of battle.

So shall the Lord Jesus Christ come in judgment. It is no new revelation, but is a revelation as old as are the ages. Before the deluge rolled over the earth, Enoch went about saying, Behold, the Lord cometh with ten thousands of his saints, to execute judgment upon all, and to convince all that are ungodly among them of all their ungodly deeds which they have ungodly committed and of all their hard speeches which ungodly sinners have spoken against Him.

That prophecy was taken up by Moses, and reiterated by Him, and by all the prophets, and by all the apostles.

But beyond the storm lies the eternal calm. The light that brightens over the hills of Galilee is the harbinger of a serene and an endless day.

Though He march through the land in indignation, and thresh the heathen in anger: yet He comes for the salvation of His people, even for the salvation of His anointed (Hab. 3:12,13). Zion shall be redeemed with judgment, and her converts with righteousness: and the destruction of the transgressors and of the sinners shall be together, and they that forsake the Lord shall be consumed.

"The tents of Judah" are to be saved first, and the reason assigned for this is, "That the glory of the house of David and the glory of the inhabitants of Jerusalem do not magnify themselves against Judah" (Zech. 12:7).

Judah delivered up her glorious King to be crucified. This priority of Judah is in keeping with the Lord's immeasurable grace. As on the day of His resurrection He appeared to Peter, who had denied Him, before He met all of the disciples together: so He saves Judah first, lifting the reproach of His death from them, before He brings the others into blessing.

He has come to keep God's oath to David, and He shall defend the inhabitants of Jerusalem; and "he that is feeble among them at that day shall be as David; and the house of David shall be as God, as the angel of the Lord before them" (Zech. 12:8).

Then follows the pouring out of the Spirit, and the making of the new covenant, under the terms of which the twelve tribes are to take possession of the land, and the house of David to be established forever.

"I will pour out upon the house of David, and upon the inhabitants of Jerusalem, the spirit of grace and of supplications: and they shall look upon me whom they have pierced, and they shall mourn for him, as one mourneth for his only son, and shall be in bitterness for him, as one that is in bitterness for his first-born" (Zech. 12: 10).

In that day, and never until that day dawns, shall there be a fountain opened to the house of David and to the inhabitants of Jerusalem for sin and for uncleanness.

In that fountain they shall wash and be clean.

> They shall survey the wondrous Cross
> On which their Prince of glory died;
> Their richest gain shall count but loss,
> And pour contempt on all their pride.

And it shall come to pass in that day, saith the Lord, that the light shall not be clear nor dark: but it shall be one day which shall be known to the Lord, not day, nor night: but it shall come to pass, that at evening time it shall be light.

CHAPTER XVII

THE KINGDOM

THE kingdom to be established here upon the earth by the Lord Jesus when He returns in glory is the kingdom that God promised to David.

We are content to rest this assertion on the obvious and natural meaning of the words contained in the promise taken in connection with the general teaching of the Old Testament about the Messiah, on the positive testimony of the prophets and the apostles, and on the authority of Christ.

The so-called "providential" coming of Jesus at the destruction of Jerusalem by Titus is an unwarranted assumption, and it passes the ingenuity of the fair-minded interpreter to understand how such unauthorized interpolations ever came to be tolerated. The necessity of an unscriptural theory is the only possible explanation.

The destruction of Jerusalem was not the restoration of the kingdom to Israel: it was the blasting of the hope inspired by all the Hebrew prophets. Instead of the fulfilment of the covenant that God made with David, it looked rather like the final abrogation of it.

The coming of the Son of man, as foretold in the prophecy of Daniel, contemplated the establishing of the Messianic kingdom by a sudden and crushing blow that should displace all the other kingdoms of the world. It was to be like a great stone falling from heaven on the feet of the great image representing the kingdoms of this world, overthrowing them completely, and grinding them to powder. So, and in no other way, was the Son of man to shatter the empires of this world and bring Israel into a place of supremacy and blessing. In this all the prophets agree.

How illusory, then, to assume that Jesus came at the destruction of Jerusalem or that He comes at death or that He has ever come at all, as the angels, after His ascension, declared He would come!

There can be no doubt, except to such as are prepossessed with other theories, that such a kingdom as Daniel represents has never yet been constituted upon the earth.

Before the smiting stone falls from heaven, the Church is removed, and then darkness covers the earth and gross darkness the peoples; but the light begins to shine over the hills of Galilee, and Israel's morning — stormy though it be — brightens into unending day.

The excision of the Church as threatened by the apostle Paul, and her removal from the earth before Israel's prophetic history now under suspension is resumed, are facts of momentous import; but their urgent and pressing claim for consideration has been ignored by those who do not discriminate and who, through want of distinction, confound Israel with the Church.

It is this failure to distinguish things that differ that can alone account for the Christian's appropriation of Israel's promises.

In neither history nor doctrine can Judaism and Christianity go on together. Israel was set aside to make way for the Church: and the Church must be removed from the earth before Israel can be restored. This is absolutely demanded by the unanswerable logic of all prophetic testimony.

Suddenly, at the end of Israel's last great sorrow, the Lord shall come. As soon as the fig tree — the symbol of Judah — shall put forth leaves, they shall know that Summer is near. The fruit of the fig tree comes with the leaves. So suddenly shall Israel's Summer displace her long Winter of sorrow.

There shall be signs too throughout the whole extent of nature. The sun shall be darkened; the moon shall not give her light; the stars shall fall from heaven, and the power of the heavens shall be shaken.

The whole creation, groaning and travailing together in pain, as it has done through the ages past, shall be in final birth-throes of that new and better era of which the prophets have spoken.

So shall come the kingdom for which the saints of God have so wearily waited and prayed.

The stone that smites the world-colossus shall become a great mountain and fill the whole earth: and instantly shall the earth respond to the presence of her glorious Lord and King.

Let the heavens rejoice, sings the exultant Spirit, and let the earth be glad; let the sea roar, and the fulness thereof; let the fields be joyful, and the trees of the wood rejoice before the Lord: for He cometh, for He cometh to judge the earth: He shall judge the world with righteousness, and the people with His truth.

The angels of God shall be summoned to worship Him; and all the hosts of heaven shall praise Him, sun and moon and stars of light. And the far-echoing voices of a great multitude shall be heard, saying, Hallelujah! Salvation and glory and power belong unto our God.

And His servants shall praise Him, and their voices shall be as the sound of many waters and of loud peals of thunder, saying, Hallelujah! The Lord our God, the Ruler of all, has become King. Let us rejoice and triumph and give Him glory!

And His name shall be called Wonderful, Counsellor, The mighty God, The Father of Eternity, The Prince of Peace. And there shall be given Him dominion, and glory, and a kingdom: and of the increase of His government and peace there shall be no end, upon the throne of David, and upon his kingdom, to order it, and to establish it with judgment and with justice from henceforth even forever. And righteousness shall be the girdle of His loins and faithfulness the girdle of His reins. Then judgment shall dwell in the wilderness, and righteousness remain in the fruitful field: and the work of righteousness shall be peace; and the effect of righteousness quietness and assurance forever.

And He shall build the temple of the Lord: even He shall build the temple of the Lord; and He shall bear the glory, and shall sit and rule upon His throne; and He shall be a priest upon His throne: and the counsel of peace shall be between them both.

And many nations shall come, and say, Come, and let us go up to the mountain of the Lord, and to the house of the God of Jacob; and He will teach us of His ways, and we will walk in His paths: for the law shall go forth from Zion, and the word of the Lord from Jerusalem.

In that day it shall be said to Jerusalem, Fear thou not: and to Zion, Let not thine hands be slack: the Lord thy God in the midst of thee is mighty; He will save, He will rejoice over thee with joy; He will rest in His love, He will joy over thee with singing.

And He will set up one Ruler over them, even David His servant: for, behold, the days come, saith the Lord, that I will perform that good thing which I have promised unto the house of Israel and to the house of Judah. In those days, and at that time, will I cause the Branch of righteousness to grow up unto David; and he shall execute judgment and righteousness in the land. In those days shall Judah be saved, and Jerusalem shall dwell safely: and this is the name wherewith she shall be called, The Lord our righteousness. For thus saith the Lord; David shall never want a man to sit upon the throne of the house of Israel. And He shall feed His flock like a shepherd; He shall gather the lambs with His arm, and carry them in His bosom, and shall gently lead those that are with young. They shall feed in the ways, and their pastures shall be in all high places; they shall not hunger nor thirst; neither shall the heat nor sun smite them: for He

18

that hath mercy on them shall lead them, even by the springs of water shall He guide them.

And an highway shall be there, and over it the redeemed shall walk, and the ransomed of the Lord shall return, and come to Zion with songs and everlasting joy upon their heads; they shall obtain joy and gladness, and sorrow and sighing shall flee away. For they shall go out with joy, and be led forth with peace: the mountains and the hills shall break forth before them into singing, and all the trees of the fields shall clap their hands.

Then shall the eyes of the blind be opened, and they shall see the King in His beauty: they shall behold the land that is very far off. They shall see Jerusalem a quiet habitation, a tabernacle that shall not be taken down; not one of the stakes thereof shall ever be removed, neither shall any of the cords thereof be broken: but there the glorious Lord will be unto them a place of broad rivers and streams; wherein shall go no galley with oars, neither shall gallant ship pass thereby: for the Lord shall be their judge, the Lord shall be their law giver, the Lord shall be their King: He will save them. And in mercy shall the throne be established: and He shall sit upon it in truth in the tabernacle of David, judging, and seeking judgment, and hasting righteousness.

The sun shall be no more their light by day; neither for brightness shall the moon give light unto them: but the Lord shall be unto them an everlasting light, and their God their glory: their sun shall no more go down upon them; neither shall their moon withdraw itself: for the Lord shall be to them an everlasting light, and the days of their mourning shall be ended.

They shall be clothed with the garments of salvation; they shall be covered with the robe of righteousness: and the Gentiles shall see their righteousness, and all kings their glory; they shall be called by a new name, which the mouth of the Lord shall name: they shall also be a crown of glory in the hand of Jehovah, and a royal diadem in the hand of their God.

They shall sing in the height of Zion; their soul shall be as a watered garden, and they shall sorrow no more forever.

Upon every dwelling place of mount Zion, and upon her assemblies there shall be a cloud and smoke by day, and the shining of a flaming fire by night: and there shall be a tabernacle for a shadow in the day time from the heat, and for a place of refuge, and for a covert from storm and from rain.

Before they call, God shall answer them, and while they are yet speaking, He will hear. He will cause the shower to come down in his season; and there shall be showers of blessing.

The heaven above shall pour down righteousness, and the earth beneath shall open and bring forth salvation.

The tree of the field shall yield her fruit, and the earth shall yield her increase, and they shall be safe in their land: they shall build houses, and shall inhabit them; they shall plant vineyards, and drink the wine thereof; they shall also make gardens, and eat the fruit of them: they shall sit every man under his vine and under his fig tree; and none shall make them afraid: for they shall not hurt nor destroy in all His holy mountain: for the earth shall be full of the knowledge of the Lord, as the waters cover the sea.

The wolf also shall dwell with the lamb, and the leopard shall lie down with the kid; and the calf and the young lion and the fatling together; and a little child shall lead them.

Violence shall no more be heard in their land; neither shall wasting nor destruction be within their borders: but they shall call their walls salvation, and their gates praise.

Even as the garden causeth the things that are sown in it to spring forth: so the Lord their God shall cause righteousness and praise to spring forth before all the nations.

The wilderness and the solitary place shall be glad for them; and the desert shall rejoice, and blossom as the rose. It shall blossom abundantly, and rejoice even with joy and singing: the glory of Lebanon shall be given unto it, the excellency of Carmel and Sharon; they shall see the glory of Jehovah, and the excellency of their God.

In the wilderness shall waters break out and streams in the desert. The parched ground — "glowing sands" in the revised version — or, better still, as in the margin, the "mirage" shall become a pool, and the thirsty land springs of water. There shall be neither illusion nor delusion: all shall be certainty and glorious reality.

The waste places of Jerusalem shall break forth into joy; they shall sing together; for Jehovah hath comforted His people: He hath made bare His holy arm in the eyes of all the nations; and all the ends of the earth shall see the salvation of God.

When the Lord shall turn again the captivity of Zion, the children of Israel shall be like them that dream. Then shall their mouth be filled with laughter, and their tongue with singing: then shall they declare among the heathen, The Lord hath done great things for us; whereof we are glad.

They have sown in tears: and they shall reap in joy. They have gone forth weeping, bearing pre-

cious seed, and they shall doubtless come again
with rejoicing, bringing their sheaves with them.

They shall sing the new song: the children of Zion
shall be joyful in their King. They shall praise
His name in the dance: they shall sing praises unto
Him with the timbrel and harp: then shall the
saints be joyful in glory. They shall praise Him
in the firmament of His power: they shall praise
Him for His mighty acts: they shall praise Him
according to His excellent greatness: they shall
praise Him with a sound of the trumpet: praise Him
with psaltery and harp; praise Him with timbrel
and dance; praise Him with the stringed instruments
and organs; praise Him upon the loud cymbals;
praise Him upon the high-sounding cymbals:
and everything throughout the whole extent of
nature that hath breath shall be called upon to
praise the Lord.

Such is the glorious kingdom that God intends to
establish here upon the earth in fulfilment of His
covenant with David.

In view of the unparalleled sublimity of the language used by Isaiah, from whose writings this delineation is chiefly taken, it is not to be wondered
at that the prophet should declare: "For since the
beginning of the world, men have not heard, nor perceived by the ear, neither hath the eye seen, O God,

beside thee, what he hath prepared for him that waiteth for him" (Isaiah 64:4).

Yet Paul, quoting this very passage, says, But God hath revealed them unto us by His Spirit.

It must be evident to the unprejudiced reader that the words used to set forth the glories of this kingdom cannot be spiritualized without impairing the force and fulness of their meaning. That one may spiritually enter into all these things none will deny, but a spiritual application that disinherits Israel of all temporal blessing is a perversion that goes far to justify the charge that sacred prophecy is an incoherent dream of Hebrew poets.

The Jews, accursed as they have been, doomed to misery and afflicted, a prey to every nation, and to unutterable grief; wandering upon the earth with aching heart and anguish of spirit and bitterness of soul; draining to the dregs the cup of their sorrow; always on the rack, stranded and stricken; these Jews, cursed and doomed and heart-scalled, in pain and in tears, in distress and in dejection, in trial and in torture, in trouble and in tribulation, in weariness and in want, in wretchedness and in woe, have clung to their national hope of restoration and blessing with the tenacity of faith that is not less marvelous than the miracle of their preservation. On the sand swept desert, where they were cradled, the silent sphinx still stands, and pro-claims, like the tolling of a silent bell, their speech-less and enduring misery.

There stand the pyramids over the dust of de-parted dynasties that would have crushed them in their infancy; but these sons of Jacob have multi-plied until, like the sand by the sea shore, they are become innumerable.

In the flaming fire of torment their hope remains inextinguishable. They wail at the walls of Jeru-salem, wretched, and dirty and miserable: but there they wail, and plead with God to look upon the desolation of many generations. And even while they wail, the strangers hiss, and wag their head, saying, Is this the city that men call The perfec-tion of beauty, The joy of the whole earth?

Over that city they wail, while her gates are sunk into the ground; her bars are broken; her king and her princes are among the Gentiles; her prophets find no vision from God; her beauty has departed; her princes are become like harts that find no pasture, and they are gone without strength before the pursuer.

The Lord has indeed covered the daughter of Zion with a cloud in His anger, and cast down from heaven unto the earth the beauty of Israel, and re-membered not His footstool in the day of His fierce anger. And yet this unconquerable people wait and hope and pray.

How beautiful then upon the mountains shall be the feet of Him that bringeth good tidings, that shall publish salvation, that shall call upon Zion to awake and put on her strength, that shall call upon Jerusalem to put on her beautiful garments that she may become the bridal city of her glorious King!

All this is yet to be because God hath sworn with an oath to establish the city of David forever and build up his throne to all generations.

We have followed the scriptural development of this promise, and have found that, taken in its literal significance, it gives coherence and consistency to Scripture, and unites in glorious harmony the prophetic voices of the ages past.

Not one stone is wanting in the arch that springs from David's throne in the past to David's throne in the future.

The argument proceeds from a divinely given premise and because it is scriptural, it is lucid and logical and without flaw; and the revelation of glory to which it leads makes the strongest plea for its acceptance.

The duration of this kingdom, according to the original promise, is measured by the words "for ever." Endless duration this cannot be: for the limit was fixed before man was created.

In the fourteenth verse of the first chapter of Genesis it is written of the sun and the moon, that they should be for "signs, and for seasons and for days and years."

Signs of what? Signs signify something, and Scripture can alone determine the significance of the signs it uses. In the seventy-second Psalm, which is a psalm of the Messianic kingdom, it is declared in the seventeenth verse, that "his name" — which must be in this instance His Messianic name — "shall endure for ever: his name shall be continued as long as the sun." It would therefore seem that the sun is here used as a sign of the duration of His Messianic reign: and the meaning of the words "for ever" is limited by the words "continued as long as the sun."

In the thirty-third chapter of Jeremiah the Lord says: "If ye can break my covenant of the day, and my covenant of the night, and that there should not be day and night in their season; then may also my covenant be broken with David my servant, that he should not have a son to reign upon his throne." Does not this warrant the belief that God's covenant with David is coterminous with His covenant of the day and night?

When day and night shall be no more: then David's throne shall be no more.

In the thirty-first chapter of Jeremiah, in connection with the making of the new covenant with Israel, it is written: "Thus saith the Lord, which giveth the sun for a light by day, and the ordinances of the moon and of the stars for a light by night, which divided the sea when the waves thereof roar; The Lord of hosts is his name: if those ordinances depart from before me, saith the Lord, then the seed of Israel also shall cease from being a nation before me for ever."

We know that these ordinances are to depart; for night shall be no more in heaven.

Therefore the duration of the kingdom extends to the new heavens and the new earth and not beyond: and the words "for ever" in II Samuel 7:16 imply no more.

The duration of the kingdom is limited for us in another way. In the fifteenth chapter of first Corinthians, the twenty-fourth verse, it is declared that, at the end, when Christ shall have put down all rule and all authority and power, then shall He deliver up the kingdom to God the Father.

The covenant of God being fulfilled, and His oath vindicated, the present framework of the heavens and the earth is dissolved: and we look beyond to the new heavens and the new earth wherein dwelleth righteousness.

CHAPTER XVIII

BEYOND

HUMAN language, in all its opulence of esthetic meaning, was forced into bankruptcy by the Hebrew prophets.

Their drain upon it, to represent the splendour of the kingdom to be established upon the earth under the sceptre of the Son of David, reduced its wealth to penury, and left it without reserve to meet any further demand that might be made upon it.

Beggared by the use of so many positive statements about the effulgence of the kingdom on earth, the insolvent speech of humanity is driven to extremity, and can only furnish negative terms in which to express the surpassing brightness of heaven. But in this way, as perhaps in no other possible way, there is given to us a conception of eternal glories which transcend, beyond all power of positive expression, the grandeur and greatness of the Messiah's kingdom.

The dreary negations of human speculation are

in pathetic contrast with those brilliant and inspiring negatives of Scripture which eliminate altogether from our conception of the eternal state the very things that give rise to the negations of transcendental philosophy.

Some of these negative expressions produce positive conceptions of wondrous significance and beauty.

The inheritance of the saints in glory is incorruptible, undefiled, and fadeth not away. The "fadeth not away" is, literally, amaranthine — a word which we have taken bodily from the Greek language into our own, and it means — "ever blooming": and the crown of glory given to one who feeds the flock is, like the inheritance, amaranthine — an ever-blooming crown.

We should remember that when the Messianic kingdom is delivered up to God the Father its positive glories abide; and these negatives of which we are thinking banish forever from it the last vestiges of the sin and the sorrow which have cursed and blighted and filled the earth with tears.

But in order to do this, and in preparation for it, there must be a dissolution of the present framework of the universe. At the end of the Messianic reign the heavens, all ablaze, shall be destroyed, and the elements shall melt in the fierce heat. But in ac-

cordance with His promise we are expecting the
new heavens and a new earth, in which righteousness
shall dwell.

The "new heavens and the new earth" are "the
old heavens and the old earth" in their resurrection
robes of glory.

On the rock-bound island of Patmos, whose shores
were washed by the undying surge of the sea, John
the aged, banished because of his testimony to
Jesus, saw the new heaven and the new earth: for
the first heaven and the first earth were passed
away; and — "there was no more sea."

The ocean, groaning as it breaks along the shore,
gives expression to the whole creation, which
groaneth and travaileth in pain, while it waits to
be delivered from the bondage of corruption into
the liberty of the glory of the children of God.

No more sea with its waste and barren waters:
gone forever to make room for permanent fruitful-
ness and abiding peace. So shall the alienated
seven eighths of God's possession return to Him,
when "that which drew from out the boundless
deep turns again home." In the Messianic kingdom
righteousness reigns; in the kingdom of the Father
righteousness dwells: so shall the work of righteousness be peace; and the effect of righteousness,
quietness and assurance forever. And God's peo-

ple shall dwell in a peaceable habitation, and in sure dwellings, and in quiet resting places.

"In my father's house" said One, who knew so well whereof He spake, "are many mansions." If it were not so, would He have told us, "I go to prepare a place for you?" And if He has gone to prepare a place for us, He will come again, and receive us unto Himself; that where He is, there we may be also.

If the heavens be the work of His fingers, if the moon and the stars were ordained by Him; and Scripture declares that they were: "For in Him was created the universe of things in heaven and on earth, things seen and things unseen, thrones, dominions, princedoms, powers — all were created, and exist, through and for Him: and He is before all things, and in and through Him the universe is a harmonious whole." If, in the framework of creation, He has so written His signature; if the heavens declare His glory, and the firmament showeth His handiwork; if He spake, and it was done; if He commanded, and it stood fast, What must that new creation be to which He has given His thought and heart and hand these years?

Baffled in its attempt to answer, the exhausted treasury of speech can only respond in negatives. But these, like the loaves and the fishes, in the hands

of Jesus, multiply as they are broken: and the redeemed are satisfied, and baskets are filled with
the fragments that remain.

Rising from the dead with incorruptible and im-
mortal bodies or, if living when Jesus comes, having the body of humiliation fashioned anew and con-
formed to the body of His glory, we shall take possession of our everlasting inheritance, and enter into
the fellowship of the redeemed of all ages. We
shall stand together on the plains of light, we shall
walk together over the radiant hills of eternity,
we shall know as we are known; and the memories
of earth shall be sanctified, when God shall have
wiped away all tears from our eyes.

"And there shall be no more death, neither
sorrow, nor crying, neither shall there be any more
pain: for the former things are passed away."

How these glowing negatives shine with a light
above the brightness of the sun!

But what about our sins? They are gone, re-
membered no more, neither by the Lord our God
nor by us. Like a thick cloud, they are blotted out;
they are behind God's back; they are cast into the
depths of the sea, and the sea has fled away and
carried them with it; and as far as the east is
from the west, so far are they removed forever
from us.

And death shall be no more; nor sorrow; nor wail of woe; nor pain; and, in their stead, life shall be forever, and joy, and song, and rapture, unto the ages of ages.

The holy city, the new Jerusalem coming down from God out of heaven, is not merely the home of the soul: it is the everlasting habitation of the whole man, spirit and soul and body, transfigured and glorified.

Of this new Jerusalem the Hebrew prophets were not suffered to speak; for it was theirs to declare the splendour of the earthly Jerusalem that is yet to be the capital city of the Messianic kingdom.

John, inspired though he be, knows not the language of heaven; and he is forced to use the stammering tongue of man to describe the city, whose builder and maker is God. But what if the fact outstrip the figure? Here language fails altogether and becomes absolutely insolvent. Even as John describes it, with what a singular fascination it holds us!

It has a radiance like that of a very precious stone — such as a jasper, or, more likely, a diamond. Its walls are massive and high, with twelve gates, and an angel guardian at each gate. And overhead, above the gates, names are inscribed, which are

19

the names of the twelve tribes of the descendants of Israel.

The walls of the city are raised on twelve foundation stones, and on these are engraved the names of the twelve apostles of the Lamb.

The plan of the city is a square, the length being the same as the breadth; and the city, measured furlong by furlong, is twelve hundred miles long; and the length and the breadth and the height of it are equal.

The walls are of jasper, and the city itself is of pure gold. The twelve foundations are beauteous with various kinds of precious stones. And the twelve gates are twelve pearls; each of these consisting of a single pearl; and the main street of the city is made of pure gold, resembling transparent glass.

The throne of God and of the Lamb is in it, and the river of the water of Life, clear as crystal, issues from the throne.

On either side of the river, midway between it and the main street of the city, is the tree of Life. It bears twelve kinds of fruit, yielding a fresh crop month by month, and the leaves of the tree are for the healing of the nations.

There is no sanctuary in the city. "For the Lord God, the Ruler of all, is its Sanctuary, and so is the

Lamb. Nor has the city any need of the sun, or of the moon, to give it light; for the glory of God has shone upon it and its lamp is the Lamb. The nations shall live their lives by its light; and the kings of the earth shall bring their glory into it. And in the day time — for there shall be no night there — the gates shall never be closed; and the glory and honor of the nations shall be brought into it. And no unclean thing shall ever enter it, neither anything that worketh abomination, nor any one that telleth lies, but only they whose names stand recorded in the Lamb's book of Life."

It would be difficult, if not impossible, to imagine a degree of glory surpassing that revealed in these final words of divine revelation.

The veil has been lifted: and before us in vivid reality are the new heavens and the new earth, which are to be the everlasting inheritance of the redeemed.

If, when we think of eternity, our heart fail, and our mind be confused, and our inheritance become indistinct and vague, it must be that, like the men on the road to Emmaus, we are slow to believe all that Scripture has so solemnly affirmed. Faith is alone able to deliver us from all uncertainty: for "faith is a well-grounded

assurance of that for which we hope, and a
conviction of the reality of things which we do
not see."

"He which testifieth these things saith, Surely
I come quickly.   Amen."

Even so, come, LORD JESUS.

INDEX

1982-83 TITLES

TITLES CURRENTLY AVAILABLE

TITLES CURRENTLY AVAILABLE